The NEW KITCHEN GARDEN

The NEW KITCHEN GARDEN

ANNA PAVORD

DORLING KINDERSLEY
LONDON • NEW YORK • SYDNEY • MOSCOW
www.dk.com

A DORLING KINDERSLEY BOOK

www.dk.com

To Vanessa, who planted a weed garden

Project Editor Pamela Brown
Art Editor Thomas Keenes
Editorial Assistant Claire Benson
Designer Kylie Mulquinn
Design Assistants Rachana Devidayal,
Deborah Swallow

Location Photographer Steven Wooster
Illustrators Valerie Hill, John Lawrence

Managing Editor Susannah Marriott
Managing Art Editor Toni Kay

Production Manager Maryann Rogers
DTP Designer Karen Ruane

Deputy Editorial Director Daphne Razazan
Senior Managing Art Editor Carole Ash

First published in Great Britain in 1996
by Dorling Kindersley Publishers Limited,
9 Henrietta Street, London WC2E 8PS

First published as a Dorling Kindersley paperback 1999

2 4 6 8 10 9 7 5 3 1

A CIP catalogue record for this book is available from
the British Library

ISBN 0 7513 0703 3

Reproduced by Euroscan, Nottingham, Great Britain
Printed and bound in Singapore by
Star Standard Industries (Pte.) Ltd.

CONTENTS

Introduction **6**

GARDEN STYLES **10**

GROWING VEGETABLES, HERBS & FRUIT **50**

FRUIT **116**

PLANNING & CULTIVATION TECHNIQUES **150**

INTRODUCTION

ORDER, COUPLED WITH PROFUSION, is the hallmark of the best kitchen gardens. If you can add to this a sense of being cut off from the real world, then you are very close to Eden. For the ultimate sense of detachment, you have to have walls, sunny walls, where pears can ripen mellifluously against warm brick. But even without the walls, even in the smallest of spaces, you can recreate a sense of abundance in your own garden by growing trained fruit trees to make living screens between one part of the plot and another, or planting exotic-looking lettuce and frilly parsley among the flowers in your border or windowbox.

SUMMER STRAWBERRIES
Think of the warmth on your tongue of a freshly picked strawberry on a summer's day. This is a fruit for sybarites.

GEOMETRY IN THE PLOT
Spreadeagled on a warm, sheltering stone wall, the apple tree, trained as an espalier, reinforces the geometrical design of this formal plot.

A dilettante gardener may grow a passable show of flowers. Vegetables signify a deeper level of commitment. To cut yourself off from growing food is to cut yourself off from a long and resonant tradition of gardening to survive. Even if you no longer have to feed yourself from your plot, without fruit and vegetables you deny yourself some of the great pleasures of gardening. Think of the sense of pride you get when sitting down to a supper that you have made entirely with produce from your own plot. You need to make the most of those moments. After the pride comes the inevitable fall, when somebody discovers a caterpillar, mummified, in the artistically arranged spears of calabrese on their plate.

It is only quite recently that vegetables and fruit have been herded into separate areas of the garden and that the kitchen garden has acquired its drear overtones: overblown cabbages and decaying runner beans. When, with increasing affluence and ease on the part of gardeners, the first flowers crept out of the physic gardens to decorate cottage plots, flowers, fruit and vegetables all grew together in happy profusion.

George Eliot set the scene in her novel *Scenes of Clerical Life* (1858): "No finical separation between flower and kitchen garden there; no monotony of enjoyment for one sense to the exclusion of another; but a charming paradisiacal mingling of all that was pleasant to the eyes and good for food. The rich flower-border running along every walk, with its endless succession of spring flowers, anemones, auriculas, wall-flowers, sweet-williams, campanulas, snapdragons and

HAPPY PROFUSION
Tall Verbena bonariensis *waves above the purple and green marbled foliage of lettuce. The sumptuous tones are reinforced by the dark leaves of a patch of beetroot beyond. Stone paths make neat divisions between the plots.*

tiger-lilies, had its taller beauties, such as moss and Provence roses, varied with espalier apple-trees; the crimson of a carnation was carried out in the lurking crimson of the neighbouring strawberry-beds; you gathered a moss-rose one moment and a bunch of carrots the next; you were in a delicious fluctuation between the scent of jasmine and the juice of gooseberries." There is no reason why you too should not be in that same state of delicious fluctuation, if you abandon some preconceived notions about the "proper" place of plants.

Perhaps you have a summer jasmine straddling an old fence at the back of a border. Perhaps the border itself has been a source of irritation. Something is wrong with it. You may decide that what it needs is a series of landmarks to punctuate its sleepiness. You could put in acanthus, but how much more fun it would be to use mop-headed standard gooseberries to bob up between the campanulas. Grown on straight metre-high stems, they have the sculptural quality of pieces of topiary, and are particularly enchanting if you leave the berries to hang and ripen until they are as richly coloured as amber. Alternatively, you could draft in some bold clumps of globe artichokes to liven up the scene. The leaves will bring to the border the drama that it needs and you will have the buttery bonus of the artichoke heads to look forward to. That is more than an acanthus will ever give you.

You may have two small plots at the end of the garden that you use for vegetables. These grow in straight parallel rows, cabbages next to lettuce, carrots next to parsley. Just by manipulating the rows of vegetables themselves, thinking about contrasts between the shape and texture of their foliage, you can make the plot start to sing. Try setting the frilly leaves of a red lettuce such as 'Lollo Rossa' against the drooping blue flags of leeks. Line out your Savoy cabbages with their swirling foliage next door to the carrots, which have leaves as good as the finest ferns.

There are several other things that you can do to improve the appearance of your plot. The first is to choose cultivars that are in themselves more decorative than the norm. There is no need to take this to ridiculous lengths. The prime purpose of a leek is to give comfort on a cold, graceless day when the buses are late and your children more than usually intractable.

CHISELLED ARTICHOKES
Every sculptor's dream, the globe artichoke makes a dramatic focal point in mixed plantings of vegetables and flowers. If you do not eat them, the beautifully chiselled buds eventually open into huge, bluish-purple thistleheads.

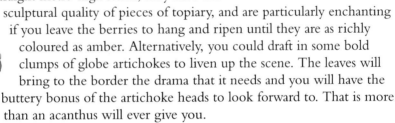

GLOSSY CHARD
Chard is a perfect foliage plant for the kitchen garden. Use the glossy crinkled leaves of a red-stemmed chard next to the feathery foliage that grows above the white bulbs of Florence fennel.

HANDSOME LEEKS
Leeks, planted in a bed of marigolds, chives, cos lettuce and red-stemmed chard, have been allowed to run up to flower, their globe-shaped heads balanced on long, strong stems.

DECORATIVE BEANS
Runner beans were originally introduced into Europe as decorative climbers. Here, a white-flowered cultivar is mixed with the red and white flowers of 'Painted Lady'.

Flavour is the prime criterion of any fruit or vegetable. But you can look for other attributes as well. Among leeks, for instance, there is an extremely handsome cultivar called 'Bleu de Solaise' (also known as 'St Victor') which is hardy and wonderful to eat. You would expect this from an old French variety, but the bonus is its foliage, leaves of a rich purplish-blue that you can use to great effect among the pale, frizzed foliage of endive. You might think of experimenting with the old-fashioned runner bean 'Painted Lady'. Runner beans were originally brought from America to Europe as decorative climbers for the flower garden, and with 'Painted Lady' you can see why. The flowers are neatly bi-coloured, red and white, charming when grown over an arch, perhaps mixed with the white flowers of a clematis. Even the prosaic Brussels sprout can dress itself up if you want it to. Try 'Rubine', which is suffused all over with a deep purplish-red, the kind of saturated colour that looks sumptuous against tall, pale cones of Chinese cabbage.

The other thing you can do is to bring flowers back into the kitchen garden, recreating the "paradisiacal mingling" that George Eliot wrote about. Line the paths with neat clumps of alpine strawberries. Set behind them a ribbon of pinks, choosing perhaps the blood-red flowers of 'Hidcote'. These contrast boldly with their own pale grey, grassy foliage, but they will also strike up an alliance with the strawberries. As you bend to pick a strawberry, the heady, spicy scent of the pinks will be where it needs to be – right under your nose.

The photographs in this book show many different ways of combining fruit, flowers and vegetables in a single plot. You might like to plant purple-headed alliums among leeks (their cousins), set purple aquilegias with your red cabbage, grow marigolds with curly kale, lay down lengths of blue cornflowers in between your fennel and carrots, scatter seed of the Californian poppy, *Eschscholzia californica,* to sprout among the onions, or use brilliant blue anchusa behind clumps of purple-leaved sage. Certain annual flowers, such as marigolds and nasturtiums, have a special affinity with vegetables, for they too can be eaten, the petals of marigolds sprinkled over a green salad, the leaves and seeds of nasturtiums used to add extra spice and bite to a sandwich.

THE COLOUR OF MARIGOLDS
A low, sprawling bush tomato, its trusses of fruit still to ripen, shares a terracotta pot with clumps of single-flowered French marigolds. English pot marigolds carry the same clear orange into the bed of basil beyond.

GOLDEN HARVEST
One of many vegetables that came into gardens from Latin America, sweet corn has been bred to adapt to cooler climates. Use the tall sheaves to make a summer screen.

George Eliot was writing about a time when the kitchen garden was at its full-blown, spectacular height. At Drumlanrig Castle, in Dumfries, Scotland, during that period, the kitchen garden contained vineries, melon houses, carnation houses and hothouses for indoor plants. There was also a glass fruithouse that was 150m (500ft) long and 5.5m (18ft) wide. A cast metal path ran down the middle with edges raised to make tracks for a railway wagon that carted muck into the glasshouse and produce out.

BRIGHTEST BLOSSOM
Safe in the cocoon of a frost-free greenhouse, this peach flowers bravely while the garden outside is still in the grip of winter. A tree needs careful training if it is to flower and fruit successfully in a confined situation such as this.

In the 1880s, the house was packed with nectarines and figs, peaches, pears and plums, all trained up wires strung from the roof. Pots of pelargoniums, begonias and other ornamentals were massed on stepped shelves against the wall. Fourteen gardeners worked for the Duke of Buccleuch at Drumlanrig under the eagle eye of David Thomson, one of the best gardeners of his day. They formed a Mutual Improvement Association and kept careful notes of the subjects they discussed at their meetings: Forcing of the Fig, Cultivation of the Raspberry, Man's Inhumanity to Man. Our pictures of Glenbervie, another old Scottish garden (see pages 16–17), show that the tradition evoked by George Eliot and enshrined in David Thomson still lives on today. It is a tradition from which we have much to learn. If you are interested in good food, there is an overwhelming reason to grow your own fruit and vegetables. Without good ingredients you cannot expect to produce good food. Commercial growers worry less about the taste of vegetables than the size and uniformity of the crop. When you are growing your own, different standards prevail. To enjoy asparagus, sweet corn and sprouting broccoli at their best, they need to go straight from plot to pot. Some produce such as French beans, strawberries and raspberries may be expensive to buy. If you have your own, you can indulge to your heart's content.

BOLD COURGETTES
While the courgette itself is just beginning to swell, you can pick off the flower and use it as a package to fill with a savoury rice stuffing. Grow both green and yellow-fruited cultivars of courgette in the decorative kitchen garden.

These are practical reasons to grow fruit and vegetables. The best reason, though, is the pleasure that they give, and the beauty that they add to the garden. Few trees in spring can match the elegiac performance of a mature pear, pouring out its heart in white blossom against the blue sky. Few flowers can produce a smell to equal the scent of a ripe greengage drooping, intoxicatingly, from a tree fanned out against a warm wall. Few foliage plants can match the bravura perfomance of a kale such as 'Chou Palmier', rising in a bold fountain of near black leaves. All these pleasures can be yours. To recreate Eden, just plant, watch and wait.

Anna Pavord

1
GARDEN STYLES

IN THIS FIRST PART OF THE BOOK you will find ideas for many different ways of combining fruit, vegetables and flowers in your garden to create effects that may be whimsically nostalgic, as in this charming display, or strictly formal, as in the design for the salad and herb plot on pages 36–37. Following each inspiring photograph is a plan showing how you can interpret each particular style in your own garden. The plans assume a never-never land where everything fruits and flowers at the same time. Your own garden will behave more sensibly, as nature intended. The plans do not take into account the exact number of cabbages or lettuce that will fit into a row. For the correct spacings at which they should be grown, check the information given in Part Two.

EXUBERANT POTAGER

POTAGER, USED IN THE ENGLISH SENSE, means posh vegetables, grown as part of a formal design and mixed with flowers, fruit or whatever else makes them look decorative as well as useful. Villandry, the great Renaissance château west of Tours in France, has the world's most famous potager. There are acres of it divided into nine equal squares, each containing a different arrangement of formal beds edged with box. The idea has since been copied all over the world.

When planning a potager, avoid too many permanent plantings of perennials that will cut down on your options for change. Interplant vegetables with annual flowers, such as cornflowers or Californian poppies, and try edging beds with violas rather than box. Use decorative structures to give plants height. You might try a wigwam of runner beans, or a clipped bay tree as in this exuberant potager at Kinoith, in south-west Ireland. Here, nasturtiums partner frilly lettuce on one side of the path, while violas romp with lettuce on the other, and a golden hop scrambles over an arbour to make a seat in the shade.

RECREATING THE POTAGER

WHEN CREATING YOUR OWN POTAGER, the first task is to draw up a design for the beds. The main danger lies in over-complication, but a central focal point will help pull the design together. Use a gazebo, a decorative frame or a dramatic plant such as a globe artichoke (left, and in plan). To furnish a potager you need three sorts of plants: some to edge the beds, some to fill them and some to give height. Plant generously to create an exuberant effect, but avoid the temptation to cram in as many different types of vegetables and flowers as you can. The pattern will be much more effective if you restrict your choice. Choose carefully, for a potager displays each vegetable like a piece of china in a cabinet. In this plan, there are combinations of vegetables that complement each other in looks or habit – purple-leaved beetroot make dark, alternating stripes through rows of feathery-topped carrots, and tomatoes sprawl under tall sheaves of sweet corn. Stick to a few edgers and use them to reinforce the symmetry of the layout. Aim, too, for a balance between vegetables and flowers. Californian poppies (eschscholzia) brighten up the onion bed in this arrangement, and cornflowers mingle with the French beans.

COURGETTE COVER-UP
The big, bold leaves of courgettes soon cover the ground, their flowers shining out brightly from beneath. If picked regularly, courgettes have a long season. Follow them with some cut-and-come-again oriental brassicas for fresh winter salads.

THE KEY ELEMENTS

MARIGOLDS TAKE OVER
Borders of orange pot marigolds keep a bed looking fresh and bright while the vegetables growing inside are picked and replanted. A neatly clipped, standard bay tree gives a sense of permanence as well as height.

SWEET CORN, TOMATOES & MARIGOLDS *Bright pot marigolds edge a mixture of tall sweet corn and low-growing bush tomatoes that do not need staking.*

HIGH DRAMA
A wigwam of willow or a wrought iron frame, used to support a mixture of runner beans and sweet peas, will add vertical impact to a bed. In a smaller garden, use it to form a centrepiece for the whole potager, where it will give the right feeling of formality.

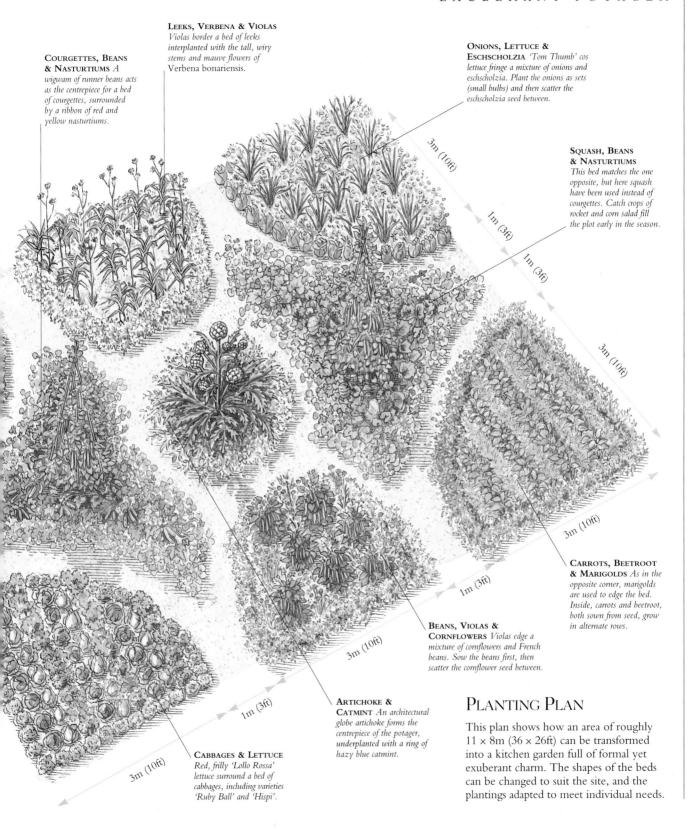

COURGETTES, BEANS & NASTURTIUMS *A wigwam of runner beans acts as the centrepiece for a bed of courgettes, surrounded by a ribbon of red and yellow nasturtiums.*

LEEKS, VERBENA & VIOLAS *Violas border a bed of leeks interplanted with the tall, wiry stems and mauve flowers of Verbena bonariensis.*

ONIONS, LETTUCE & ESCHSCHOLZIA *'Tom Thumb' cos lettuce fringe a mixture of onions and eschscholzia. Plant the onions as sets (small bulbs) and then scatter the eschscholzia seed between.*

SQUASH, BEANS & NASTURTIUMS *This bed matches the one opposite, but here squash have been used instead of courgettes. Catch crops of rocket and corn salad fill the plot early in the season.*

CARROTS, BEETROOT & MARIGOLDS *As in the opposite corner, marigolds are used to edge the bed. Inside, carrots and beetroot, both sown from seed, grow in alternate rows.*

BEANS, VIOLAS & CORNFLOWERS *Violas edge a mixture of cornflowers and French beans. Sow the beans first, then scatter the cornflower seed between.*

ARTICHOKE & CATMINT *An architectural globe artichoke forms the centrepiece of the potager, underplanted with a ring of hazy blue catmint.*

CABBAGES & LETTUCE *Red, frilly 'Lollo Rossa' lettuce surround a bed of cabbages, including varieties 'Ruby Ball' and 'Hispi'.*

3m (10ft)
1m (3ft)
1m (3ft)
3m (10ft)
3m (10ft)
1m (3ft)
3m (10ft)
1m (3ft)
3m (10ft)

PLANTING PLAN

This plan shows how an area of roughly 11 × 8m (36 × 26ft) can be transformed into a kitchen garden full of formal yet exuberant charm. The shapes of the beds can be changed to suit the site, and the plantings adapted to meet individual needs.

TRADITIONAL KITCHEN GARDEN

THE TRADITIONAL KITCHEN GARDEN, walled around with stone or brick, is an oasis of order in a chaotic world. Here, ruler-straight paths divide the space into neat, beautifully tended plots. Beans and cauliflowers, onions and peas grow in rows running from north to south to catch the best of the weather. Although this is primarily a place for the production of food, flowers are not entirely banished. Broad bands of catmint border paths under garlands of rambling roses; other flowers are grown purely for cutting. There will undoubtedly be perfectly trained fruit trees, spreading their arms over a sunny wall or perhaps used to make espaliered hedges along the edges of the plots. When you walk through a door into one of these private places, you jettison any timetable constructed around dentists' appointments, car services or the possible arrival of trains, and tune into a deeply established pattern of sowing and growing, then harvesting and sowing again.

RECREATING THE KITCHEN GARDEN

MOST TRADITIONAL WALLED kitchen gardens are of a size that needs to be divided into smaller areas. This plan shows just one quarter of a garden that has been split into four equal plots. The way the plots themselves are organized is entirely a matter of personal taste. Here, the vegetables are grown in conventional rows, but you might prefer to divide each plot into a series of raised beds, with narrow paths of beaten earth running between. Gnarled espaliers with outstretched, lichen-covered branches are a feature of old kitchen gardens. Like the fan-trained greengages on these walls, once established they are easy to prune each summer. You could also grow a screen of espaliered apples and pears on two sides of this vegetable plot. Annual flowers, such as larkspur, are grown in trellis-patterned beds to provide flowers for cutting. The paths can be of grass, gravel or hoggin (rolled aggregate). They used, once, to be made of ash, spewed in vast quantity from the greenhouse boiler. The greenhouse here is emphatically not a space for living, in the manner of a modern conservatory. It is a forcing house, a larder, a growing space, although it will provide welcome shelter in winter and early spring when you can loiter there, sowing seeds and dreaming of the harvest to come.

THE KEY ELEMENTS

FRAGILE SPRING
The peach and nectarine blossom in early spring is one of the delights of the greenhouse. Once, producing such tender fruit was an essential part of the gardener's job.

BOXED BORDERS
An edging of box, arranged in a geometric pattern, breaks up the length of the side border. Each diamond can be used to grow a different type, or colour, of flower.

GREENHOUSE *This is an ornamental yet very practical place. A floor laid with tiles or stone is easy to hose down in summer. This helps deter red spider mite and whitefly.*

GERANIUMS *Wherever room can be found in the greenhouse, fill it with old clay pots planted up with geraniums or elegant apricot clivias.*

TUNNEL OF BEANS *Train climbing French and runner beans on long hazel poles, tied over the path, to create a colourful, productive and shady tunnel.*

7.5m (25ft)

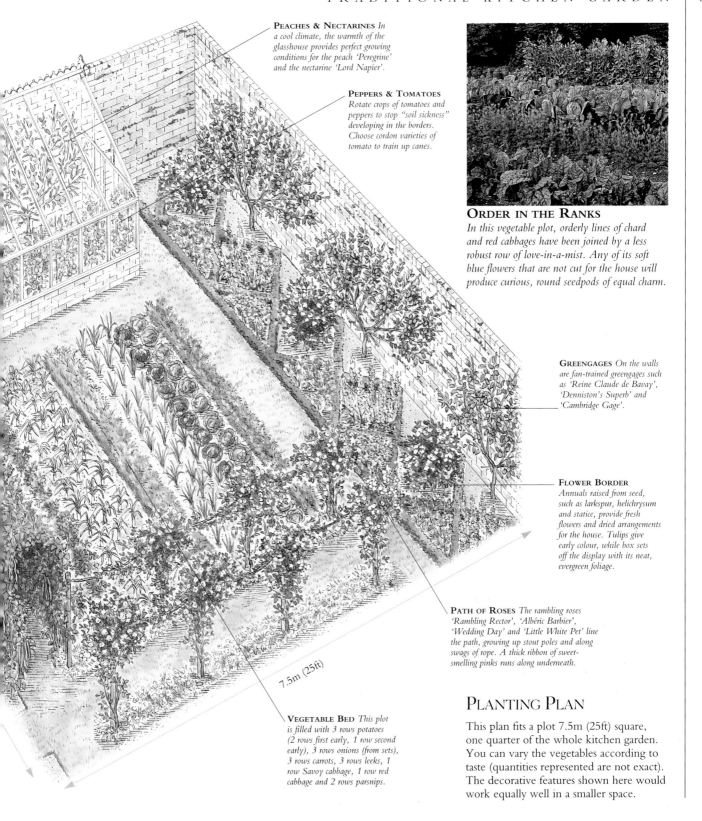

PEACHES & NECTARINES *In a cool climate, the warmth of the glasshouse provides perfect growing conditions for the peach 'Peregrine' and the nectarine 'Lord Napier'.*

PEPPERS & TOMATOES *Rotate crops of tomatoes and peppers to stop "soil sickness" developing in the borders. Choose cordon varieties of tomato to train up canes.*

ORDER IN THE RANKS

In this vegetable plot, orderly lines of chard and red cabbages have been joined by a less robust row of love-in-a-mist. Any of its soft blue flowers that are not cut for the house will produce curious, round seedpods of equal charm.

GREENGAGES *On the walls are fan-trained greengages such as 'Reine Claude de Bavay', 'Denniston's Superb' and 'Cambridge Gage'.*

FLOWER BORDER *Annuals raised from seed, such as larkspur, helichrysum and statice, provide fresh flowers and dried arrangements for the house. Tulips give early colour, while box sets off the display with its neat, evergreen foliage.*

PATH OF ROSES *The rambling roses 'Rambling Rector', 'Albéric Barbier', 'Wedding Day' and 'Little White Pet' line the path, growing up stout poles and along swags of rope. A thick ribbon of sweet-smelling pinks runs along underneath.*

7.5m (25ft)

VEGETABLE BED *This plot is filled with 3 rows potatoes (2 rows first early, 1 row second early), 3 rows onions (from sets), 3 rows carrots, 3 rows leeks, 1 row Savoy cabbage, 1 row red cabbage and 2 rows parsnips.*

PLANTING PLAN

This plan fits a plot 7.5m (25ft) square, one quarter of the whole kitchen garden. You can vary the vegetables according to taste (quantities represented are not exact). The decorative features shown here would work equally well in a smaller space.

IN THE BORDER

OCCASIONAL DRAMA is what you want in a herbaceous border, to wake up the sleepy hordes of geraniums and well-bred campanulas. There is no reason why vegetables and fruit should not provide that drama as easily as flowers. The best borders, as gardeners are told a thousand times, are those that include plenty of good foliage. Only the slightest shift of focus is needed before you reach for a scarlet-stemmed chard instead of a bergenia, plant a globe artichoke rather than an acanthus, or fill a gap with a frilly-leaved lettuce rather than a hosta. What could be more dramatic spearing through a mound of bright red verbena than the elegant, drooping leaves of leeks, especially the French purple-leaved cultivar 'Bleu de Solaise'? So be bold and cast aside inhibition. Liberate your leeks and let their flags fly among your flowers.

SCARLET AFFAIR
The stems of ruby chard glow with a particular brilliance. These have been planted a sensible distance from the path edge so that when the leaves splay out from the centre of the plant, they do not get in the way. If well watered, this is also a striking plant for containers.

WICKER WORKS
A wicker tripod provides support for runner beans (purple-splashed French beans would make a good alternative) between purple Verbena bonariensis *and the fluffy heads of thalictrum. Further along, feathery bronze fennel partners a variegated iris.*

COLOURS OF KALE

Ornamental kales such as this have leaves of many colours – pink, purple, sea-green, grey or cream. Although it would not be your first choice for cooking, this will make a decorative feature in an ornamental potager, and grows well in pots and windowboxes.

PARSLEY AND SAGE

The sage's cool grey foliage makes a perfect foil for crisply curled parsley. With their contrasts of texture and tone, these two herbs both enliven the front of the border. Flat-leaved parsley, which is not such a bright green, would be less successful.

DESIRABLE THISTLES

Globe artichokes and cardoons are both dramatic plants in a border, but you must not put any other plant too close. Despite being ruthless smotherers, the plants have great style and presence. If you can bear not to eat the artichokes, they open out into huge purple thistleheads.

FORMAL FRUIT GARDEN

A BEAUTIFULLY TRAINED ESPALIER APPLE, with a row of Chinese chives at its foot, reinforces the horizontal lines of the stonework on this sunny barn wall. In cold areas, a wall such as this offers protection for the blossom against late frosts, and its stored warmth hastens the ripening of the fruit.

The charm of trained fruit trees lies in their formal precision and they can be used to great effect in a garden, either against a wall or tied to strong parallel wires stretched between posts. Grown like this, both apples and pears will make a protective screen around a fruit garden, filled with raspberries, strawberries and currants. The practical reason for growing soft fruit together is that you can net the whole lot against birds. Do not believe anyone who tells you that if you plant extra for the birds, both you and they will be happy. They will be delirious at the prospect of more food, but you will be left without a strawberry to your name. To enhance the decorative air of the plot, you could introduce some sort of arbour at the centre. Find a rubber hawk to sit on the top and it may save you the trouble of a net.

MAKING A FRUIT GARDEN

GROUPING FRUIT TOGETHER gives you the chance to arrange it in a decorative yet practical and productive way. The whole plot can be screened from the rest of the garden, as in this plan, by apples and pears trained as espaliers. Winter will reveal the geometry of their bare branches; then follows blossom and luscious fruit. Raspberry canes are generally planted in wide parallel rows, but in a squarish plot you could plant two lines from corner to corner giving four generous triangles to fill with soft fruit. Put a standard gooseberry in each, staking the bushes firmly for they are top heavy, especially when laden with berries. Plant two of the triangles with currants – blackcurrants in one and a mixture of white and redcurrants (above) in the other – and edge with alpine strawberries. That leaves two triangles for growing ordinary, large-fruited strawberries. Since they rarely crop well after three years, it is essential to keep producing new plants from their runners to grow in fresh ground. Use the two triangles as strawberry beds and whenever there is a spare patch in one of them, sow an assortment of annual flowers for cutting. For the best crops, mulch the ground regularly with thick layers of compost or manure.

ESPALIERED PEARS
Since few pears are self-fertile, plant two varieties to ensure pollination. Avoid planting where frosts may ruin blossom and subsequent fruit.

THE KEY ELEMENTS

RASPBERRIES *Grow one line of summer-fruiting raspberries and one of an autumn-fruiting variety. This row of 'Glen Moy' will provide abundant fruit in summer, followed by a later crop from the row of 'Autumn Bliss'.*

7.5m (25ft)

A DECORATIVE CAGE
If you grow soft fruit in one patch, you can easily net it against the predations of birds and squirrels. This highly ornamental octagonal structure stays in place all year. The netting is fixed to it as soon as the fruit starts to ripen.

STRAWBERRY TIME
It is essential to net strawberries well before the fruit turns red. Here, sappy boughs of hazel have been bent over the plants to provide a pleasingly natural way of holding the netting in place.

STRAWBERRIES *Use two of the triangles for strawberries, starting plants off in one and transferring rooted runners to the other when the original plants begin to flag, after about three years.*

SPRING PEARS
The delicate white flowers of pear are the most attractive of all fruit blossoms. A beautifully trained espalier shows them to perfection. Try to include pears in your garden, whether to screen a fruit plot or herb patch or to decorate a lawn.

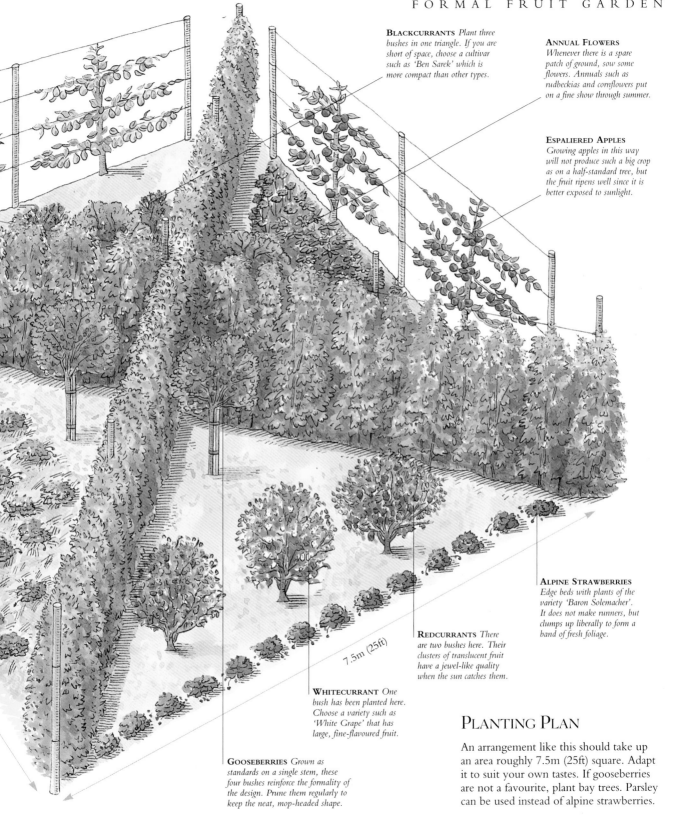

BLACKCURRANTS *Plant three bushes in one triangle. If you are short of space, choose a cultivar such as 'Ben Sarek' which is more compact than other types.*

ANNUAL FLOWERS *Whenever there is a spare patch of ground, sow some flowers. Annuals such as rudbeckias and cornflowers put on a fine show through summer.*

ESPALIERED APPLES *Growing apples in this way will not produce such a big crop as on a half-standard tree, but the fruit ripens well since it is better exposed to sunlight.*

ALPINE STRAWBERRIES *Edge beds with plants of the variety 'Baron Solemacher'. It does not make runners, but clumps up liberally to form a band of fresh foliage.*

7.5m (25ft)

REDCURRANTS *There are two bushes here. Their clusters of translucent fruit have a jewel-like quality when the sun catches them.*

WHITECURRANT *One bush has been planted here. Choose a variety such as 'White Grape' that has large, fine-flavoured fruit.*

GOOSEBERRIES *Grown as standards on a single stem, these four bushes reinforce the formality of the design. Prune them regularly to keep the neat, mop-headed shape.*

PLANTING PLAN

An arrangement like this should take up an area roughly 7.5m (25ft) square. Adapt it to suit your own tastes. If gooseberries are not a favourite, plant bay trees. Parsley can be used instead of alpine strawberries.

AN ALCOHOLIC HEDGE

FOR TAKING AWAY the backs of your knees, there is nothing like a slug of sloe gin. In country areas, sloes are a common component of mixed hedgerows, but there is no reason why they should not be planted in town. They could be part of an alcoholic hedge, mixed with elder for champagne and wine, cherry plums to make into liqueur, and hazelnuts to nibble along with your drink. Sloes are the fruit of the blackthorn, whose spiny shoots make a hedge that neither animals nor vandals can push through. The wood is dark, a counterfoil to the wreaths of white blossom that cover it in spring before the leaves come out. Elder grows so easily it is practically a weed, but if you prune out the oldest growths each year it can be kept within bounds. You can make champagne from the flat creamy flowerheads that appear in early summer; the berries, in early autumn, provide a second excuse for a binge. The cherry plum, or myrobalan, has fruit twice the size of sloes and half as bitter, too fiddly for pies but good for liqueur or wine, which becomes more like port the longer you keep it. Hazels will bear decorative catkins as well as providing nuts. Once the hedge is fairly well established, you could add to its wine-making potential by planting blackberries at intervals, then training and tying in the shoots.

SLOE WORK
Soused in gin, sloes make a highly intoxicating drink. Pick them in early winter, pull off the stems and prick with a darning needle. Drop into an empty gin bottle with 125g (4oz) sugar. When nearly full, dribble in enough gin to cover, screw on the top and steep for a year.

THE KEY ELEMENTS

The sloe or blackthorn, *Prunus spinosa*, makes a shrubby sort of tree, rarely more than 3.5m (12ft) tall. Young plants get off to the best start when they are 30–45cm (12–18in) high. Set them about 45cm (18in) from their nearest neighbour, preferably in autumn. Elder, *Sambucus nigra*, grows quickly to about the same height and is easily grown from cuttings taken in late autumn. For a more decorative effect, choose the variety 'Aurea', although its golden foliage turns green as summer wears on. The best coloured leaves, unfortunately, come from cutting the elder hard back each winter which means losing the flowers and hence the champagne. The ferny-leaved form *Sambucus laciniata* does not need such

drastic treatment but is not vigorous. Plant elders about 4m (14ft) apart, hazels at a similar distance. Both can be kept within bounds if branches are removed from the base at regular intervals. The cherry plum, *Prunus cerasifera*, is more tree-like and taller than the sloe, but you can trim it to size. Its white flowers appear in late winter and early spring, giving, together with the sloe, a long season of blossom. Set plants about 60cm (24in) apart. Once the hedge has reached about 1.2m (4ft), add a blackberry or two. Try 'Bedford Giant' for flavour, or cut-leaved 'Oregon Thornless' for decorative effect.

HONOUR YOUR ELDERS
For the best berries, give elders a site that is reasonably shady and damp, plus an annual mulch of home-made compost.

PLANTING PLAN

This plan shows a range of trees and shrubs that could be used in a hedge about 4m (14ft) long. Choose plants to provide the raw materials for your favourite brews and adjust quantities according to the length of hedge required. If possible, make the planting strip about 1m (3ft) wide and set plants in a zigzag pattern, some at the front and some at the back, to make a hedge that is reasonably thick.

FRESH AS A HAZELNUT

The taste of creamy, fresh hazelnuts, the fruit of Corylus avellana *or* C. maxima, *is quite unlike anything that has been kept in store. You will have to race the squirrels to pick them, and the squirrels will probably get there first.*

CHERRY PLUMS *The tree blossoms in early spring with white flowers slightly larger than the sloe's. The fruit is usually ready to pick in late summer. Prune, if necessary, in winter.*

ELDERBERRIES *Soon after the berries hang their heads and ripen, the leaves begin to turn a soft pinkish-purple, the colour of watered-down wine.*

BLACKTHORN *Planted at regular intervals, this will make a tough, spiny, impenetrable hedge. It needs cutting back from time to time in order to restrict its girth as much as its height.*

SLOES *The blackthorn's small, hard fruit are about the size of a grape and consist mostly of stone. They gradually turn purple in late summer but will remain on the tree for a long time.*

HAZELNUTS *Clusters of nuts decorate the hedge from late summer on. In late winter and early spring, it will be hung with delicate catkins.*

ELDERFLOWERS *Spring turns into summer as heads of elderflower light up the hedgerow with lacy patches of cream. As well as making excellent champagne, the flowers give gooseberry jam a delicious muscat flavour.*

BLACKBERRIES *Cultivated types produce larger, earlier, less pippy fruit than wild brambles. Each year, cut out the stems that bore the fruit and tie in the new ones that spring from the base.*

FOXGLOVES *Tallest of the naturalized flowers that grow at the foot of this hedge are the foxgloves in early summer. At ground level, violets, cowslips and daisies scatter their flowers through the grass.*

VEGETABLE PATCHWORK

VEGETABLES PLANTED IN BOLD BLOCKS have much more impact than those planted in single rows. This plot, inspired by the paintings of Mondrian, has been divided into a series of rectangular beds of different sizes and proportions to make a vegetable patchwork. In this way you can build up contrasts of colour and texture just as you do in a flower border. Hazel poles are lashed together to make the outdoor equivalent of a room divider: this one has been supporting a crop of scrambling peas, but it could equally well be used for climbing French beans or flowers. The annual climber *Cobaea scandens* would give the plot an exotic touch. Tall stems of sweet corn make a living hedge to screen this part of the garden from the lawn beyond, but Jerusalem artichokes could be used in the same way. The main paths are wide and paved and are connected by much narrower routes of beaten earth so that you can get in to pick or weed the vegetables. The beds, none of them too wide to be tended from one path or another, are also practical, as they make it easy to plan a year-to-year rotation of crops.

MAKING A PATCHWORK

THIS KIND OF LAYOUT will lend itself to any garden, whatever the size or however awkward the shape. It uses plants that look good in combination with each other and that will supply meals for most of the year. You can vary the quantities or substitute personal favourites. Choose the most decorative vegetables such as bright ruby chard or courgettes with glowing golden flowers (left). Grow lettuce such as frilly, burnished 'Lollo Rossa' next to the ferny foliage of carrots or the blue ribbons of leeks. Here, the patchwork is made up entirely of vegetables and herbs, but for greater contrast of colour, add flowers. Orange pot marigolds could replace one bed of parsley, or a stand of cheerful sunflowers could be planted instead of the red-stemmed chard. If you do use flowers, choose annuals rather than more permanent perennials that occupy the ground from year to year. The wide divisions between the beds are proper paths, made from paving slabs or other hard material such as brick. The narrow paths can be left as beaten earth, although on heavy ground you might find a dressing of bark or woodchips helps to mop up the damp. None of the crops in this planting will need support, but you could introduce a screen alongside one of the paths and use it to prop up a crop of peas.

THE KEY ELEMENTS

ACCENT ON SHAPE
Try to make the most of contrasting textures and forms when planning the plot. Above, the spiky, upright leaves of leeks emphasize the soft, rounded shapes of butterhead lettuce.

EXPLOITING YOUR SPACE
Underplant tall growers like sweet corn with ground-huggers such as fiery nasturtiums, whose peppery leaves and red or yellow flowers can be used to enliven a summer salad.

PLANTING PLAN

Designed for a plot roughly 7.5 × 4.9m (25 × 16ft), this plan shows the challenging variety of vegetables and herbs that can be combined in patchwork planting; quantities represented are not exact.

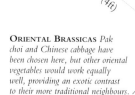

LETTUCE *Use this block to grow a crisphead type that adds texture to the salad bowl and garden alike.*

ONIONS *The slender strappy foliage of onions looks much more decorative set against the chunky shapes of oriental brassicas.*

1.2m (4ft)

2.5m (8ft)

ORIENTAL BRASSICAS *Pak choi and Chinese cabbage have been chosen here, but other oriental vegetables would work equally well, providing an exotic contrast to their more traditional neighbours.*

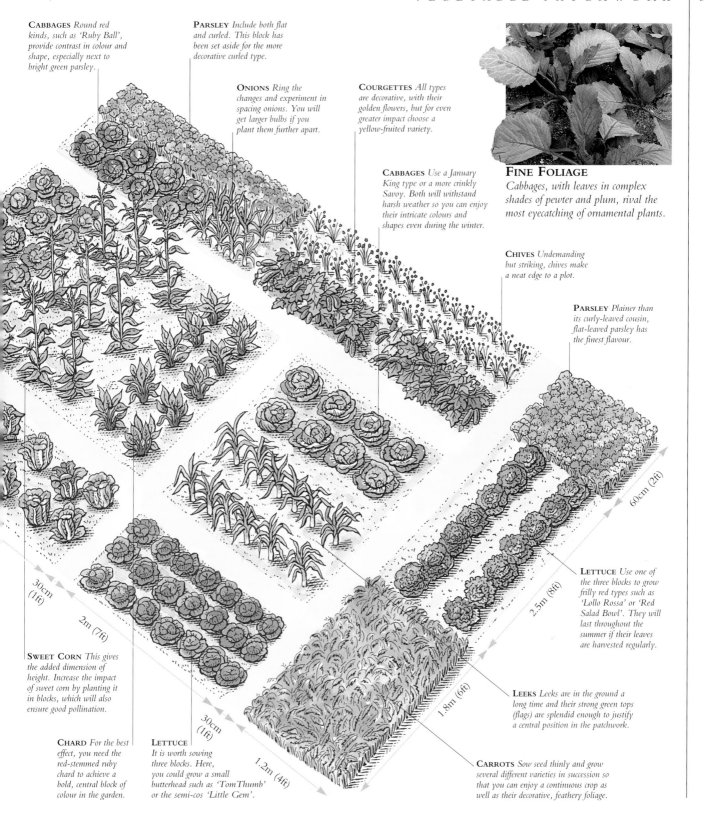

CABBAGES *Round red kinds, such as 'Ruby Ball', provide contrast in colour and shape, especially next to bright green parsley.*

PARSLEY *Include both flat and curled. This block has been set aside for the more decorative curled type.*

ONIONS *Ring the changes and experiment in spacing onions. You will get larger bulbs if you plant them further apart.*

COURGETTES *All types are decorative, with their golden flowers, but for even greater impact choose a yellow-fruited variety.*

CABBAGES *Use a January King type or a more crinkly Savoy. Both will withstand harsh weather so you can enjoy their intricate colours and shapes even during the winter.*

FINE FOLIAGE

Cabbages, with leaves in complex shades of pewter and plum, rival the most eyecatching of ornamental plants.

CHIVES *Undemanding but striking, chives make a neat edge to a plot.*

PARSLEY *Plainer than its curly-leaved cousin, flat-leaved parsley has the finest flavour.*

LETTUCE *Use one of the three blocks to grow frilly red types such as 'Lollo Rossa' or 'Red Salad Bowl'. They will last throughout the summer if their leaves are harvested regularly.*

LEEKS *Leeks are in the ground a long time and their strong green tops (flags) are splendid enough to justify a central position in the patchwork.*

CARROTS *Sow seed thinly and grow several different varieties in succession so that you can enjoy a continuous crop as well as their decorative, feathery foliage.*

SWEET CORN *This gives the added dimension of height. Increase the impact of sweet corn by planting it in blocks, which will also ensure good pollination.*

CHARD *For the best effect, you need the red-stemmed ruby chard to achieve a bold, central block of colour in the garden.*

LETTUCE *It is worth sowing three blocks. Here, you could grow a small butterhead such as 'TomThumb' or the semi-cos 'Little Gem'.*

30cm (1ft)

2m (7ft)

30cm (1ft)

1.2m (4ft)

1.8m (6ft)

2.5m (8ft)

60cm (2ft)

DECORATIVE COMBINATIONS

SHAPE, FORM, COLOUR AND TEXTURE are the attributes you have in mind when combining plants in a flower border. You put together those that will enhance each other's characteristics, perhaps using a broad-leaved hosta to set off the elegant fronds of a fern. Vegetables, herbs and fruit are no less diverse in their qualities. Of course they are grown to eat, but while they are growing your pleasure can be heightened by combining them in equally telling ways. For hosta, think cabbage. For fern, think carrot. Edge the onion bed with violas and pepper the patch with leeks. If you leave the leeks in place, they will eventually run up to flower, producing huge, silvery heads like those of an allium. That is not surprising, for alliums is what they are.

STRAWBERRY BAND

Alpine strawberries make a broad, low edging for a bed of spiky lavender. Choose a variety such as 'Baron Solemacher' that clumps up rather than sending out runners. The strawberry is not evergreen but the leaves stay fresh over a long period.

VERSATILE LEEKS

Instead of being harvested, these leeks have been allowed to run up to flower, the silvery-lilac globes balanced on strong, hollow stems. Marigolds have self-seeded between lettuce and red chard, while golden marjoram makes a striking contrast with purple sage.

CABBAGES ARE KINGS

For form, colour and texture, you can scarcely find a better plant than a cabbage. Swirling skirts of leaves surround the tightly folded hearts of these red cabbages, protected by tall screens of Verbena bonariensis, *a short-lived, strong-stemmed perennial.*

VIOLAS AND LETTUCE

The long, elegant fingers of an oak-leaf lettuce brush against the irrepressible Viola *'Jackanapes'. This viola is ideal along the margin of a path because, although it is exuberant, it does not get too big or straggly. More aggressive plants will attack your feet.*

RED SPROUTS WITH YELLOW POPPIES

The late-maturing Brussels sprout 'Rubine' has sprouts as richly dark as its leaves, well set off here by the bright blooms of the Californian poppy, Eschscholzia californica. *This is an annual that will perpetuate itself by self-seeding wherever there is a patch of bare earth.*

SALAD & HERB PLOT

A SALAD PLOT COMBINED with a scattering of the most useful culinary herbs – parsley, chives, mint and coriander – will, with a little planning, provide a long succession of crops for a gourmet gardener.

Lettuce in all their forms – cos, loose-leaf, butterhead and crisphead – provide the bulk of the planting, but for a smooth sequence you need a small back-up plot or greenhouse to raise seedlings for transplanting at the appropriate time. This small formal area, part of a larger garden, has the benefit of a sheltering wall of Cotswold stone that gives crops an early start to the season. A pot of runner beans and variegated horseradish forms the centrepiece and the edgings are a mixture of plain and variegated box. For extra ornamental effect, let flowers such as nemophila (baby blue eyes), pink opium poppies and purple *Verbena* 'La France' grow among the salad leaves. The poppies will self-seed themselves but the others need replacing each year. This is, in the main, a late spring and summer garden, although some salads, especially if given the protection of cloches, will continue through the winter.

MAKING A SALAD & HERB PLOT

IN A FORMAL DESIGN SUCH AS THIS, you need to think carefully about a suitable centrepiece. You could use a wigwam of runner beans or sweet peas, or a big clay pot of scented-leaved geraniums. You could also use a tall, architectural plant such as angelica, as in this plan. Angelica is splendidly statuesque with bright, light green foliage. It is biennial and in its second year throws up huge, rounded flowerheads of pale yellow-green. There is a dramatic purple-stemmed form called *A. gigas*. To add a little colour, a few purely ornamental flowers – pink opium poppies (left), blue nemophila and purple verbena – have been sprinkled among the red and green lettuce. For both decorative and practical reasons, other salad crops have been included. Endive, rocket, corn salad and oriental mizuna will all help to extend the season. Edging plants need to be compact. Floppers will swish wetly around your ankles or smother crops. Box, as shown on the preceding page, is a traditional edging plant, but it is hungry. The two edgings used in this design are less demanding: germander and violas. Germander, *Teucrium chamaedrys*, is an evergreen sub-shrub rarely more than 23cm (9in) high. The little oval leaves are shining green on top, grey underneath, and the tiny pink flower spikes last from mid to late summer.

PLANTING PLAN

This is a salad-lover's garden, designed to extend the season for picking fresh leaves for as long as possible. It measures just over 7m (24ft) square, but a simplified version could be fitted into a smaller space or the beds used for another range of crops.

LETTUCE *The three varieties here give a long season: crisp 'Saladin', well-flavoured 'Little Gem' and solid-headed 'Merveille de Quatre Saisons', all in a viola edging.*

2.2m (7ft 6in)

50cm (1ft 8in)

1.8m (6ft)

CORN SALAD, ENDIVE, PARSLEY, VERBENA & POPPIES *Here are rows of corn salad, the curly endive 'Sally', flat-leaved parsley, and Verbena 'La France', with opium poppies and an edging of germander.*

THE KEY ELEMENTS

LETTUCE PAGODAS
When red 'Lollo Rossa' lettuce are past their best for eating, they become even better looking and grow into decorative pagodas. Here, they rise out of a bed of nasturtiums and green lettuce.

SALAD DAYS
Lettuce come in so many shapes and colours that you can plan a pretty yet practical salad patch with nothing else. Mix seed of green and red loose-leaf types for a speckled effect and put them next to a neat butterhead type.

HEAVENLY ANGELICA
The round green flowerheads look magnificent on top of the towering stems. Later, the seedheads can be dried for decoration. The stems can be crystallized and used in sweet dishes or to decorate cakes.

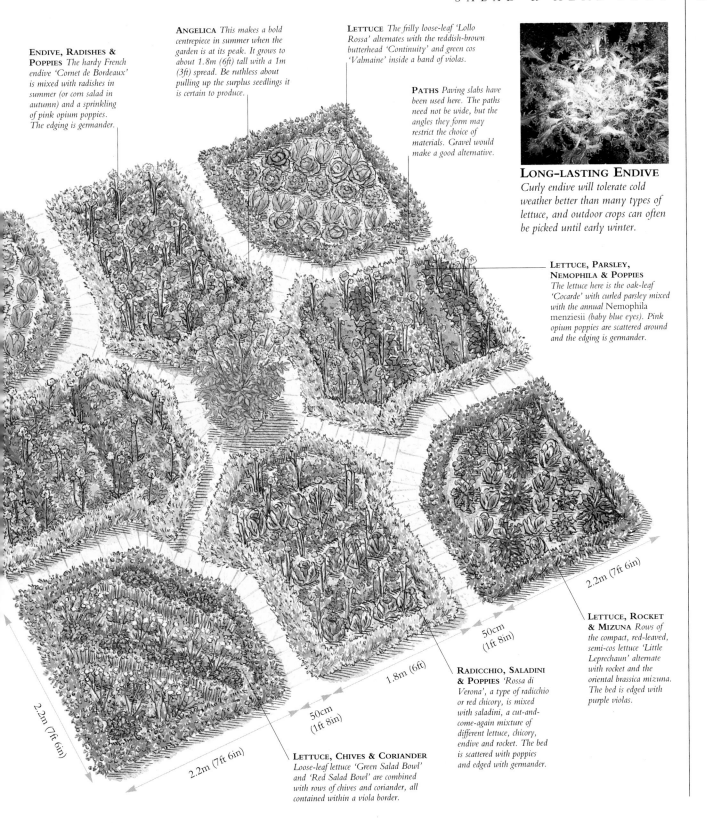

ENDIVE, RADISHES & POPPIES *The hardy French endive 'Cornet de Bordeaux' is mixed with radishes in summer (or corn salad in autumn) and a sprinkling of pink opium poppies. The edging is germander.*

ANGELICA *This makes a bold centrepiece in summer when the garden is at its peak. It grows to about 1.8m (6ft) tall with a 1m (3ft) spread. Be ruthless about pulling up the surplus seedlings it is certain to produce.*

LETTUCE *The frilly loose-leaf 'Lollo Rossa' alternates with the reddish-brown butterhead 'Continuity' and green cos 'Valmaine' inside a band of violas.*

PATHS *Paving slabs have been used here. The paths need not be wide, but the angles they form may restrict the choice of materials. Gravel would make a good alternative.*

LONG-LASTING ENDIVE
Curly endive will tolerate cold weather better than many types of lettuce, and outdoor crops can often be picked until early winter.

LETTUCE, PARSLEY, NEMOPHILA & POPPIES *The lettuce here is the oak-leaf 'Cocarde' with curled parsley mixed with the annual Nemophila menziesii (baby blue eyes). Pink opium poppies are scattered around and the edging is germander.*

LETTUCE, ROCKET & MIZUNA *Rows of the compact, red-leaved, semi-cos lettuce 'Little Leprechaun' alternate with rocket and the oriental brassica mizuna. The bed is edged with purple violas.*

RADICCHIO, SALADINI & POPPIES *'Rossa di Verona', a type of radicchio or red chicory, is mixed with saladini, a cut-and-come-again mixture of different lettuce, chicory, endive and rocket. The bed is scattered with poppies and edged with germander.*

LETTUCE, CHIVES & CORIANDER *Loose-leaf lettuce 'Green Salad Bowl' and 'Red Salad Bowl' are combined with rows of chives and coriander, all contained within a viola border.*

2.2m (7ft 6in)

2.2m (7ft 6in)

2.2m (7ft 6in)

50cm (1ft 8in)

50cm (1ft 8in)

50cm (1ft 8in)

1.8m (6ft)

COTTAGE GARDEN

PROFUSION AND A CERTAIN HAPPY randomness
should be the order of the day in a cottage garden.
Here, vegetables are kings of the castle while
flowers grow hugger-mugger in small patches
wherever space can be found. Paths are narrow so
that as much room as possible can be given over to
the production of food, and are covered in straw
to stop the ground getting muddy. Shallots have
been laid out to dry on one side of the path,
strawberries line the other. Country hedgerows
yield the hazel, willow and sweet chestnut needed
to make the screen, nearly submerged beneath a
tumbling hop, and the wigwam that could support
a crop of runner beans. True cottage gardens were
made by instinct and fuelled by necessity. Seed for
the following season would be saved from the best
of the year's crops. By this means, cottage
gardeners gradually developed strains of vegetables
that suited their particular growing conditions.
Nowadays, they may introduce plants with a
more foreign flavour. In this garden, the feathery
leaves of Florence fennel nudge a more prosaic
crop of parsnips.

RECREATING THE COTTAGE GARDEN

IN THIS PLAN FOR A STYLIZED cottage garden, a meandering path makes its way past beds of vegetables, bordered and interspersed with flowers, to the simple woven seat that occupies a sheltered, sunny corner. A second path leads in through an arch in a willow screen covered with hops and blackberries. Next to it, a stand of hollyhocks makes a welcoming entrance. Protecting the garden from cold winds is a mixed hedge of elder, hazel, honeysuckle, ash, willow and hawthorn. The honeysuckle is there for its swoony scent; the rest provide nuts and berries and sticks for the garden. In front of the hedge, a succession of biennials – foxgloves, honesty, mulleins and evening primroses – will seed themselves from year to year. In the left-hand corner, a fine topiary peacock gazes blandly at the view. In the other corner, next to the seat, a pear tree is planted for its bountiful white blossom and tempting fruit, while an old moss rose provides sweetly scented flowers for a buttonhole. The paths are of beaten earth, covered with straw, which is cheap and easy to find in the country. The crops either side are mostly traditional. There is a big bed of peas and potatoes, both of which can be stored for winter use. The wigwam of beans rises from a sprawling patch of bush tomatoes and marrow, while other beds contain onions, leeks, parsnips, cabbages, sprouts and kale.

TOPIARY PEACOCK
Yew is best for large clipped shapes such as this sprightly bird.

VEGETABLES *In this bed, carrots, kale, beans, beetroot and Brussels sprouts have been joined by some marigolds and a patch of herbs.*

6m (20ft)

TOMATOES, MARROWS & ONIONS *Use bush tomatoes that do not require staking. The marrow leaves will keep down weeds. Next to them, the onions need a bed of their own.*

THE KEY ELEMENTS

ONION ARCH
The arch that forms part of the woven willow screen can be put to all kinds of additional uses. Here, it has been hung with a rope of onions that are finishing drying in the sun.

HANDSOME KALE
Kale should find a place in every cottage garden. It has a long season, can be picked in the roughest winter weather and rarely fails to produce a handsome head of crinkled leaves.

PLANTING PLAN

With its easy informality, a cottage garden is the most adaptable of styles. This mix of vegetables, flowers, fruit, topiary and willow furniture fills an area 6 × 7.5m (20 × 25ft). Draw on the ideas to fill a space any size or shape.

BOUNDARY HEDGE
A mixture of useful native species includes willow and hazel for sticks and honeysuckle for scent.

PEAR TREE, ROSE & FLOWERS *A pear tree shades the seat and bears inviting fruit, while in front is an old-fashioned moss rose and space for growing annual flowers. A mixture of biennials lines the foot of the hedge.*

TAKE A SEAT
A seat, made from willow, chestnut and hazel, has a natural, easy charm – the very place to take a drink and watch the sun go down.

BLACKBERRIES & HOPS
These cover a screen woven from willow cut from the hedge. Choose a blackberry variety such as 'Oregon Thornless' that has pretty, finely cut leaves.

VEGETABLES *Lettuce, leeks, parsnips and red cabbage fill this bed, together with Florence fennel, a recent arrival in the cottage garden patch.*

PATH EDGINGS *Strawberries and double daisies line the paths. In the centre, they are joined by patches of nasturtiums.*

HOLLYHOCKS *The tall flower spikes, in faded shades of plum and pink, make a picture-book entrance at the side of the arch.*

7.5m (25ft)

PEAS & POTATOES *These were both staples of a cottager's diet. The peas would have been dried before being stored for the winter. Now they will be stashed in the freezer.*

PATHS *Made of beaten earth, these are covered with straw that can be raked up each season, put on the compost heap and replaced with a fresh layer.*

BEAN WIGWAM *The wigwam is made of willow gathered from the hedge and is used to support a crop of scarlet runner beans.*

BOLD AS A MARROW
Stripy marrows, growing larger and larger by the minute, put on a bold display, although they can soon outstrip their allotted corner.

THE CITY LARDER

EVEN IF YOU LIVE with your head in the clouds, 17 floors up in a block of flats, you may still be able to surround yourself with the fruits of your own labour by making a mini kitchen garden in pots and grow bags on a balcony. Hungry vegetables such as cauliflowers and celery will never be happy in these conditions, but lettuce, tomatoes, peppers and aubergines adapt well to life in the concrete jungle. Cucumbers, French beans and courgettes are other possibilities, together with cut-and-come-again salad crops that can be sown at intervals through the season. Even hanging baskets can be pressed into service: some bush tomatoes will crop happily in a basket, provided you attend to the feeding and watering. In a hot, dry summer you may have to water containers twice a day. Herbs such as marjoram, savory, sage and thyme grow easily in terracotta pots. Parsley and chives need a little more attention, for they both hate to dry out. Basil can be grown in small pots on a kitchen windowsill, where it will thrive on regular liquid feeds. An indoor windowsill is ideal, too, for crops of mustard and cress, which can be sown on damp tissue paper laid in seed trays. This is also the place to set up a little production line of sprouting bean shoots. Use them fresh in salads or whirl them in a wok.

TUMBLING TOMATOES
Bush tomatoes have a natural inclination to droop and sprawl, a useful habit in a hanging basket. Mix in some stripy French marigolds to add interest while the fruit is still green, although once the tomatoes start to ripen they will have colour enough of their own.

THE KEY ELEMENTS

An assortment of tubs, pots, baskets and grow bags will transform a small space into an attractive yet efficient growing area. Most of the crops in this plan are in grow bags: one contains tomatoes and lettuce, another French beans, a third cut-and-come-again salad crops. On an exposed balcony, you may need to put up heavy mesh netting inside the railings to filter the wind. Grow bags are quite shallow and dry out quickly, so you need to be particular about watering and feeding. A concrete floor makes a cold base. Insulate the grow bags by slipping some polystyrene tiles under them. Tomatoes are greedy, so they should have first turn in a grow bag. You can use it a second time for a less

demanding crop such as lettuce. Ease out the roots of the previous crop and fork over the compost. Do not feed new plants until they are well established or you may get a build-up of unhelpful salts that will eventually retard growth rather than promote it. Even the most hastily constructed salad or dish of pasta is improved by a whiff of basil. You can easily grow plants on a windowsill, where they will get plenty of light. From time to time, soak the pots in the sink, adding a few drops of liquid fertilizer to the water.

JUMBO DISPLAY
For the greatest impact you need a profusion of plants in pots of every shape, height and size. Grow scented-leaved geraniums, to perfume the air, as well as culinary herbs such as sage. In a crowded space all will need special care.

PLANTING PLAN

This plan shows how a mouthwatering range of vegetables, fruit and herbs can be fitted on to a balcony only 2 × 1.5m (7 × 5ft). The growing methods used here can be adapted to the smallest of spaces, from roof gardens to minute backyards. Even the windowsill inside has been put to productive use, with pots of aromatic basil and jars of sprouting seeds.

AN EDIBLE WINDOWBOX
Just lean out of the window to pick the strawberries, lettuce, tomatoes and cabbages that have been included in this planting, designed to make the best possible use of limited space.

BASIL, SPROUTING SEEDS, MUSTARD & CRESS *Fill the windowsill inside with trays of mustard and cress, pots of basil and jars of sprouting seed such as mung beans or fenugreek.*

BALLERINA APPLE TREE *On this new type of tree, the fruit forms directly on a single upright stem. It is ideal for a site like this, underplanted with spring bulbs and trailing lobelia.*

TOMATOES *Choose a bush variety, such as 'Tumbler' or 'Phyra', whose cherry-sized tomatoes will cascade elegantly from the basket. If you remember to water and feed regularly you will be rewarded with a delicious crop.*

TOMATOES *Plant cordon types in grow bags. Instead of using stakes, train them up the railings or tie them to a purpose-made frame.*

CUT-AND-COME-AGAIN SALADS *Sprinkle a mixture of rocket, mizuna and saladini seed over a grow bag and keep cutting the leaves as they sprout.*

PARSLEY *The tightly curled kind is the easiest to grow in a pot. Put it in a shady corner where the compost is less inclined to dry out.*

PEPPERS *These will thrive in a pot, given shelter and sun. Raise seedlings indoors, or buy ready-grown plants to pot into large containers.*

LETTUCE *Grow an oak-leaf type around the tomatoes, and pick the leaves a few at a time.*

CHILLIES *As with peppers, the best crops in cool climates often come from pot-grown plants. Choose a variety such as 'Yellow Cayenne' or the prolific 'Apache' which may bear up to 100 chillies.*

FRENCH BEANS *Use bush varieties and sow seed inside in mid-spring, singly in 7cm (3in) pots. The plants should be ready to set out in a grow bag in late spring. Up to 12 plants will fit into one bag. Make sure that they are always kept well watered.*

PURPLE SAGE & CHIVES *Chive flowers look especially good next to the purple leaves of sage. Trim the sage regularly to prevent it getting straggly.*

MEDITERRANEAN COURTYARD

LEMONS AND LARGE TERRACOTTA POTS are the quintessential elements of a warm, sunny courtyard: the kind of garden you might make by the Mediterranean, in California, western Australia perhaps, or any other place where winters are kind and hard frosts as rare as sunshine in Siberia. A courtyard by its very nature will be a sheltered place, probably enclosed on two sides by the arms of the house to which it belongs. Here, a retaining wall, pierced with railings through which a patch of sunflowers peer, will break the force of winds coming from any other quarter. The paving that covers the courtyard is randomly laid, with sufficient cracks to encourage the growth of creeping thymes, marjoram or camomile. Flowers, such as monkey-faced violas or the little Spanish daisy *Erigeron karvinskianus*, can also seed themselves casually between the slabs. Although the area will probably be used primarily as an outdoor room, with chairs for lounging and a shady arbour for meals, there is still plenty of space on the walls for fan-trained peach trees, nectarines and figs. If, when drawing up your own plan, you can add a small wall fountain, perhaps a benign lion's mask dripping into a stone trough beneath, you will be getting very close to Eden, Mediterranean style.

THE TANG OF LEMONS

The fruit on a citrus tree look curiously unreal, as though they might have been modelled from wax. Lemons can take up to a year to ripen. When they finally turn from green to yellow, the following season's flowers are beginning to open their thick white petals to scent the air.

THE KEY ELEMENTS

The courtyard in the plan opposite contains two separate areas, linked by a long, low step. The area by the house is paved with large, random stone slabs, and the lower level is covered in gravel. Pots are an important feature: three handsome lemon trees in pots march along the stone kerb. Bay trees in pots stand either side of the railings, let into the retaining wall to give a view of the landscape beyond. A pomegranate sits in a large pot by the house, while in the sunny gravelled area, massed lavender fills another swagged terracotta container. Shallow pots of fleshy-leaved aeoniums or sempervivums can be grouped wherever there is space. One door from the house opens directly into a shadowy arbour, made from rough poles lashed together, with a vine trained up and over it to make a green living roof. A passion flower, *Cobaea scandens* and summer jasmine bring extra colour and scent to the sitting-out area. A whole series of flowers colonizes the gravel and enjoys this sun-baked patch. Sunflowers fill the space between the bay trees, while iris, agapanthus and gazanias sprawl in relaxed clumps elsewhere. In spring, the area is carpeted by dwarf bulbs – species tulips, crocus and bright de Caen anemones.

POTTED HIGHLIGHTS

Citrus trees in handsomely decorated pots give a garden a decidedly sunny air. Lemons can be left outside all year in a frost-free courtyard. They need no regular pruning, although you can trim them to shape, if necessary.

PLANTING PLAN

The shape and aspect of your courtyard will, to some extent, determine the choice of plants. This plan shows one way of creating a relaxing space filled with the scent of fruit, herbs and flowers.

ARBOUR *Made by a grapevine scrambling over a lattice of rough wooden poles, the arbour creates a relaxed eating area. A passion flower, Cobaea scandens and summer jasmine climb up the three support poles at the front.*

ON THE VINE

Vines are ideal plants to shade a sunny terrace. Trained over a lattice roof, their soft, refreshing leaves create a cool, dappled light. The bunches of fruit will hang temptingly through the criss-cross of wooden rafters.

FLOWERS *Choose flowers such as iris and agapanthus that positively like to bake and will not droop if they spend a week without water.*

NECTARINE *Trained fruit trees can be used in a courtyard like wall-hangings in a room. Through the seasons a nectarine will provide a decorative sequence of blossom, foliage and then fruit.*

LAVENDER *Plant one of the taller varieties, such as Lavandula angustifolia, for maximum effect and place it so that you can catch its scent whenever you pass. Cut it back hard after flowering to keep it in good shape.*

SUNFLOWERS *With their golden heads always turned toward the sun, a group of sunflowers puts on a bold show through the railings. When the flowers have finished, dry the heads. The seeds can be eaten raw or roasted.*

POMEGRANATE *This small tree will have clusters of showy scarlet flowers all summer long. Its fruit, ready in autumn, can be used to make a delicious jelly.*

WISTERIA *The variety chosen here has white flowers that help give the courtyard a cool elegance in the heat of the sun.*

FIG *A fan-trained fig tree not only provides melting, sensuous fruit, but also clothes the wall with splendid architectural foliage.*

LEMON TREES *The row of three lemon trees in pots signals the change in levels between the paved area and the semi-circle of gravel.*

BAYS *Two bay trees, with tops trimmed into neat balls, are placed either side of the railings, planted in large terracotta pots. Their clear-cut outlines stand out well among the more complex shapes of other plants in the courtyard.*

PEACH *A fan-trained peach will produce a first-rate crop in a warm, sheltered spot. An apricot would be equally at home in a courtyard such as this.*

FLAGSTONES *Tiny violas, daisies, aromatic thyme and marjoram creep among the large, randomly laid paving stones.*

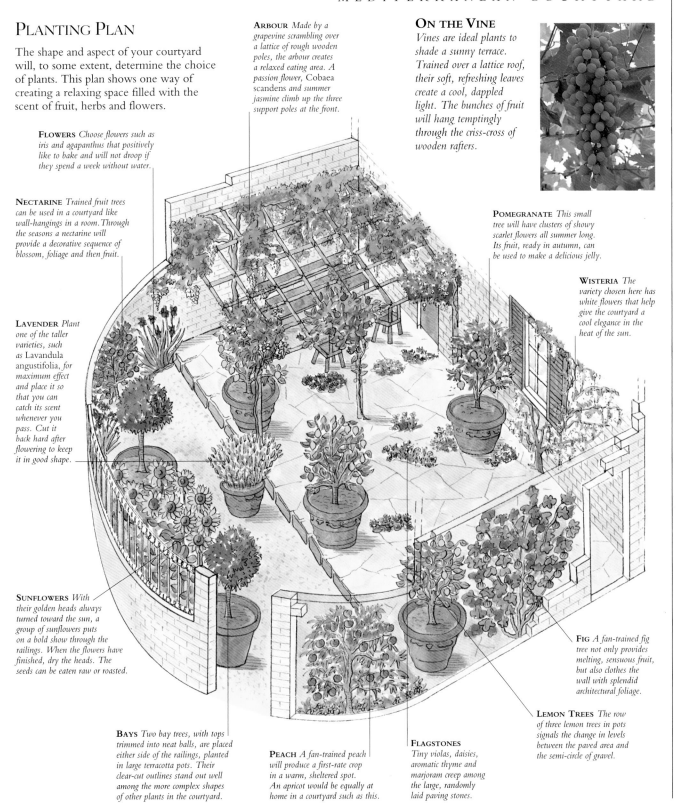

FORMAL HERB GARDEN

HOW MANY OF US when we plant hyssop, the aromatic herb that flowers in midsummer in blue, white and pink, really believe we are going to brew hyssop tea or produce hyssop honey? We just like the idea that one day we might. Growing hyssop reassures us that we have not entirely cut ourselves adrift from a tradition of folk knowledge and thrifty housekeeping. But it is a pretty plant and in the big formal herb garden at Kinoith, in Ireland, herbs grown for their looks, such as hyssop and bergamot, are mixed with culinary herbs such as sage. Massive buttresses of purple-leaved sage prop up a showy cardoon, and nasturtiums cavort at the feet of a monumental stand of lovage.

The low box hedges that edge all the beds emphasize the garden's formal layout and provide solid frames for the tumbling plants inside. Evergreens such as box and sage offer year-round interest and form. Three different kinds of sage (an excellent foliage plant in or out of a herb garden) are used in the plan overleaf, where the emphasis is on herbs that are not just decorative but are most necessary for a keen cook.

MAKING A HERB GARDEN

THE MOST USEFUL HERBS are those needed for cooking: thyme, basil, parsley, sage and their kind. This design for a formal plot is planted with a collection for the kitchen, although if you wanted to create a bolder, more decorative effect, it would be easy to introduce some flowering herbs, such as bright blue hyssop, hazy lavender or pink germander. The beds are edged alternately with tightly curled parsley and chives (left), with mop-headed standard roses marking the corners. In the centre is a clipped bay tree, but it could be a small fountain with a simple jet of water, a statue or an urn tumbling with scented-leaved geraniums. Herbs can be split roughly into two kinds: the Mediterranean aromatics such as thyme, rosemary and marjoram that like hot sun and grow in poor soil, and others such as mint, borage and parsley that need a cooler, richer soil to thrive. If one side of your projected herb patch is much warmer than the other, save it for the Mediterranean sunbathers. Paths in a herb garden need only be wide enough to shuffle along to pluck and weed. Brick, laid on edge, always looks satisfying. Gravel, as suggested in this plan, is simple to use but needs low wooden edgings to keep it off the beds. If the ground is not too sticky, leave the paths as bare beaten earth.

PLANTING PLAN

This mixture of annual herbs – which you can vary from season to season – and more permanent plants to give height and form has been chosen to fill a plot roughly 2.6m (8ft 4in) square. The design, however, can be expanded or shrunk to fill the space available.

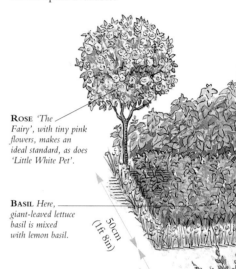

ROSE 'The Fairy', with tiny pink flowers, makes an ideal standard, as does 'Little White Pet'.

BASIL Here, giant-leaved lettuce basil is mixed with lemon basil.

50cm (1ft 8in)

30cm (1ft)

MINTS In this bed, spearmint grows with gingermint, variegated applemint and purplish eau de cologne mint.

1m (3ft)

THE KEY ELEMENTS

SAGE COMPANIONS
The deep velvety leaves of purple sage combine well with amber and yellow. For extra colour, add orange pot marigolds or, as here, grow sage next to the golden pea flowers of dyer's greenweed (Genista tinctoria).

CHIVE EDGINGS
Chives make a neat edging for paths. Cut down the rows in turn so that one will be newly sheared, the second resprouting, the third nearly ready to use, and the fourth at its peak for picking.

MIXED MINTS
Mints have a bad name for putting themselves where they are not wanted. Plant a mixture of plain and variegated types in a bed together, where they can battle it out with each other.

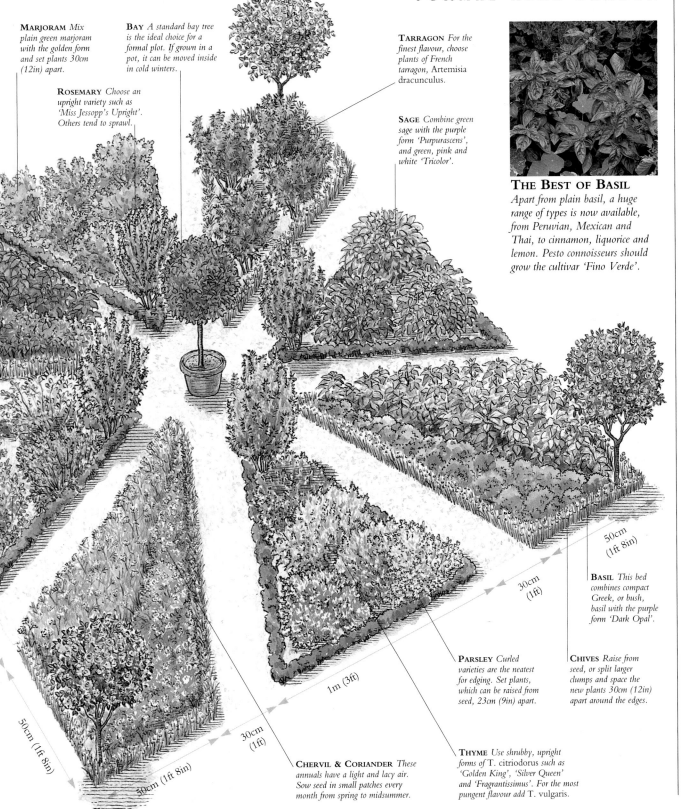

MARJORAM *Mix plain green marjoram with the golden form and set plants 30cm (12in) apart.*

ROSEMARY *Choose an upright variety such as 'Miss Jessopp's Upright'. Others tend to sprawl.*

BAY *A standard bay tree is the ideal choice for a formal plot. If grown in a pot, it can be moved inside in cold winters.*

TARRAGON *For the finest flavour, choose plants of French tarragon, Artemisia dracunculus.*

SAGE *Combine green sage with the purple form 'Purpurascens', and green, pink and white 'Tricolor'.*

THE BEST OF BASIL

Apart from plain basil, a huge range of types is now available, from Peruvian, Mexican and Thai, to cinnamon, liquorice and lemon. Pesto connoisseurs should grow the cultivar 'Fino Verde'.

BASIL *This bed combines compact Greek, or bush, basil with the purple form 'Dark Opal'.*

CHIVES *Raise from seed, or split larger clumps and space the new plants 30cm (12in) apart around the edges.*

PARSLEY *Curled varieties are the neatest for edging. Set plants, which can be raised from seed, 23cm (9in) apart.*

THYME *Use shrubby, upright forms of T. citriodorus such as 'Golden King', 'Silver Queen' and 'Fragrantissimus'. For the most pungent flavour add T. vulgaris.*

CHERVIL & CORIANDER *These annuals have a light and lacy air. Sow seed in small patches every month from spring to midsummer.*

50cm (1ft 8in)

30cm (1ft)

1m (3ft)

30cm (1ft)

50cm (1ft 8in)

50cm (1ft 8in)

50cm (1ft 8in)

2

GROWING
VEGETABLES,
HERBS & FRUIT

THE FOLLOWING PAGES give all the information you need to be able
to grow a wide range of vegetables, herbs and fruit to combine
with flowers in a decorative kitchen garden. Cultivation techniques
include full instructions on choosing the right place for each crop,
advice on sowing, transplanting, thinning and harvesting, as well as
highlighting likely pests and diseases. There are details, too, for
pruning and training fruit. You may already know which types of
vegetables and fruit you want to grow. If you are not sure, you will
find plenty here to inspire you.

VEGETABLES & HERBS

IF ON A MAP OF THE WORLD you drew lines showing how different foods had travelled from their countries of origin, you would end up with a pattern more complex than a spider's web. Before the discovery of the Americas, the vegetable diet in Europe relied heavily on peas and beans. The New World proved a happy hunting ground, as maize and tomatoes as well as potatoes enriched gardens on this side of the Atlantic. Some vegetables travelled in the opposite direction. In the pages ahead you can learn how to grow more than 50 different vegetables and 20 different herbs. Stars highlight the best plants for a decorative kitchen garden.

LEAF & SALAD VEGETABLES

These include some of the lushest vegetables in the kitchen garden: winter cabbages in red and plum, crisp oriental brassicas and elegantly curled kale. Among this group you will find the ingredients for summer salads: cos lettuce, frizzy endive and peppery rocket, as well as a host of other leafy delights such as purslane, watercress and mizuna. Many leaf vegetables are high in vitamins.

FRUITING & FLOWERING VEGETABLES

Warm oranges, yellows and reds characterize the showiest members of this tribe, pumpkins and squash. Along with courgettes, marrows and cucumbers, they belong to the diverse family of cucurbits, originating in South and Central America. Tomatoes belong in this group, too, as does sweet corn. And here you will find the most dramatic vegetables – the artichoke and the cardoon, whose sculpted leaves rise from the ground in fountains of silver-grey.

PODDED VEGETABLES

The obliging pea and bean family produces two types of food, seeds and pods. You eat either or both, depending on when you gather the crop. This is not a large group, but in nutritional terms it is an important one, and the climbing members can be used to great decorative effect.

BULB, STEM & ROOT VEGETABLES

Although this group does not include the most eyecatching vegetables, it contains some kitchen staples: onions, garlic, potatoes and carrots. There are some gourmet treats here, too, such as asparagus, for gardeners to indulge themselves. Leeks and carrots, in particular, can be grown with flowers to create some superb combinations.

HERBS

All the most useful herbs are to be found in this section, divided into annuals, which must be sown fresh each year, and perennials, which will provide years of pleasure.

STAR PLANTS
❀ Especially decorative plants (see also page 200)

KEY TO CULTIVATION CHARTS
🌱 Sow inside ➡ Transplant
🌱 Sow outside ✂ Harvest

LEAF & SALAD VEGETABLES

SHOCK WAVES SPREAD THROUGH the florists' world back in the 1950s when the renowned flower arranger Constance Spry first put cabbage leaves among her delphiniums. But she saw what vegetable gardeners had always known: for texture, form, substance, and diversity, there is nothing like a cabbage leaf. Unless it is a lettuce leaf. These two vegetables provide endless opportunities for the gardener. For rich combinations seek out the black kale, sometimes called 'Chou Palmier', with narrow, upright leaves that are as sumptuously textured as tapestry. Combine it with wobbling heads of allium, purple iris, or deep blue columbines. Plant bronze fennel between rows of red cabbage, and sprinkle cornflowers among the endives.

CRIMPED KALE

The superbly handsome kale 'Chou Palmier', with its dark fronds, grows like a miniature palm tree. The texture, bubbly and finely crimped, is like that of a Savoy cabbage, and in France this kale has long been grown as an ornamental plant.

IN THE PINK

Pinks and purples complement each other in this planting that includes young plants of the cabbage 'Red Drumhead', the frilly rosettes of the lettuce 'Lollo Rossa', and the flowering heads of chives. Curly-leaved parsley and parsnip foliage fill in the spaces.

BRIGHTEST CHARD

Cold weather turns the leaves of ruby chard a rich purple, making a dramatic setting for the bright red midribs. Try to arrange these plants so that light shines through the leaves, and keep them away from other strong tones to enjoy the singing colour of the stems.

OUT OF THE EAST

Pak choi, seen here with young flowering shoots, is one of many oriental vegetables increasingly being grown in Western gardens. Its shiny, rounded leaves, crunchy stems, and its flowerheads, which may be produced in the first year of growth, are all edible.

THE RED AND THE GREEN

Dark loose-leaf lettuce have been allowed to run up to seed, making spires among the chunky shapes of green loose-leaf lettuce. The lettuce patch is surrounded by a thick border of nasturtiums. Here, the variety 'Alaska' has been chosen for its cream and green marbled leaves.

CABBAGES *Brassica oleracea* Capitata Group

CABBAGES MAKE SOME PEOPLE THINK only of clubroot and caterpillars. But once you have grown your own, they start to assume personalities. Where space is limited, the winter kinds are the ones to go for. For the pleasure of looking at them as well as eating them, you need the Savoy varieties, with leaves more intricately puckered than smocking. The outer leaves make a chiselled, swirling skirt around the core. January King types are less tactile but their plum and grey colouring is more complex, while the red and Dutch white varieties provide the neatest outlines in a small plot.

Cultivation

Savoy cabbages are extremely hardy. Planted out in midsummer, they can be harvested from autumn through until the very end of winter. Cultivars of the January King type need to be set out in early summer and are ready by midwinter. Red cabbages and the solid Dutch white types can be planted out in early summer and harvested in early winter. Both store well under cover.

SITE AND SOIL All brassicas are hearty eaters. They like ground that is rich and fertile, well manured in the autumn before planting. The ground need not be deeply dug before planting as they prefer firmness around the roots. Cabbages will not thrive in shade, nor in soils with a pH less than 7.

SOWING Sow seed in shallow drills outside (see page 170), or raise seedlings indoors in trays, prick them out and grow on in individual pots before transplanting (see page 168). You can buy young plants in early summer, but then you will have to accept someone else's choice of varieties. These may not be the most decorative.

THINNING AND TRANSPLANTING Thin seedlings to 7cm (3in) apart. In early summer, lift the plants to set in their final growing positions. Use a trowel so that you cause least disturbance to the rootball, and set them about 60cm (24in) apart, slightly deeper than they were before (see page 171). Water them in well. When the water has drained away, firm the soil around the plants with your feet.

ROUTINE CARE Cabbages sit a long time in the ground working up to their grand winter performance. Extra rations, particularly nitrogen, should be offered during the long growing period.

YIELD AND HARVESTING Size varies enormously with growing conditions. Heads may weigh anything from 500g (1lb) to 1.5kg (3lb) each. Red and white cabbages should be cut by midwinter and stored in a cool, frost-free place. Savoys and January King types are cut as needed.

PESTS AND DISEASES Clubroot is the worst problem (see page 193). Try to prevent it by growing on a different patch each year and do not compost cabbage plants. Liming helps: clubroot is less of a problem on alkaline soils (see page 161). Pigeons may attack the crop in winter unless it is protected by netting. Jump on caterpillars unless you are squeamish. Damage caused by the cabbage root fly is not obvious at first because it happens underground (see opposite and page 191).

RECOMMENDED CULTIVARS

SAVOY
'Ice Queen': *tight, solid heads.*
'Julius': *early, vigorous, bright green heads.*
JANUARY KING
'January King Hardy Late Stock 3': *characteristic red-tinged hearts.*
DUTCH WHITE
'Polinius': *large heads that will stand outside in mild winters.*
RED CABBAGE
'Ruby Ball': *early and compact.*

	SPRING			SUMMER			AUTUMN			WINTER		
	Early	Mid	Late	Early	Mid	Late	Early	Mid	Late	Early	Mid	Late
	⚘	⚘	➡	➡				✀	✀	✀	✀	✀
	⚘	⚘	➡							✀	✀	

☐ Savoy/January King	☐ Red/Dutch white

DUTCH WHITE CABBAGE

❀ **SAVOY CABBAGE**

❀ **RED CABBAGE**

❀ **JANUARY KING CABBAGE**

PREVENTING ROOT FLY

Place a circle of roofing felt or carpet underlay around young plants to deter the cabbage root fly from laying its eggs next to the stem. Its maggots feast on the roots.

ORIENTAL BRASSICAS

PAK CHOI, CHINESE CABBAGE, KOMATSUNA, MIZUNA and oriental mustard are still strangers in the average vegetable garden. Chinese cabbage, in fact, looks rather like a chunky lettuce, while mizuna, a relation of European cabbages and sprouts, has such delicately divided leaves that it is pretty enough to use as a foliage plant in its own right. Mix it in a tub with trailing lobelia or set it among the bright yellow daisy flowers of *Chrysanthemum segetum*. You could plant up a whole container of oriental specialities: white-flowered Chinese chives, mizuna, coriander, a Chinese cabbage and perhaps some chrysanthemum greens. These look like ordinary garden chrysanthemums but it is the leaf that you eat.

Cultivation

The easiest way to grow these brassicas in a decorative kitchen garden is as a cut-and-come-again crop, sometimes called oriental saladini. Sow seed of pak choi (*Brassica rapa* var. *chinensis*), loose-leaf Chinese cabbage (*B. rapa* var. *pekinensis*), mizuna (*B. rapa* var. *nipposinica*) and komatsuna, also known as spinach mustard (*B. rapa* var. *perviridis*), mixed together in roughly equal quantities, and cut at seedling stage. For extra variety, add an ornamental lettuce such as 'Red Salad Bowl' and an oriental mustard (*Brassica juncea*) to give spice to the mix. Late summer and autumn sowings will provide a succession of baby leaves for winter salads. Most oriental brassicas are fast growing and in spring will provide a speedy follow-on from winter crops such as carrots or parsnips.

SITE AND SOIL Oriental brassicas need fertile, moisture-retentive soil and an endless supply of water.

SOWING Cut-and-come-again crops can be sown over a long season from spring until autumn (see pages 170–71). Broadcast the seed over a bed or sow in wide drills. For individual crops, sow seed in drills, little and often, about 1cm (½in) deep, scattering it thinly. Or you can sow groups of 3–4 seeds at 10cm (4in) intervals along the row and then thin to leave the strongest seedling. The earliest sowings do best under a floating mulch (see page 166) to warm the soil. Avoid sowing pak choi or Chinese cabbage too early as they have a tendency to bolt (run up to flower). Low temperatures when seeds are germinating or lack of moisture as the plants are growing are the most likely causes.

THINNING Thin seedlings as necessary (see page 171). Cut-and-come-again crops need little thinning. Leave plenty of space, up to 30cm (12in), between large vegetables such as Chinese cabbage that are growing individually in rows.

ROUTINE CARE Keep plants well watered at all times. This will also encourage fresh growth on cut-and-come-again crops.

YIELD AND HARVESTING In ideal conditions, pak choi may be ready to pick 6 weeks after sowing, komatsuna after 8, Chinese cabbage after 8–10 and mizuna after 10. Oriental mustards take 6–13 weeks. Harvest promptly as these vegetables do not stand long in an ideal state. You can usually start picking cut-and-come-again crops after a month and then take 3 later cuts. Cut above the base of the leaves (see page 63) to ensure the plants resprout.

PESTS AND DISEASES Unfortunately, the cabbage root fly is just as partial to Eastern brassicas as it is to Western ones, so take precautions (see pages 57 and 191).

RECOMMENDED CULTIVARS

There are no cultivars of most of these vegetables but there are big differences in the performance of seed depending on where it was gathered. There is some evidence that seed from plants grown in central and northern China is most likely to succeed in European gardens. The loose-leaf Chinese cabbage **'Santo'** *is a good variety for a cut-and-come-again crop.*

IN THE KITCHEN

The leaves of Chinese cabbage blend well in a raw salad of lettuce, green pepper, celery, mooli radish and tomato. They also make a delicious warm salad, stir-fried and mixed with orange.

HOT CHINESE CABBAGE AND ORANGE SALAD
Serves 4

half a head of Chinese cabbage
2 large oranges
2 tbsp white wine vinegar
4 tbsp olive oil
1 large clove garlic, crushed

1 Slice the cabbage lengthways into several sections and then chop into 2cm (1in) pieces.

2 Peel one of the oranges, cut into quarters lengthways and slice thinly. Squeeze the juice from the other orange and mix with the vinegar.

3 Heat the oil with the garlic in a frying pan. Add the cabbage and keep stirring until it just turns limp.

4 Pour over the vinegar and orange juice and let the mixture bubble for a minute or two. Add the sliced orange and serve immediately.

CULINARY NOTES

⚜ The flavour of most oriental vegetables intensifies as the leaves age. This is particularly pronounced with the mustards. In salads of Chinese greens, use young leaves, both for their texture and subtle taste. Chinese cabbage will keep for up to 2 months in the salad compartment of a refrigerator. Clean well before storing as slugs are extremely partial to it.

⚜ With oriental brassicas, brief, fast cooking in a wok gives the best results. Chinese cooks often blanch vegetables before frying, as this takes the edge off any bitterness.

❀ Pak Choi

Chinese Cabbage

Oriental Mustard

KOMATSUNA

Komatsuna, or spinach mustard, has the flavour of cabbage combined with spinach. It grows well in a range of temperatures and is less inclined to bolt than Chinese cabbage.

❀ MIZUNA

Mizuna greens are wonderfully versatile. They look especially decorative in a potager or lining the edges of paths, and grow well in a range of temperatures from summer heat to winter cold.

BRUSSELS SPROUTS & KALE
Brassica oleracea Gemmifera & Acephala Groups

SPROUTS AND BRUSSELS GO TOGETHER like tea and China. The Belgians discovered the first sprout plant around 1750 and have made sure the rest of the world does not forget it. One sprout plant tends to look much like another, but there is a reddish-green type called 'Rubine' that can be used to decorative effect in the winter garden. Kales are the oldest kind of cabbage, and are sometimes dismissed (unfairly) as cattle fodder. They are bulky, hardy vegetables, bearing the kind of names – 'Ragged Jack' and 'Hungry Gap' – that remind you of the less picturesque side of cottage gardening. Kale does not make a head, as a cabbage does; instead the leaves splay out like a palm tree. The curly kinds can be used as tall foliage plants in a border. Experiment with the handsome 'Russian Red' or the stunningly elegant black variety, 'Chou Palmier'.

BRUSSELS SPROUTS

❀ **KALE**

Cultivation

Kale is a handsome vegetable and adds a dramatic focus to the kitchen garden in winter and early spring but you need a back-up patch where you can bring on young plants before setting them out.

SITE AND SOIL Brussels sprouts do best in medium to heavy soil that is well drained, firm and fertile, but not recently manured. Too much nitrogen makes the buttons "blow" (become very loose and elongated). The pH should be around 6.5. Kale will tolerate poorer soil.

SOWING Sow seed of Brussels sprouts outside in shallow drills in a seedbed (see page 170), just under 1cm (½in) deep. Sow early-maturing varieties in early spring, late-maturing varieties in mid-spring. Kale can be sown in late spring in the same way. Keep seedlings well watered.

TRANSPLANTING Lift young plants with as much soil as possible around the rootballs (see page 171). Plant sprouts out in their final position in early summer, setting them 60cm (24in) apart each way. If you prefer small sprouts, reduce the spacing. Kale plants can be transplanted in midsummer, about 8 weeks after sowing. Plant tall types 75cm (30in) apart each way. Water plants well until established.

ROUTINE CARE Earth up sprouts as they grow (see page 167), to keep them stable.

YIELD AND HARVESTING Expect about 1kg (2lb) of sprouts from a plant and the same weight of shoots or young leaves from kale. Sprouts can be picked from early autumn until midwinter. Start picking from the bottom upwards. Kale can be cropped from late autumn to early spring.

PESTS AND DISEASES The worst problem is clubroot (see page 193). Aphids also have a habit of hiding themselves in the tightly packed sprout buttons (see page 190).

RECOMMENDED CULTIVARS

BRUSSELS SPROUTS
'Noisette': *gourmet sprouts of French breeding.* **'Peer Gynt'**: *reliable, with a long season.* **'Rubine'**: *well-flavoured red sprouts.*
KALE
'Chou Palmier': *elegant, upright, dark leaves.* **'Dwarf Green Curled'**: *wide-spreading, curly leaves.* **'Pentland Brig'**: *masses of succulent shoots in late winter.* **'Russian Red'**: *purple leaves with red ribs.*

SPRING			SUMMER			AUTUMN			WINTER		
Early	Mid	Late	Early	Mid	Late	Early	Mid	Late	Early	Mid	Late
♣	♣		➡			✣	✣	✣	✣	✣	
	♣		➡				✣	✣	✣	✣	✣
✣											

☐ Brussels sprouts	☐ Kale

SPINACH *Spinacia oleracea*

SPINACH HAS TWO USEFUL ATTRIBUTES. It will grow in light shade if the ground is moist, and it grows very fast. True spinach is an annual and the one aim of an annual is to set seed and perpetuate itself. In hot, dry conditions, this works against the spinach fancier. Instead of pausing to produce a feast of leaves, the plant races on up to maturity, leaving only an unusable crop of creamish-green seed.

Cultivation

Little and often is the best way to sow spinach. It is most likely to succeed in rich, damp soil, in cool conditions. Feast on it in spring and autumn and do not expect too much from the crops of high summer. On hot, dry soils, New Zealand spinach (a different, non-hardy species, with smaller, fleshy leaves) is more likely to succeed. These are the greens that the intrepid 18th-century voyager Captain Cook collected by the boatload in New Zealand to stop his sailors getting scurvy.

SITE AND SOIL Spinach is a great gobbler of nitrogen. Ground can scarcely be too rich for it. It tolerates light shade, but not dryness. New Zealand spinach is more tolerant of dry, poor conditions.

SOWING For a summer crop, sow seed every 2–3 weeks from early to late spring, setting it not more than 1.5cm (¾in) deep in rows 30cm (12in) apart. For a winter crop, sow late summer to early autumn. Sow seed of New Zealand spinach 1cm (½in) deep in drills 38cm (15in) apart.

THINNING Thin summer spinach to 15cm (6in) between plants, and winter crops to 23cm (9in). Thin New Zealand spinach seedlings to 20cm (8in) apart.

ROUTINE CARE Spinach must never be short of water and on hungry soils extra feeding is also beneficial. In exposed areas, winter crops may need cloches.

YIELD AND HARVESTING Expect about 2.5–5kg (5–10lb) from a 3m (10ft) row.

SPINACH

NEW ZEALAND SPINACH

PESTS AND DISEASES Downy mildew is the most prevalent disease (see page 193). Thin plants to allow good air circulation.

RECOMMENDED CULTIVARS

‘Secundo’: *quick-growing, resistant to mildew.*
‘Sigmaleaf’: *good resistance to bolting.*
New Zealand: *named cultivars not available.*

SPRING			SUMMER			AUTUMN			WINTER		
Early	Mid	Late	Early	Mid	Late	Early	Mid	Late	Early	Mid	Late
♧	♧	♧		♧	♧						
	✂	✂				✂	✂		✂		
		♧	♧	♧✂	✂	✂					

☐ Spinach		☐ New Zealand spinach	

IN THE KITCHEN

Spinach can be used in many different ways: in a soufflé, served as a simple purée, or combined with spices as a tangy stuffing. This recipe is excellent inside a boned-and-rolled shoulder of lamb. You can also pile it into an earthenware dish and cook it in the oven alongside a roast chicken.

ROAST LAMB WITH SPINACH FORCEMEAT
Serves 4–6

½ large, mild onion, finely chopped
30g (1oz) butter
250g (8oz) spinach, washed
250g (8oz) good sausagemeat
1 egg, beaten
1 tbsp finely chopped parsley
salt and black pepper
nutmeg and mace, to taste
1.75–2kg (3½–4lb) shoulder of lamb (boned weight)

1 Preheat the oven to 180°C/350°F/gas mark 4. Sauté the onion gently in the butter until it has become soft and transparent.

2 In a clean pan, cook the spinach until limp (it will cook in the moisture remaining on the leaves after washing), then chop finely.

3 Combine the onion and spinach with the sausagemeat, egg, parsley, seasoning and spices in a large bowl and mix well. Use this mixture to stuff the boned shoulder of lamb, spreading the stuffing over the flattened-out joint. Roll it up like a Swiss roll and secure firmly with skewers or string.

4 Weigh the stuffed joint and roast it in the oven, allowing 20–25 minutes for each 0.5kg (1lb), plus a final 20–25 minutes. Let the joint stand for 10 minutes before carving.

LETTUCE *Lactuca sativa*

OF ALL DECORATIVE VEGETABLES, lettuce is the most versatile, because it presents itself in so many different guises and adapts itself to so many uses in the garden. The ferny, frilly, loose-leaf kinds can be used as foliage plants between bright groups of annual flowers or to add bulk to billowing, daisy-covered argyranthemums in a windowbox. You can plant a variety such as 'Red Salad Bowl' to line paths or edge a raised bed, or a small butterhead like 'Tom Thumb', all heart, to fill beds in a modest parterre. Crisp, crunchy 'Windermere' will frame tomatoes in a grow bag.

Cultivation

There are four types of lettuce to choose from: soft butterheads, upright cos, dense crispheads, and long-lasting loose-leaf varieties. Differences between them have as much to do with texture as with taste and it is useful to grow several kinds, bearing in mind that cos types usually take longer to mature than butterheads, and loose-leaf varieties can be cut at an earlier age. Seed keeps from one year to the next, so it is not too expensive to experiment.

SITE AND SOIL Lettuce grows best on soil that is light and fertile, but retains moisture. It does not mind partial shade.

SOWING In theory, if you sow seed every fortnight from spring until midsummer, you should have a non-stop supply until autumn. Autumn and winter crops require a cold frame or greenhouse. In practice, lettuce either bolts or sulks and you end up with the usual chaos of feast or famine. Unpredictable weather is the most frequent cause of unpredictable crops. In hot weather, germination is erratic; in drought, growth is sluggish. Sow seed little and often, directly outside (see page 170), 1cm (½in) deep, in rows 15cm (6in) apart for small cultivars like 'Little Gem', 30cm (12in) apart for large types like 'Lollo Rossa'.

THINNING Thin small cultivars to 15cm (6in) apart and large types to 30cm (12in) apart. Make the first thinning about a month after sowing when seedlings are 5cm (2in) tall (see page 171). Thinnings transplant well at the start of the season. Once it turns hot and dry, it is hard to persuade them to settle.

ROUTINE CARE Lettuce needs plenty of water while growing, but not too much feeding: scientific tests have shown that excess nitrogen makes it bitter. Water in the morning rather than the evening, when leaves dry off quickly and are less prone to attacks of downy mildew.

YIELD AND HARVESTING A 3m (10ft) row gives roughly 10–20 lettuce. Harvest loose-leaf types a few leaves at a time.

PESTS AND DISEASES Slugs, aphids, cutworms, downy mildew and grey mould can all be problems (see pages 190–93).

RECOMMENDED CULTIVARS

BUTTERHEAD
'All the Year Round': *very long season.*
'Tom Thumb': *small but large hearted.*
COS
'English Cos': *classic long, stiff leaves with a particularly good flavour.* **'Little Gem'**: *small semi-cos, fast-growing, the best of its kind.*
CRISPHEAD
'Iceberg': *crunchy texture and long-lasting.*
'Windermere': *medium heads, fine quality.*
LOOSE-LEAF
'Lollo Rossa': *crisp, frilly, red-tinged leaves.*
'Red Salad Bowl': *will last a long time if the leaves are picked regularly.*

	SPRING			SUMMER			AUTUMN			WINTER		
	Early	Mid	Late	Early	Mid	Late	Early	Mid	Late	Early	Mid	Late
							🥬	🥬	🥬	🥬	🥬	
										✂	✂	✂
	✂	✂	✂									
											🪴	🪴
	🥬	🥬	🥬	🥬	🥬							
	➡	➡	✂	✂	✂	✂	✂	✂	✂			
	☐ Greenhouse or cold frame					☐ Outdoor or cloche						

IN THE KITCHEN

John Parkinson, the 17th-century grand-daddy of all garden writers, recommended lettuce for "Monkes, Nunnes and the like of people . . . to keep them chase". Poor Nunnes: lettuce on its own is not much of a diet. Like pastry, it is a background for livelier ingredients such as walnut oil, olives, hard-boiled eggs and anchovies or bacon and blue cheese.

LETTUCE, BACON AND BLUE CHEESE SALAD
Serves 4

250g (8oz) smoked bacon
1 crisphead lettuce (such as 'Iceberg')
1 bunch watercress
500g (1lb) small tomatoes
2 avocados
4 tbsp lemon juice
250g (8oz) Gorgonzola cheese, finely sliced
4 tbsp olive oil
2 tbsp red wine vinegar
1 tsp grainy mustard
2 tbsp clear honey

1 Grill the bacon until it is crisp and chop it finely.
2 Wash the lettuce and watercress and gently pat dry the leaves. Halve the tomatoes and mix with the bacon, lettuce and watercress.
3 Peel and slice the avocados and dress them with lemon juice to prevent discoloration. Add them to the salad with the cheese.
4 Make a dressing by combining the remaining ingredients. Pour over the salad just before serving.

CULINARY NOTES

❧ Use the small, inner leaves of cos lettuce as crunchy scoops for dips.
❧ Braise lettuce leaves with fresh young peas, some chopped onion, a knob of butter and a little water for the French classic *petits pois à l'étuvée*.

❀ SEMI-COS
LETTUCE
'Little Gem'

BUTTERHEAD
LETTUCE
'All the Year
Round'

COS
LETTUCE
'English Cos'

❀ LOOSE-LEAF
LETTUCE
'Lollo Rossa'

❀ CRISPHEAD
LETTUCE
'Iceberg'

CUT-AND-COME-AGAIN
*This method of growing salad
leaves is ideal for a small garden.
Choose loose-leaf varieties and
start cropping when the plants are
7–15cm (3–6in) high, cutting
them just above the lowest leaves.
They will then resprout from the
remaining 3cm (1½in) of stem.*

OTHER SALAD LEAVES

WATERCRESS, PURSLANE, CORN SALAD, AND MUSTARD AND CRESS are all useful extras to add a tang to a sandwich or salad bowl. In the garden, you can grow them as catch crops between slower-growing vegetables. As the seeds germinate fast – mustard and cress can be cut within two weeks of sowing – you can use them to make instant edgings or to "paint" patterns in a bed. Mark out a diamond trellis in the earth and sow along the lines of the pattern. Children like seeing their initials rise magically from the ground. The sharp-tasting, fleshy leaves of summer purslane are best used as a seedling cut-and-come-again crop. It needs a warm spot to grow well. Corn salad, or lamb's lettuce, is very hardy and is best eaten as a winter substitute for lettuce. Watercress, too, is at its best in winter and can be grown without running water, although it is not quite as succulent.

WATERCRESS

Cultivation

However smoothly you try to plan the production of these salad crops, sowings either catch up with each other or else dawdle like recalcitrant runners to widen the gap between themselves and the crop in front. Sow little but often.

SITE AND SOIL You would not want to give over your best ground to these crops. They must make do with what they are given. Watercress, however, will only succeed in a moist, shady bed and is happiest of all growing in a stream.

SOWING Watercress (*Rorippa nasturtium-aquaticum*) is best grown from rooted cuttings rather than seed (stems readily produce roots in a jar of water). Take out a narrow trench, 5cm (2in) deep, with a hoe and fill it with water until really soggy. Dribble sand along it about 2cm (1in) deep and then, using a dibber, make small holes about 15cm (6in) apart. Drop in the cuttings and keep well watered. Summer purslane (*Portulaca oleracea*) can be sown outdoors in early summer. Broadcast seed (see page 171) for a cut-and-come-again crop. Sow corn salad (*Valerianella locusta*) in late spring for a summer crop or in late summer for leaves to cut in winter. Sow seed thinly, just under 1cm (½in) deep, in a drill if you want to transplant seedlings (see pages 170–71). Broadcast seed over a wide drill or bed for a cut-and-come-again crop. Corn salad is slow to resprout, so is often better transplanted to grow to maturity. Set out young plants

10cm (4in) apart, in rows 30cm (12in) apart. Sow small quantities of mustard and cress (*Sinapis alba* and *Lepidium sativum*) at weekly intervals for a continuous supply. It grows well on wads of damp newspaper, paper tissues or towels on a windowsill. You can sow outside in drills (see page 170), barely covering the seed with soil. Rape seed (*Brassica napus*) is often substituted for true mustard. If growing this crop inside, wait 3 days, then sprinkle the mustard or rape seed on top of the cress so that they germinate together.

THINNING Thin corn salad to about 10cm (4in) apart. Summer purslane will not need thinning if harvested as seedlings, nor will mustard and cress, nor watercress if planted at the spacing given above.

ROUTINE CARE Watering and weeding are all that is required.

YIELD AND HARVESTING Yield depends on the time of year and the stage at which you harvest. You can gather individual leaves from watercress, summer purslane and corn salad or cut down the whole plant. Snip mustard and cress with scissors.

PESTS AND DISEASES These crops are generally free of trouble.

There are no cultivars to recommend as none has been selected.

SUMMER PURSLANE

CORN SALAD

MUSTARD   **CRESS**

CHARD & LEAF BEET
Beta vulgaris Cicla Group

RED-STEMMED CHARD HAS A DRAMATIC BEAUTY in the vegetable garden, but it needs to be grown carefully. If you can nurse it through the early stages without upsetting it, it will develop into a superb plant. Its glowing red stems are topped by luxuriant foliage, either green or, in the variety 'Burgundy Chard', deep purplish-ruby. The leaf stalks are broad and meaty and you eat these and the leaves separately. Chard is used to magnificent effect in the vast potager at Villandry in France, where the ruby stems are set off against deep red roses and blue spikes of *Salvia superba*. Leaf beet, or perpetual spinach as it is sometimes called, has a much smaller midrib. It is often used as a substitute for true spinach, a much trickier crop to grow, but the flavour is not nearly so fine.

❀ **RED-STEMMED CHARD**

WHITE-STEMMED CHARD

LEAF BEET

Cultivation

Chard is a biennial and can usually be cropped over a long period before running to seed in its second season. Once through the ticklish early stages, it will stand quite well in drought conditions, but if checked in the first two or three months of its life, it will forget all about being a biennial and run straight up to seed. Chard enthusiasts say that the steamed stalks, especially of white-stemmed varieties, are as good as asparagus, but the taste is more watery, less concentrated. Leaf beet, often called perpetual spinach or spinach beet, is also biennial and fairly tolerant of drought. This makes it a useful, if coarse-flavoured, alternative to true spinach, especially on ground that does not easily retain moisture.

SITE AND SOIL Chard and leaf beet like fertile soil, rich in nitrogen. Add plenty of farmyard manure or compost. If it can be arranged, they make good follow-on crops after peas or beans in a crop rotation.

SOWING Sow chard and leaf beet from late spring to midsummer, setting the seed no deeper than 1.5cm (¾in) in rows that are 38–45cm (15–18in) apart (see page 170). The plants should then crop through the winter until late spring of the following year when they will start to run to seed. Both chard and leaf beet will run to seed in the same year if they are sown too early.

THINNING These grow into fairly large plants, so allow room for them to develop.

Thin seedlings to at least 30cm (12in) apart in the row (see page 171).

ROUTINE CARE The early stages are by far the most critical, especially for chard. Keep the young plants growing as smoothly as possible by providing sufficient water and plenty of liquid feeds. Mulch to conserve moisture.

YIELD AND HARVESTING Expect about 3.5kg (7lb) from a 3m (10ft) row. Pull, rather than cut, the stems as required. Take care not to take too many leaves from any one plant at a time, especially in the middle of winter, or the plant may not be able to recover.

PESTS AND DISEASES These are generally easily grown, trouble-free crops.

RECOMMENDED CULTIVARS

CHARD
'Burgundy Chard': *purplish-red stems.*
'Feurio': *red stems, good resistance to bolting.*
'Rhubarb Chard': *bright scarlet ribs.*
'Italian': *white stems, dark green foliage.*
LEAF BEET
Also sometimes listed in catalogues as perpetual spinach or spinach beet. Named cultivars are not generally available.

SPRING			SUMMER			AUTUMN			WINTER		
Early	Mid	Late	Early	Mid	Late	Early	Mid	Late	Early	Mid	Late
				⚘	⚘	✂	✂	✂	✂	✂	✂
✂	✂	✂									

CHICORY & ENDIVE
Cichorium intybus & C. endivia

THESE ARE DESIGNER VEGETABLES *PAR EXCELLENCE*, and you could fill a whole potager with decorative combinations of this one group, contrasting the smooth leaves of chicory with a shaggy endive, or playing with the marbled colours of the red chicories, often called radicchio. The names are muddling. In France, curly endive is called *chicorée frisée* and Belgian chicory, which looks like a small cream bomb, is called endive. In growing terms, the major difference is that endive is an annual. Chicory is not and, in its second year, produces tall sheaves of attractive blue flowers.

Cultivation

To blanch or not to blanch, that is the question. Blanching alleviates the bitterness characteristic of both these crops. With Belgian chicory it is essential. With the curly types of endive you can experiment. The French use chic little caps, like berets, to blanch the hearts. An upturned plate does the same thing, but less stylishly.

SITE AND SOIL Both crops need fertile, well-drained soil, preferably in full sun.

SOWING Sow seed of Belgian/blanched chicory in early to midsummer, dribbling the seed as thinly as possible, 1cm (½in) deep, in rows 30cm (12in) apart. Seed of unblanched (sugar loaf) types should be sown at the same depth and spacing. Sow in midsummer or plants may run to seed. Red chicory/radicchio can be sown from mid-spring to midsummer, using early or late-maturing cultivars. Sow 1cm (½in) deep in rows 25–30cm (10–12in) apart. Sow curly endive from late spring to mid-summer (earlier sowings often run to seed). You can also sow in late summer under glass for a winter crop. Sow 1cm (½in) deep in rows 25–38cm (10–15in) apart.

THINNING Thin Belgian chicory to 23cm (9in) apart and unblanched and red chicory/radicchio to 25–30cm (10–12in) apart. This spacing will also suit most endives, but the very large types need to be 30–38cm (12–15in) apart.

ROUTINE CARE Weed and water well.

FORCING AND BLANCHING Belgian chicory can be forced and blanched outdoors (see page 167) but it is more usually done inside where it gives quicker results. Lift the roots in early winter, discarding any very thin ones. Trim leaves 2cm (1in) above the neck and pack the roots flat in a box of sand, taking them out to force a few at a time. Cut off sideshoots and shorten the main roots to 15cm (6in). Plant them upright in moist soil, fitting 3–6 in a 23cm (9in) pot (see page 167). Invert another pot over the first and store. In an airing cupboard, chicons (the blanched heads) develop in about 3 weeks. In a cool cellar – not below 10°C (50°F) – forcing will take longer. See opposite for blanching curly endive.

YIELD AND HARVESTING Expect about 3kg (6lb) of Belgian chicory, or 10–15 heads of unblanched chicory or endive from a 3m (10ft) row. Cut forced chicons when they are 12–15cm (5–6in) long. Pick a few leaves at a time from unblanched chicory and endive. If you cut whole heads, leave 2cm (1in) or so of the neck, which will then resprout.

PESTS AND DISEASES Chicory and endive are robust and usually trouble-free.

RECOMMENDED CULTIVARS

BELGIAN/BLANCHED CHICORY
'Witloof': *traditional cultivar for forcing.*
UNBLANCHED CHICORY
'Sugar Loaf'/'Pain de Sucre': *large and fast-growing.***'Bianca di Milano'**: *can be used as a cut-and-come-again crop.*
RED CHICORY/RADICCHIO
'Alouette'/'Chioggia': *early, with red and white leaves.***'Palla Rossa'**: *neat, wine-red leaves for winter salads.***'Variegata di Castelfranco'**: *wonderfully decorative old variety, with green, red and white leaves.*
CURLY ENDIVE
'Wallonne': *traditional, hardy, French curled variety with a large, tightly packed head.*

✿ RED CHICORY/RADICCHIO

BELGIAN/BLANCHED CHICORY

	SPRING			SUMMER			AUTUMN			WINTER		
	Early	Mid	Late	Early	Mid	Late	Early	Mid	Late	Early	Mid	Late
Belgian/blanched chicory				sow	sow					harvest	harvest	harvest
Unblanched chicory	harvest											
Unblanched chicory					sow		harvest	harvest	harvest	harvest		
Red chicory/radicchio	sow	sow	sow	sow								
Red chicory/radicchio							harvest	harvest	harvest	harvest	harvest	
Curly endive	sow	sow	sow	sow (pot)								
Curly endive							harvest	harvest	harvest	harvest	harvest	harvest

☐ Belgian/blanched chicory		☐ Red chicory/radicchio
☐ Unblanched chicory		☐ Curly endive

BLANCHING CURLY ENDIVE
*Blanch endive, when nearly fully grown,
with a plate for about 10 days to whiten the
centre. The leaves must be dry or rot may set
in. Cover with a cloche to keep off any rain.*

❀ **CURLY ENDIVE**

**UNBLANCHED/
SUGAR LOAF
CHICORY**

ROCKET *Eruca vesicaria*

ROCKET (OR ROQUETTE IF YOU ARE BEING POSH), grown in pots or
windowboxes, makes an ideal salad crop in city gardens. It runs to seed
quickly in hot weather and is best sown frequently in small quantities. The
deeply lobed leaves should be picked while still very young, and have a
piquant, spicy taste that quickly wakes up a bland gathering of lettuce.

ROCKET

Cultivation

Rocket grows fast so you will need several
patches growing at once: one to cut, one
to cultivate, and one to come on behind.
SITE AND SOIL No special preferences.
SOWING Rocket is a hardy annual. It can
withstand a mild winter and will germinate
at low temperatures. Broadcast seed from
early spring to late summer (see page 171).

ROUTINE CARE Keep well weeded.
YIELD AND HARVESTING Pick leaves
regularly, harvesting a few at a time.
Alternatively, cut an entire plant about
3cm (1½in) above the soil, leaving
the neck to sprout new leaves.
PESTS AND DISEASES Flea beetle may
attack seedlings (see page 191).

There are no recommended cultivars.

FRUITING & FLOWERING VEGETABLES

CAULIFLOWERS AND BROCCOLI APART, this group of plants hates frost. In cold areas, they cannot go out until early summer, but once planted they grow rapidly and peak in a rich harvest of golds, greens and oranges in autumn. Courgettes, marrows, pumpkins and squash can be used to great effect trailing over the ground between upright blocks of sweet corn or securely tied cordon tomatoes. In this respect, they are natural companions, one needing vertical space, the other, horizontal. Squash can be striped, spotted, shiny pewter-grey or as vivid as a setting sun. This family alone could make a splendidly decorative summer bed.

PUMPKIN HARVEST

Each large enough to serve as Cinderella's coach, these pumpkins are being cured in the sun before they are stored. Enormous cultivars such as these 'Atlantic Giant' types are showy, but cooks may find the smaller types more useful in the kitchen.

PLANT SCULPTURE

A whole avenue of globe artichokes lines this narrow border. Spectacular plants at their peak, with sculpted, arching foliage, they leave little room for less robust crops to grow around them. In a smaller space, use a single plant as a centrepiece for a potager or a herb garden.

GLOSSY AUBERGINE

Few plants can boast of fruit so glossily polished as the aubergine. In cool areas it succeeds best in a greenhouse border. In warm areas, you can grow aubergines in containers. Group them with pots of chillies and trailing cascades of cherry tomatoes.

FLOWERING SQUASH

The trailing growths of pumpkins and squash can easily be trained over arches or supports like this wigwam of bamboo canes. Use cultivars with smallish fruit. The extraordinary shapes and colours of many of the squash will make a spectacular end to the season.

CREAM OF THE CAULIFLOWERS

The smooth curds of unblemished cauliflower have the strange texture of an underwater sponge, the heart protected by great, contrasting leaves of green. But cauliflower is not an easy crop to grow well and, like many other brassicas, needs a long growing period before it comes to fruition.

CAULIFLOWERS
Brassica oleracea Botrytis Group

IF YOU CAN GROW A GOOD CAULIFLOWER you can award yourself maximum merit stars. They are not easy vegetables to bring to crisp perfection, and will produce only small, misshapen heads if their growth is checked in any way. Cauliflowers are generally creamy white, the heads surrounded by a crisp green frill of leaves, but there are also lime-green and purple varieties. With a careful choice of cultivars, you could be harvesting cauliflowers during most months of the year, but then you would tie up a great deal of ground for long periods. In a small garden, fast-maturing mini-cauliflowers are probably the most useful.

CREAM CAULIFLOWER

Cultivation

Cauliflower cultivars have been bred to be ready for harvesting at different times of year but some, such as the spring varieties, take almost 12 months to reach maturity. Late summer and autumn cauliflowers are better suited to most gardens. 'Dok Elgon', sown in early spring for harvesting at the end of summer, is a safe choice. Mini-cauliflowers are the most useful for filling small beds in a potager.

SITE AND SOIL Cauliflowers prefer a more alkaline soil than most of the other members of the brassica family. Acid soils, even when they are limed, may not produce worthwhile crops. Cauliflowers must have soil that is deeply dug and fertile, with sufficient moisture to enable them to grow smoothly and productively.

SOWING Sow seed thinly in drills in a seedbed outside, 1cm (½in) deep (see page 170). Sow late summer varieties in early or mid-spring and autumn cauliflowers in late spring.

TRANSPLANTING After 6–8 weeks cauliflowers should be transplanted to their final growing positions (see page 171). Water the seedlings well beforehand and keep as much earth as possible around the roots. Allow at least 60cm (24in) between plants in the row and space the rows 60cm (24in) apart. Mini-cauliflowers can be grown much closer. Plant them about 15cm (6in) apart each way.

ROUTINE CARE Water frequently throughout the growing season and keep well weeded. Mulch to conserve moisture in the soil.

YIELD AND HARVESTING You will get about 6 cauliflowers from a 3m (10ft) row, but the size of each may vary greatly. Cut while the heads are still firm before the florets start to grow away from the core.

PESTS AND DISEASES As with cabbages, cabbage root fly and clubroot are the worst problem (see pages 57, 191 and 193). If necessary, protect from pigeons by putting netting over the crop and pick off caterpillars.

RECOMMENDED CULTIVARS

SUMMER
'Alpha 5': *sow mid-spring for a late summer crop.* **'Aubade'**: *solid, smooth heads, excellent flavour.* **'Dok Elgon'**: *well-packed, round heads; ready in autumn if sown late spring.*

AUTUMN
'Limelight': *bright green heads, easy to grow.* **'Plana'**: *strong-growing with heavy, deep heads.* **'Rosalind'**: *deep purple, but turns green when cooked, fairly fast-maturing.*

MINI-CAULIFLOWERS
'Bambi': *compact habit, short, upright foliage.* **'Garant'**: *10cm (4in) heads after 3 months' growing.* **'Predominant'**: *takes slightly longer to mature than 'Garant'.*

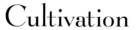

GREEN CAULIFLOWER

SPRING			SUMMER			AUTUMN			WINTER		
Early	Mid	Late	Early	Mid	Late	Early	Mid	Late	Early	Mid	Late
♧	♧	♧									
			➡	➡	➡	✂	✂	✂	✂		

CALABRESE & BROCCOLI
Brassica oleracea Italica Group

THE COLOURS OF CALABRESE AND BROCCOLI are similar to those of the cauliflower family: lime green, white and purple. Calabrese is a summer vegetable with one heavy, central head. The prettiest are the 'Romanesco' types. The sprouting broccolis have masses of small florets, produced over a long season from late winter, but they need to spend nearly a year in the ground which, in a small garden, may make them difficult to accommodate. The names are Italian, but it is likely that these vegetables arrived from the eastern Mediterranean during the 17th century. Philip Miller, who wrote one of the first gardening dictionaries in England in 1724, called broccoli "Italian asparagus"; if you eat the first of the crop with some hollandaise sauce on the side, it is hard to decide which is the more ambrosial.

CALABRESE

SPROUTING BROCCOLI

Cultivation

In character the two plants are very different. Calabrese goes in for one big extrovert gesture, while sprouting broccoli twitters into life with a shower of possibilities but has the greater staying power. Eventually, by late spring, its sprigs will only be matchstick-sized. When its season starts, however, there is little else to beat it in the vegetable garden.

SITE AND SOIL Calabrese will cope with less luscious soil than cauliflowers, although the best crops come from well-dug, well-fed ground. Both thrive in warm, well-drained sites.

SOWING Sow small quantities of calabrese in succession from early spring to midsummer. Sow 2 or 3 seeds at "stations" 15cm (6in) apart to avoid the need for transplanting, which encourages them to run to seed. Keep the rows 30cm (12in) apart and sow seed 1cm (½in) deep (see page 170). Sow broccoli thinly in drills, at the same depth, in mid-spring.

THINNING AND TRANSPLANTING Thin calabrese seedlings to leave one strong plant at each station (see page 171). Transplant broccoli from early to midsummer (see page 171), setting the plants at least 60cm (24in) apart in rows that are also 60cm (24in) apart.

ROUTINE CARE Make sure that plants are never short of water. Broccoli may need earthing up (see page 167) as it develops.

YIELD AND HARVESTING Expect 3–4kg (6–8lb) from a 3m (10ft) row. Calabrese is ready from summer to autumn, broccoli from late winter to spring.

PESTS AND DISEASES As with cabbages, these plants may suffer from cabbage root fly and clubroot (see pages 57, 191 and 193). Green caterpillars are well camouflaged on calabrese. Soak heads in salt water before cooking. Net broccoli to protect it from winter attack by pigeons.

RECOMMENDED CULTIVARS

CALABRESE
'Shogun': *large, blue-green heads on a plant that is tolerant of a wide range of soils.*
'Romanesco': *handsome, lime-green heads.*
BROCCOLI
'Early Purple Sprouting': *the hardiest type, producing a succession of tender shoots.*
'Early White Sprouting': *the white equivalent, but less prolific.*

SPRING			SUMMER			AUTUMN			WINTER		
Early	Mid	Late	Early	Mid	Late	Early	Mid	Late	Early	Mid	Late
♣	♣	♣	♣	♣							
			✂	✂	✂	✂	✂				
	♣		➡	➡							✂
✂	✂										

☐ Calabrese	☐ Broccoli

DECORATIVE CALABRESE
With its cone-shaped clusters of tiny flowers grouped in a geometric dome, 'Romanesco' is the most striking of all the calabrese varieties. Harvest it from summer to early autumn.

COURGETTES & MARROWS
Cucurbita pepo

COURGETTES ARE ZUCCHINI under a different name and they have the frightening capacity to metamorphose into marrows if you go on holiday at the wrong time. Marrows have heroic status among gardeners who are also showmen – there is always a class for the heaviest marrow at a British horticultural show. But in the kitchen garden (and even more so in the kitchen) there is little to recommend them, unless you want to camouflage a chainlink fence or some other unsightly boundary. Courgettes are best grown from seed of hybrid bush cultivars and are easier to manage in a confined space. The golden flowers glow richly among the sober foliage, and yellow-fruited varieties make an even greater impact.

Cultivation

Courgettes and marrows are thirsty beasts, so any device you can think of to conserve water will be advantageous. The traditional method is to build a shallow, circular wall of earth about 60cm (24in) in diameter around each plant. When you water, the water stays where you want it. Mulching is also very beneficial: it suppresses weeds as well as conserving moisture.

SITE AND SOIL Rich, moisture-retentive soil will give the best results. Plants can cope with partial shade if necessary.

SOWING Seed will not germinate at temperatures lower than 13°C (56°F). Either sow inside (see page 168), one seed to a 7cm (3in) pot, and grow on in the pot until late spring/early summer. After hardening off, plants can be set outside. Or be patient and sow directly outside in late spring or early summer (see page 170), setting the seed 2cm (1in) deep and 1–1.2m (3–4ft) apart each way. Set upside-down jam jars over the seeds to protect them from mice and to act as mini-greenhouses.

TRANSPLANTING If you have sown seed inside, set the plants out when they have 3 or 4 proper leaves, and danger of frost has passed (see page 169). Leave room for the plants to develop. Bush courgettes will need 1–1.2m (3–4ft) each way, trailing marrows should have slightly more.

ROUTINE CARE Courgettes and marrows must be fed and well watered. There are two critical periods: when the plants are first set out, and when they are flowering and forming fruit. Once they have become established, their huge leaves will smother any weeds. They will also smother other crops. Do not put less competitive plants, like carrots, too close.

YIELD AND HARVESTING Expect about 4 marrows and four times as many courgettes from each plant. If you want a monster marrow, pick off all fruit except one. Courgettes need to be picked regularly to keep the plants cropping.

PESTS AND DISEASES If fruit wither rather than develop, attend more carefully to watering and feeding. The plants will soon respond. Slugs may eat young plants. Cucumber mosaic virus can mottle the foliage but you will have to live with it as there is no cure (see page 194).

RECOMMENDED CULTIVARS

COURGETTES
'Ambassador': *dark green courgettes with glossy skin.*
'Brimmer': *succulent and well flavoured.*
'De Nice à Fruit Rond': *pale green, round fruit, very good flavour.*
'Gold Rush': *yellow fruit, not as heavy a cropper as green types but beautifully decorative.*

MARROWS
'Long Green Trailing': *large, dark green fruit with paler stripes.*

SPRING			SUMMER			AUTUMN			WINTER		
Early	Mid	Late	Early	Mid	Late	Early	Mid	Late	Early	Mid	Late
🌱	🌱	🌱									
		➡	➡	✄	✄	✄	✄				

IN THE KITCHEN

Ratatouille is one of the classics of the kitchen and, as with all classic dishes, there are many variations. This is my own favourite.

RATATOUILLE
Serves 4

1 large aubergine, cubed
salt
3 tbsp olive oil
2 onions, sliced
2 cloves garlic, crushed
500g (1lb) tomatoes, skinned and quartered
3 courgettes, chopped
1 green pepper, deseeded and chopped
2 tbsp mixed fresh herbs (preferably including thyme and basil), finely chopped
2 tbsp tomato purée
salt and black pepper

1 Sprinkle the aubergine with salt in a colander and leave for 30 minutes so that the bitter juices drain away. Rinse and pat dry.

2 Heat the olive oil in a large pan and cook the onion and garlic until slightly coloured. Add the aubergine to the onion mixture, cooking it gently for 5 minutes.

3 Add the tomatoes, courgettes, pepper and herbs, and cook for 15 minutes, stirring occasionally. Stir in the tomato purée, let it heat through and check the seasoning.

CULINARY NOTES

❧ For the most intense flavour, pick courgettes when they are still small. Slice them lengthways and chargrill them.

❧ The flowers have little taste, but you can pick them just as they are fully open and use them as tiny packages to stuff with a rice and meat filling, well flavoured with herbs. Bake with a covering of home-made tomato sauce.

❀ **COURGETTE FLOWERS**

❀ **GREEN COURGETTE**

MARROW

❀ **YELLOW COURGETTES**

PUMPKINS & SQUASH
Cucurbita maxima, C. moschata & C. pepo

"SQUASH NEVER FAIL TO REACH MATURITY. You can spray them with acid, beat them with sticks and burn them; they love it," wrote the American humorist S. J. Perelman. So, secure in the knowledge that you will have to work hard to stop them growing, you can think instead about which of the staggering variety of pumpkins and squash you would like to have in the garden. The smaller ones can be grown over fences and strongly built arches, or trailing through the tall stems of sweet corn. There are two main kinds: summer squash, which are eaten as soon as they are ready, and winter squash and pumpkins, which need to be "cured" in the sun to harden their skins if they are to store successfully through the winter.

Cultivation

In essence, you raise pumpkins and squash in the same way as courgettes and marrows, which are members of the same family, the cucurbits. They are no hardier and the plants cannot be set out in the open until all danger of frost has passed.

SITE AND SOIL Choose an open, sunny site in ground that is rich and well fed but also well drained. Pumpkins and squash grow most happily where the soil is slightly acid to neutral.

SOWING Sow indoors from mid-spring onward, pressing the seeds on edge 2cm (1in) deep into individual 7cm (3in) pots (see page 168). Cover with polythene and keep at a temperature of 15–18°C (60–65°F) until the seeds have germinated. This should take no more than a week.

TRANSPLANTING In early summer, once the soil outside has warmed up, set out the hardened-off plants (see page 169), raising ridged circles of soil around them to retain water. Set them at least 1.2m (4ft) apart and far away from less robust crops, such as carrots, which they may smother. Sweet corn, with its upright growth, will not be bothered by the territorial habits of squash.

ROUTINE CARE These are hungry and thirsty plants. Food is best supplied by incorporating plenty of compost or manure into the ground before planting. Drink must be lavishly provided. The smothering foliage of pumpkins and squash will take care of any weeds.

YIELD AND HARVESTING The yield depends entirely on the type of pumpkin or squash that you are growing. The little pancake-shaped ones should be cut when they are just 7cm (3in) across. Cut the summer squash as you need them. Dry off the winter squash and pumpkins until the skins are hard and the fruit sounds hollow when tapped. Then store them in a frost-free, cool shed.

PESTS AND DISEASES Generally trouble-free, although slugs may be tempted by young plants when they are first set out.

RECOMMENDED CULTIVARS

PUMPKINS
'Autumn Gold': *smaller, more manageable fruit than the giant, record-breaking varieties.*
SUMMER SQUASH
'Custard White': *pale, scallop-edged fruit.*
'Spaghetti Squash': *spaghetti strands of flesh in pale, oval fruit.*
'Sunburst': *yellow, pancake-shaped squash.*
WINTER SQUASH
'Buttercup': *firm, sweet flesh in a grey-green skin.* **'Butternut'**: *creamy fruit, bred to mature early in cooler climates.*
'Little Gem': *apple-sized fruit that ripen from green to gold.* **'Red Kuri'**: *big, teardrop-shaped, orange fruit.* **'Turk's Turban'**: *intricately shaped squash that are marked with orange, red, green and cream.*

	SPRING			SUMMER			AUTUMN			WINTER		
	Early	Mid	Late	Early	Mid	Late	Early	Mid	Late	Early	Mid	Late
		🌱	🌱	🌱								
				➡	➡	✂	✂					

IN THE KITCHEN

For this soup you need a beautiful, unblemished fruit to use as a natural tureen. Do not be too ambitious as regards size – a monster may buckle under its own weight.

PUMPKIN OR SQUASH SOUP
Serves 4

1 pumpkin or winter squash, ideally about 20cm (8in) high and wide
2 tbsp softened butter
salt and black pepper
1 medium onion, finely sliced
60g (2oz) long grain rice
900ml (1½ pints) good chicken stock
freshly grated nutmeg or ground cumin
to garnish: 6 bacon rashers, grilled until crisp and finely chopped, and 3 tbsp crumbled mozzarella cheese

1 Cut a lid from the stalk end of the pumpkin or squash and scoop out the seeds (see below). Rub butter on to the flesh inside. Season, and add the onion and rice.

2 Bring the stock to the boil in a saucepan. Settle the pumpkin or squash in a big roasting tray, pour the stock inside it and put on the lid. Bake for 2 hours at 190°C/375°F/gas mark 5.

3 Remove the pumpkin or squash from the oven, take off the lid and scrape some of the softened flesh from the walls into the soup and mix it in.

4 Correct seasoning and add either nutmeg or cumin to taste. Garnish with the bacon and mozzarella and serve.

CULINARY NOTES

◊ Do not waste the seeds when you prepare pumpkins for cooking. Spread them on a baking sheet, sprinkle lightly with salt and bake in the oven for 20 minutes at 190°C/375°F/gas mark 5.

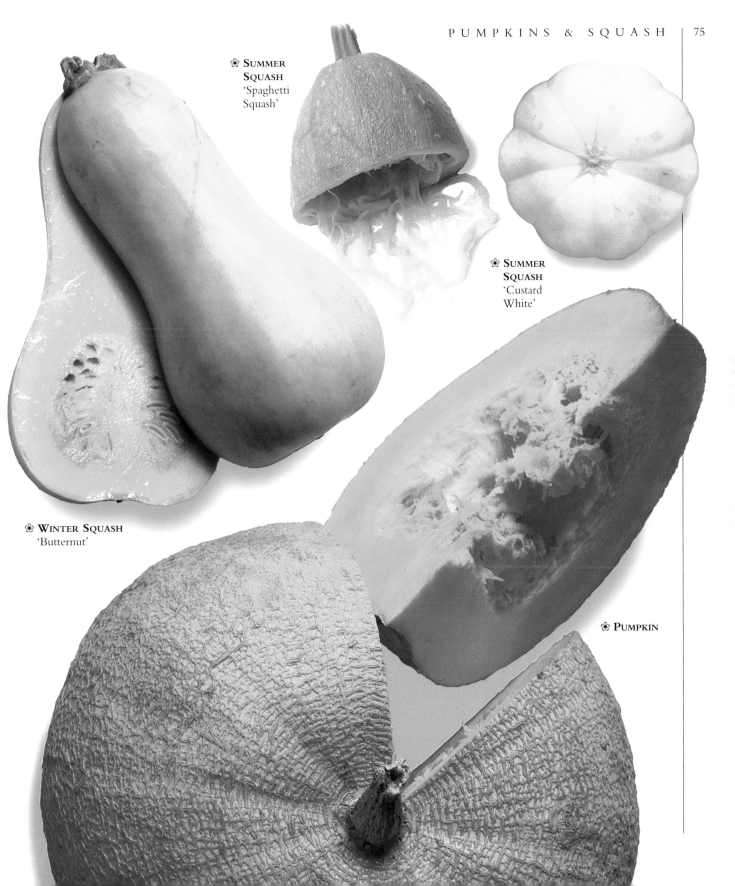

❀ **SUMMER SQUASH**
'Spaghetti Squash'

❀ **SUMMER SQUASH**
'Custard White'

❀ **WINTER SQUASH**
'Butternut'

❀ **PUMPKIN**

AUBERGINES, PEPPERS & CHILLIES
Solanum melongena & Capsicum spp.

NOTHING LOOKS QUITE SO UNREAL in a vegetable garden as a waxy aubergine, smooth, glossy and enigmatic. The standard type is deep purple, almost black, but the white-skinned kind is more likely to have given the aubergine its common name of egg-plant. There are also pretty striped varieties – streaked with cream and maroon – that you sometimes see in France and Italy. Set the dark, lustrous fruit of aubergines close to the brilliant red of peppers or chillies. All three crops do well in grow bags in a sunny spot but are unlikely to succeed outside in cool areas. Try them in a cold frame or greenhouse. In late spring you can buy young plants which saves the bother of raising them from seed. They need no complicated staking and, as long as you take care over the watering and feeding, look their best grouped in mellow clay pots.

AUBERGINE

Cultivation

If you can grow tomatoes, you should be able to grow aubergines, peppers and chillies. And like tomatoes, especially the cherry types, they are particularly well suited to patio gardening. Plants are most vulnerable when they are young, but you may find you can persuade them to grow outdoors if you wrap them up at night with polythene or fleece (see page 166) for the first couple of weeks. Aubergines have a longer growing season than peppers and need about 5 months to complete the full cycle from seed to fruit. They are also less hardy than peppers and chillies.

SITE AND SOIL Shelter is all important, especially if you are growing plants in open ground. If you are using grow bags outside, push them up against a sunny wall for extra warmth. Cloches, polytunnels, frames and greenhouses provide their own protection.

SOWING Sow seed in trays or pots indoors (see page 168), 1–2cm (½–1in) deep, in a heat of about 21°C (70°F) from late winter. For aubergines you need to maintain a growing temperature for the seedlings of 15–18°C (60–65°F). Pepper and chilli seedlings need to be kept at 12–15°C (55–60°F).

TRANSPLANTING Prick out the seedlings (see page 169) when they are about 5cm (2in) high, into separate 7cm (3in) pots to grow on. Gradually lower the growing temperature, harden off the seedlings (see page 169) and plant in their permanent positions in late spring or early summer when the first flowers appear, spacing them about 45cm (18in) apart. Alternatively, move them into larger pots, setting each plant in a pot at least 23cm (9in) wide.

ROUTINE CARE Keep the plants well watered, particularly when the fruit has begun to set. Tomato feed is a good booster for plants growing in containers. Pinch out the growing tips of aubergines, peppers and chillies when the plants are about 38cm (15in) high.

YIELD AND HARVESTING Expect about 4 aubergines on each plant, slightly more from the peppers, and about 20 chillies on a plant. Green peppers will ripen and turn red if they get enough warmth in early autumn.

PESTS AND DISEASES Whitefly and red spider mite (see pages 190 and 191) are the chief pests if you are growing under glass. Keep the atmosphere as damp as possible. A car vacuum cleaner quickly disposes of whitefly when they are on the wing.

RECOMMENDED CULTIVARS

AUBERGINES
'Black Beauty': *well-flavoured, pear-shaped fruit, early to ripen.* **'Moneymaker'**: *prolific cultivar with long, well-flavoured aubergines.*

PEPPERS
'Bell Boy': *thick-walled, bulbous fruit.*
'Canape': *early, good outdoors in mild areas.*
'New Ace': *dependable cultivar, early to set fruit, heavy-cropping.*

CHILLIES
'Yellow Cayenne': *relatively large chilli, hot and suitable for drying, good in containers.*
'Jalapeño': *smooth, bullet-shaped fruit.*
'Apache': *prolific, small, cayenne type, sometimes producing 100 fruits on a single plant. Excellent for containers.*

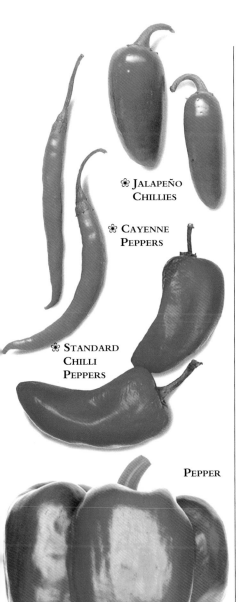

**❀ JALAPEÑO
CHILLIES**

**❀ CAYENNE
PEPPERS**

**❀ STANDARD
CHILLI
PEPPERS**

PEPPER

CUCUMBERS
Cucumis sativus

THERE ARE TWO KINDS OF CUCUMBER, beauty and the beast, although Japanese breeders are trying hard to make the warty outdoor beast as attractive as the smooth indoor beauty. Cucumbers were one of the crops Victorian growers minded about to an extraordinary degree. A kinked cucumber was a sign of moral slackness and gardeners fixed glass tubes over newly set fruit to ensure they grew straight as rulers. Outdoor cucumbers can be trained up tripods as decorative centrepieces.

**OUTDOOR
CUCUMBER**

**INDOOR
CUCUMBER**

Cultivation

Outdoor "ridge" cucumbers (so-called because they were planted on ridges to ensure good drainage) are hardier, easier to grow and less prone to attack by pests and diseases than the greenhouse types. Indoor, or greenhouse, cucumbers will only do well if you can keep both heat and humidity at almost tropical levels.
SITE AND SOIL Cucumbers like a very rich soil, well larded with manure or compost. They lap up water faster than camels and must never be allowed to dry out. In sheltered sites, they will grow in dappled shade. The compact variety 'Bush Crop' does well in pots or grow bags.
SOWING Sow seed indoors from early spring, 2cm (1in) deep, setting it on edge in individual 7cm (3in) pots (see page 168). Cover with polythene until it germinates. Keep plants growing well, repotting if necessary, to put outside after the last frost. Seed can also be sown directly outside in early summer, covering it with jam jars for protection. Set it no deeper than 2cm (1in), 60cm (24in) apart.
TRANSPLANTING Harden off indoor-raised plants (see page 169) and set out in early summer at least 60cm (24in) apart.
ROUTINE CARE Water frequently – lack of water is the most usual reason for fruit failing to develop.
YIELD AND HARVESTING An outdoor cucumber may produce about 10 fruit, an indoor one probably twice as many. Pick fruit regularly.
PESTS AND DISEASES Aphids may attack plants in the open; under glass, they are prey to red spider mite (see pages 190 and 191). Cucumber mosaic virus is the most serious disease (see page 194). Leaves may become so mottled and misshapen that plants die. There is no cure.

RECOMMENDED CULTIVARS

OUTDOOR
'Burpless Tasty Green': *one of the best of the "improved" types, with smooth fruit.*
'Kyoto': *best grown up a tripod or other support to display the very long, very thin fruit.*
INDOOR
'Fenumex': *all-female flowers producing superb fruit that are never bitter.*
'Telegraph Improved': *traditional, prolific variety with well-flavoured fruit.*

SPRING			SUMMER			AUTUMN			WINTER		
Early	Mid	Late	Early	Mid	Late	Early	Mid	Late	Early	Mid	Late
											🪴
🌱	🌱	➡	➡		✂	✂	✂				

SPRING			SUMMER			AUTUMN			WINTER		
Early	Mid	Late	Early	Mid	Late	Early	Mid	Late	Early	Mid	Late
🌱	🌱	🌱	🌿								
			➡	✂	✂	✂	✂				

SWEET CORN *Zea mays*

TALL SHEAVES OF SWEET CORN provide an authentic hint of harvest in the late summer garden. It is a stately plant and an anciently cultivated one: husks found in caves in Mexico and Peru suggest that people were growing and eating it by 3500BC. Breeders have been working hard to make it as happy in cool northern climates as it is in its Latin American home. Whereas a traditional variety might take over 80 days to reach maturity in the States, a modern cultivar will ripen in under 60. Growth in most European countries, though, is slower than this. Interplant it with low-growing courgettes or squash to make the best use of limited space.

Cultivation

Pollination is the key to fat, well-filled cobs, and since sweet corn is wind-pollinated, it is best planted in blocks rather than rows. The pollen from the male tassels at the top of the plant then has the best possible chance of reaching the silky tassels of the female flowers. New "supersweet" cultivars have been bred for extra succulence but are slightly tender. They must be grown on their own to avoid cross-pollination with unimproved varieties which would make them lose some of their sweetness.

SITE AND SOIL Sweet corn needs a warm, sheltered site and grows best on deep, well-drained, fertile and slightly acid soils.

SOWING Climate dictates how you should proceed. In warm areas, sow seed direct into the soil in late spring (see page 170), about 2cm (1in) deep, in a block pattern. Set a few seeds together at each growing point, about 35cm (14in) apart, and thin out weaker seedlings after germination. Seed will not germinate in soil temperatures below 10°C (50°F), but you can use a floating mulch (see page 166) to warm up the ground beforehand or set jam jars over the seeds to act as miniature greenhouses. In cold areas, sow seed in gentle heat – 15–18°C (60–65°F) – inside in mid-spring, setting it no more than 2cm (1in) deep in individual 7cm (3in) pots (see page 168). Make sure that seedlings are thoroughly hardened off before transplanting.

TRANSPLANTING Set out the plants (see page 169) when all danger of frost has passed, spacing them in a block about 35cm (14in) apart in each direction. For baby corn, it is essential to use a cultivar that has been bred to mature early and also to set the plants no more than 15cm (6in) apart.

ROUTINE CARE Little water will be needed until the cobs start to swell. Sweet corn is usually sturdily self-supporting, but in exposed areas you may need to earth up the plants when they are 30cm (12in) high (see page 167).

YIELD AND HARVESTING Expect no more than 1 or 2 cobs from each plant. Do not leave them toughening on the stem. Pick them when the silky tassels begin to turn brown and the juice that oozes from the kernels, if they are pressed, is milky (see right). Use as quickly as possible after picking. Sugar in the cobs turns rapidly to starch once they are picked, although the conversion process is slower in new "supersweet" cultivars.

PESTS AND DISEASES Mice are the most troublesome pest, feasting daintily on seed that has been sown direct into the ground. Upturned jam jars placed over the seeds provide protection.

RECOMMENDED CULTIVARS

'Candle': *a "supersweet" cultivar with long cobs on plants of medium height.* **'Sundance'**: *one of the best cultivars for maturing early, suitable for cooler climates with shorter summers.*

❀ SWEET CORN

	SPRING			SUMMER			AUTUMN			WINTER		
	Early	Mid	Late	Early	Mid	Late	Early	Mid	Late	Early	Mid	Late
		🪴	⚘									
				➡	➡		✂	✂	✂			

TESTING FOR RIPENESS

Once the creamy tassel has turned brown, turn back the sheath and press one of the kernels with your nail. A milky liquid will ooze out when the cob is ripe; if under-ripe, the juice is watery; if over-ripe, it looks thick and starchy.

GLOBE ARTICHOKES & CARDOONS
Cynara scolymus & C. cardunculus

A GLOBE ARTICHOKE has the right dramatic credentials to be a star of the kitchen garden. With its jagged, greyish-green leaves and showy, fat flowerbuds – the edible part – it looks as though it has been sculpted by one of the builders of the Parthenon. Unfortunately, it is an all-or-nothing plant. It looks stunning from late spring to mid-autumn, when it will spread over a metre in all directions, but once it is reduced to nothing by the first frosts, it is a big nothing. Cardoons are equally handsome, but it is the fleshy leaf bases, tied up and blanched, that you eat, not the flowerbuds.

❀ GLOBE ARTICHOKE

❀ CARDOON

Cultivation

Seed-raised plants are very variable so globe artichokes are generally grown from rooted offsets, propagated from types that are known to have good flowerheads. If you leave the buds too long before picking, they open into spectacular great thistleheads of bluish-purple. These dry well for winter flower arrangements. Cardoons can be raised from seed or offsets. They are generally available from garden centres but are usually to be found among the ornamental plants. They have smaller, more prickly flowerheads that also look superb dried.

SITE AND SOIL In the great artichoke-growing areas of France (Brittany) and Italy (the coastal plain around Brindisi), the soil is light and the climate mild. A combination of heavy soils and cold winters is likely to be too much for these plants. In very hot areas, artichokes will tolerate shade, but elsewhere they should have sun, as should cardoons.

PLANTING Young offsets of both artichokes and cardoons should be planted shallowly, with only as much of the base below ground as is needed to keep them upright. New offsets quickly develop a sustaining root system. Set them out in late spring, about 1.2m (4ft) apart each way, and keep them well watered until they are established.

ROUTINE CARE Offsets may produce small flowerheads late in the season of their first year. Pick these off both artichokes and cardoons to encourage the plants to develop more sideshoots. Where winters are hard, protect established plants by packing them with straw. Mulch

thickly with manure in spring. Plants are not long-lived. After 3–4 years replace old clumps with the new offsets that they produce (see page 172). Begin blanching cardoons in spring (see below). The process takes about 3 weeks.

YIELD AND HARVESTING Expect about 10 artichokes from an established plant. Cut the terminal "king" bud first, with 5cm (2in) of stem attached. The head should be large, but the scales not yet opening away from the centre. While the artichokes are still young, the inside of the cooked stem is very succulent. Peel back the stringy outside and nibble out the innards.

PESTS AND DISEASES Artichokes and cardoons tend to be disease-free, although aphids can be a problem on developing flowerheads (see page 190). More problematic than any pest or disease is the question of winter wet, which, combined with cold, may rot the plants entirely.

RECOMMENDED CULTIVARS

GLOBE ARTICHOKES
'Green Globe': *flattish, rounded head with blunt-ended scales.*
'Vert de Laon': *excellent flavour.*
CARDOONS
'Gigante di Romagna': *an Italian favourite for blanching.*
'Plein Blanc Enorme': *a French selection that produces succulent leaf bases.*

BLANCHING CARDOONS
Put in a stake, and blanch cardoons in late spring when they are about 45cm (18in) high. Tie the leaves in a bundle with soft string, wrap them in newspaper and then black polythene.

TOMATOES *Lycopersicon esculentum*

FOR THE DECORATIVE VEGETABLE GARDEN, outdoor tomatoes, either of the bush or the cordon type, will be your first choice. They are simplicity itself to manage and the flavour of the new cultivars, especially when buffed up by hours of sunshine, is outstanding. Once planted – in tubs, grow bags or even hanging baskets – the bush varieties can be left to their own devices. The cordon types, trained up tall canes, make good centrepieces for decorative schemes, especially if you contrast a yellow-fruited cultivar like 'Yellow Perfection' with the stripy 'Tigerella'.

Cultivation

Not all tomatoes are suitable for growing outside in cold areas, so check you are buying the right cultivar for your purpose.
SITE AND SOIL For cropping outdoors, choose a sunny, sheltered site. The soil should be fertile, well drained and well manured. If you are growing cordon types in grow bags or pots, put them by a protecting wall. Detrimental salts and diseases build up in greenhouse borders if tomatoes are grown too often in the same spot, so rotate crops or use grow bags.
SOWING In a greenhouse, you can get a crop of tomatoes off to an early start, but with outdoor plants nothing is gained by sowing too soon, since plants cannot be put outside until danger of frost is past. Scatter seed thinly on the surface of a 12cm (5in) pot of compost and cover lightly with more compost or vermiculite (see page 168). Cover with clingfilm to retain moisture during germination, and keep at a temperature of 15–18°C (60–65°F). When the seedlings develop their first true leaves, prick them out into individual 7cm (3in) pots (see page 169).
TRANSPLANTING First, plants must be thoroughly hardened off (see page 169). Set cordons 38–45cm (15–18in) apart, and bush types 45–60cm (18–24in) apart.
ROUTINE CARE Bush tomatoes need little attention, but sideshoots on cordons must be nipped out regularly (see opposite). Cordons also need to be staked and tied in. "Stop" them by nipping out the tip of the main stem in mid to late summer. In cold areas, this may be after about 3 trusses (clusters of tomatoes) have set fruit, in warmer areas there will be more. Do not stop bush varieties. Overwatering and overfeeding have a detrimental effect on flavour, and irregular watering is the most common cause of blossom end rot (see page 192). In open ground, no extra feeding should be necessary, but plants in containers, especially hanging baskets, need plenty to eat and drink.
YIELD AND HARVESTING Expect 2–4kg (4–8lb) of fruit per plant, more from cordon than from bush types. For the best flavour, leave the tomatoes to ripen fully on the plant.
PESTS AND DISEASES In greenhouses, whitefly is the chief irritation. Small slugs nibble outdoor bush tomatoes. Watch out, too, for blight, grey mould/*Botrytis* and stem rot (see pages 191–94).

RECOMMENDED CULTIVARS

GREENHOUSE TOMATOES
'Counter': *good disease resistance; produces high yield of well-flavoured fruit (cordon).*
'Dombello': *beefsteak variety with fleshy fruit on disease-resistant plants (cordon).*
'Roma': *heavy-cropping plum tomato (bush).*
OUTDOOR TOMATOES
'Gardener's Delight': *small but exceptionally sweet fruit (cordon).*
'Phyra': *"cherry" type that thrives in pots, tubs and windowboxes (bush).*
'Tigerella': *distinctive striped fruit, early and well flavoured (cordon).*
'Tornado': *heavy-cropping, suitable for tubs (bush).* **'Yellow Perfection'**: *early, prolific, but with a tendency to burst the skin (cordon).*

SPRING			SUMMER			AUTUMN			WINTER		
Early	Mid	Late	Early	Mid	Late	Early	Mid	Late	Early	Mid	Late
🌱	🌱	➡	➡	✂	✂	✂	✂				

❀ STANDARD TOMATO

❀ SMALL, EXTRA-SWEET TOMATOES

❀ YELLOW TOMATOES

❀ PLUM TOMATO

❀ CHERRY TOMATOES

❀ STRIPED TOMATOES

PINCHING OUT SHOOTS
Pinch out sideshoots as they develop in the leaf axils of cordon types to prevent unwanted growth.

PINCHING OUT THE TOP
In mid to late summer, nip out the tip of the main stem of cordon types to stop more flowers from forming.

❀ BEEFSTEAK TOMATO

PODDED VEGETABLES

THE SCRAMBLING HABIT of some peas and beans can
be used to good effect in the decorative kitchen garden,
whether trained over a tunnel made from hazel sticks
or up a tripod. Runner beans hold on by twining; the
exploratory tendrils of peas grasp any useful prop as
tightly as a baby's fist. All the podded vegetables are
attractive in bloom, but not all are as showy as the
runner bean with its blazing red flowers. The broad
bean, although a beefy-looking plant, has delicate
flowers marked with black on white. Bean pods may
be purple, green, cream, yellow or striped. There is
also a wonderful strain of French beans (look for the
cultivars 'Rob Roy' and 'Rob Splash') with cream pods
that are streaked with bright pink or purple.

INTO THE TUNNEL

*Two different runner beans,
'Painted Lady' and 'White
Achievement', have been trained
over this hazel tunnel, straddling
a path. A border of tall purple
alliums, the striped rose
'Ferdinand Pichard' and catmint
crowd the space at their feet.*

SWEET BEANS

*Rows of broad beans and peas,
scrambling up a support of chicken
wire, are backed by decorative
sweet peas. For scent, these are
unparalleled, but if you bend your
nose to the more workaday broad
bean, you will find that this too
has sweet-smelling flowers.*

THE COLOUR PURPLE

The dark purple that suffuses the foliage of this climbing French bean is intensified in the pods and flowers. The colour disappears when it is cooked, but you can use it to great effect with dark red dahlias, such as 'Bishop of Llandaff', and clumps of bronze fennel.

BEANS WITH A PAST

The runner bean 'Painted Lady', with its red and white flowers, was being grown in kitchen gardens 150 years ago. It is a decorative climber, but also produces a heavy crop of well-flavoured beans. Grow it over an arch with white-flowered 'White Achievement' and clematis.

SOCIABLE CLIMBERS

Red-flowered runner beans are combined with pink, white and purple sweet peas on this tripod, which is nearly matched in height by the tall, flowering stems of red orach, Atriplex hortensis 'Rubra'. The orach is a fast-growing annual that self-seeds vigorously.

PEAS & MANGETOUT *Pisum sativum*

EARLY VISITORS TO TROY, where Heinrich Schliemann excavated Priam's fabled palace, were said to have been fed on peas from the great king's larder. One huge storage jar contained more than 180kg (400lb), which had remained perfectly preserved for 3,000 years. Priam's peas would have been tall-growing types. In the decorative kitchen garden, low-growing cultivars such as the mangetout 'Dwarf Sweet Green', which grows up to 75cm (30in), or the even smaller 'Waverex Petit Pois', can be used to make low, informal hedges around plots. Tall varieties, such as the pretty, purple-flowered mangetout 'Carouby de Maussane', will scramble up a screen or centrepiece to 1.5m (5ft). 'Alderman', a shelling pea from the Victorian era, is another tall type worth growing for its fine flavour. Wrinkle-seeded peas provide the sweetest crop, but round-seeded ones are the hardiest.

Cultivation

All seed sowing is a kind of horticultural futures market, and gamblers will not mind risking a row of winter-sown peas in the hope of a particularly early crop the following spring. Peas for winter sowing must be the round-seeded kind. From spring on, you can then sow any type at 3–4 week intervals until early summer.
SITE AND SOIL Peas positively like cool, damp summers. Soil should be fertile and well dug. Provided there is plenty of moisture, they do not mind some shade.
SOWING Sow seed 3–5cm (1½–2in) deep and 5–7cm (2–3in) apart. If growing a straight row, as in a pea hedge, take out a wide drill (see page 170) about 5cm (2in) deep and the width of a spade. Sow the seed about 5cm (2in) apart. Cover with soil and tread down. Protect with wire netting against birds.
ROUTINE CARE Provide some form of support for tall cultivars, either netting or hazel pea-sticks which, if woven together at the top, make a decorative feature. Semi-leafless peas, in which many of the leaves have been modified into tendrils, need less staking (see opposite). If you have used wire netting to protect seed, you can bend this up into an inverted V-shaped ridge to support low-growing cultivars rising through it. In a potager, try growing peas in combination with broad beans, which will support the crop.
YIELD AND HARVESTING Expect 5kg (10lb) from a 3m (10ft) row. Pick peas regularly to encourage more to form. Pick mangetout while the peas are visible only as tiny swellings. When the crop has finished, chop off the stems leaving the roots in the ground. Their nitrogen-bearing nodules will help enrich the soil.
PESTS AND DISEASES Birds and mice are the most serious pests (see page 191).

RECOMMENDED CULTIVARS

SHELLING PEAS
'Coral': *high-yielding and early (wrinkled)*.
'Douce Provence': *fairly hardy and sweet (round)*. **'Hurst Green Shaft'**: *superb, sweet peas maturing over a long time (wrinkled)*.
MANGETOUT
'Edula': *can be shelled if left to mature*.
'Oregon Sugar Pod': *fine flavour, over 1m (3ft) tall*. **'Reuzensuiker'**: *quite compact plants*. **'Sugar Snap'**: *fleshy pods, long season*.

	SPRING			SUMMER			AUTUMN			WINTER		
	Early	Mid	Late	Early	Mid	Late	Early	Mid	Late	Early	Mid	Late
								⚘				⚘
	⚘	✂	✂									
	⚘	⚘	⚘	⚘								
				✂	✂	✂	✂					
	⚘	⚘	⚘	⚘								
				✂	✂	✂	✂					

☐ Round seed	☐ Mangetout
☐ Wrinkled seed	

IN THE KITCHEN

If only a small amount of peas is available, use them as a first course, braised in the French way with some shredded lettuce leaves, finely chopped carrot and spring onion. Here are some ways to combine peas with other vegetables.

PEAS AND CUCUMBER
Serves 4
1 cucumber, peeled
1–1.5kg (2–3lb) peas, shelled
60g (2oz) butter
sprig of mint, chopped
salt and black pepper
1 tsp sugar

1 Cut the cucumber into 3cm (1½in) chunks, then into batons. Sprinkle with salt in a colander, leave to drain for 30 minutes, rinse and pat dry.
2 Bring 1cm (½in) water to the boil. Add the cucumber, peas, butter and mint. Season, add sugar and cook for 5 minutes, until tender.

PEAS SPICED WITH CUMIN
Serves 4
1½ tsp whole cumin seeds
2 dried hot red chillies
3 tbsp vegetable oil
175g (6oz) onions, chopped
175g (6oz) carrots, diced
175g (6oz) peas, shelled
175g (6oz) potatoes, cooked and diced
salt and ½ tsp sugar, or to taste
1 spring onion, finely sliced

1 Fry the cumin and chillies in the oil for a few seconds, then add the onions and cook until soft. Add the carrots and peas and cook for a further 5 minutes, until tender.
2 Add the potatoes, salt and sugar, and cook for a few minutes until the potato is heated through. Remove the chillies before serving, and garnish with the spring onion.

SUPPORTING PEAS

1 *Once the seedlings develop tendrils, push pea-sticks firmly into the soil. Position them 10cm (4in) apart, outside the peas.*

2 *The tendrils twine around the sticks as the peas grow. If you are growing a tall cultivar, make sure the sticks are long enough.*

MANGETOUT

SHELLING PEAS

MANGETOUT
'Sugar Snap'

SEMI-LEAFLESS PEAS
Peas of this kind need little staking. The tendrils wind around their neighbours rather than sticks and the whole mass becomes virtually self-supporting – group therapy in the vegetable garden.

RUNNER BEANS *Phaseolus coccineus*

IN THE WILD, runner beans grow in the Mexican mountains together with dahlias, begonias and lobelias. There is no reason why you should not make your own beans feel comfortably at home by providing similar companions. The hummingbirds that pollinate the flowers in Mexico will be in short supply in most gardens. Fortunately, bumblebees have learned the trick of opening the petals and provide an efficient pod-setting service. Use runner beans scrambling up a taut net to make a quick summer screen in the garden. They will soon grow up to 3m (10ft). Grow them up tripods in a flower border, or use them to cover an arbour, where they can twine happily among clematis or late summer nasturtiums and the flame-coloured climber *Eccremocarpus scaber*.

❀ RUNNER BEANS

Cultivation

Runner beans are not difficult to grow, but in some seasons they seem reluctant to set fruit. Spraying the flowers with water does not help as much as keeping the roots sufficiently moist. Less easy to cope with are pollen beetles, which move on to runner beans (and sweet peas) when oil-seed rape has finished flowering. Sitting in the keel of the flower, they discourage visiting bumblebees and the flowers are left unpollinated.

SITE AND SOIL Start thinking about the site 6 months before you sow, and dig masses of well-rotted manure or compost into the soil. Runner beans are deep-rooted and their roots like to feel the journey has been worthwhile. Some shade is beneficial, provided the ground is fertile.

SOWING Do not be in a hurry to sow direct into the ground, as the soil temperature must be at least 10°C (50°F) for the seeds to germinate. This is usually not until the very end of spring. Set seeds 15cm (6in) apart (see page 170) at the foot of a row of poles or netting, or around the base of a wigwam. You can push on the crop by sowing seed inside in big boxes or individual 7cm (3in) pots (see page 168) and setting out plants from late spring.

TRANSPLANTING Runner beans are tender, so do not transplant indoor-sown beans while there is any danger of frost. Set out plants 15cm (6in) apart (see page 169), or space them regularly around a wigwam or some other support that they can climb.

ROUTINE CARE Water liberally, especially as the plants come into flower. Mulching will help to conserve moisture and keep down weeds.

YIELD AND HARVESTING Expect about 1kg (2lb) of beans from each plant. Pick the pods before the beans have started to swell inside. If you leave mature pods on the plants, they will not feel they have to produce more.

PESTS AND DISEASES Diseases are uncommon but flowers may be unwilling to set. If so, pay attention to the watering. Nothing, however, will deter pollen beetles.

RECOMMENDED CULTIVARS

'Achievement': *red flowers producing long pods*. **'Enorma'**: *long pods of excellent quality*. **'Kelvedon Marvel'**: *heavy cropper, early-maturing*. **'Liberty'**: *smooth, fleshy pods, but can be stringy if not picked quickly*.

SPRING			SUMMER			AUTUMN			WINTER		
Early	Mid	Late	Early	Mid	Late	Early	Mid	Late	Early	Mid	Late
🌱	🌱	🌱									
		➡	➡	✂	✂	✂	✂				

MAKING THE MOST OF BEANS
Grow runner beans up tripods or wigwams to make a superb feature in the vegetable patch or the flower border. When the plants were first introduced into Europe in the 17th century they were grown for ornament rather than food.

FRENCH & HARICOT BEANS
Phaseolus vulgaris

FRENCH BEANS ARE NOT REALLY FRENCH. Like runners, they are American beans, brought to Europe by the Spanish conquistadores. These beans, wrote the early herbalist John Gerard, "boiled together before they be ripe, and buttered, and so eaten with their cods, are exceeding delicate meat, and do not ingender wind as the other pulses do". French beans may climb or they may grow as bushes. They may have flat pods or rounded. They may be green, purple, yellow, or wonderfully speckled as in the old Dutch variety 'Dragon Tongue' that has cream pods flecked with purple. The beans of some types can be eaten either green (when they are known as flageolets), or dried (when they are known as haricots).

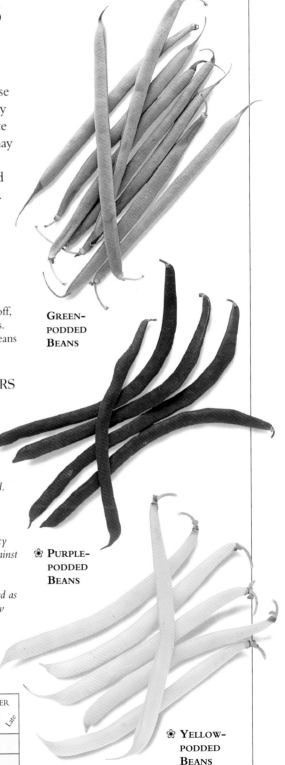

GREEN-PODDED BEANS

❀ **PURPLE-PODDED BEANS**

❀ **YELLOW-PODDED BEANS**

Cultivation

By nature, these are fast-growing annuals and it is a waste of seed to sow it in cold, dank ground. Compact bush varieties will crop successfully in pots and grow bags; climbing types will need canes or other support.

SITE AND SOIL French beans like rich, light soil, which can be neutral or slightly acid. They do best in a sheltered position.

SOWING For early crops, sow seed indoors in deep boxes or individual 7cm (3in) pots so that plants can be set out after the last frost (see page 168). When the soil temperature has reached 13°C (56°F), sow outside at regular intervals from late spring until midsummer (see page 170). Set seed 3cm (1½in) deep, in staggered rows, so that plants grow about 23cm (9in) apart in the rows. They germinate in 1–2 weeks.

TRANSPLANTING The shock to the system holds back transplants, and plants set out from seed sown indoors may crop no sooner than a later sowing outside. Water the transplants well (see page 169).

ROUTINE CARE Earth up the stems of young plants as they grow to give them extra support (see page 167). Provide support for climbers and short twiggy sticks to prop up bush varieties which tend to get top heavy when laden with beans. Keep the soil moist throughout the growing period, but especially when the plants come into flower.

YIELD AND HARVESTING Expect 4kg (8lb) of beans from a 3m (10ft) row. For fresh beans, pick the pods frequently while they are still succulent. For dry haricot beans, leave the pods on the plant until the end of the season. Hang the stems under cover until the pods have dried off, shell the beans and store in air-tight jars.

PESTS AND DISEASES As for runner beans (see opposite).

RECOMMENDED CULTIVARS

GREEN-PODDED BUSH
'Delinel': *fine texture and flavour.*
'Pros Gitana': *round, sweet pods.*

PURPLE-PODDED BUSH
'Purple Queen': *the glossy purple turns green when cooked, but the flavour of the purple cultivars is unparalleled.*
'Purple Teepee': *productive and quick to mature.*

YELLOW-PODDED BUSH
'Kinghorn Wax': *stringless, round, waxy beans.* **'Rocquencourt'**: *yellow pods against dark green foliage. Good in cold areas.*

CLIMBING
'Blue Lake': *excellent flavour, can be used as haricot.* **'Or du Rhin'**: *broad, flat, yellow pods, late and black-seeded.*

HARICOT
'Brown Dutch': *floury texture, fine flavour.* **'Chevrier Vert'**: *old French flageolet, use seeds fresh or dried.*

SPRING			SUMMER			AUTUMN			WINTER		
Early	Mid	Late	Early	Mid	Late	Early	Mid	Late	Early	Mid	Late
		🌱	🌿	🌿	🌿						
		➡	➡	✄	✄	✄	✄				

BROAD BEANS *Vicia faba*

BEFORE POTATOES CAME SAILING WITH RALEIGH across the Atlantic from the Americas, beans, such as broad beans, had long provided the staple carbohydrate for those living in the cooler parts of Europe. Broad beans are useful in a decorative vegetable garden because from winter-grown seeds you will get an early summer crop. This can then be cleared away to make room for another vegetable such as ornamental kale, which would benefit from the nodules of nitrogen left in the soil by the beans' obliging root system. The plants themselves can be tall or short, depending on cultivar. All have pleasant, glaucous foliage and black-and-white lipped flowers that have a surprisingly sweet smell.

❀ **LONG-PODDED BROAD BEANS**

❀ **SHORT-PODDED BROAD BEANS**

Cultivation

Broad beans are the hardiest of the whole bean family and can survive a winter outside, if mice, slugs and birds will let them. An autumn sowing gives the earliest crop, but you may find it safer to sow seed in boxes or trays and keep them in a cold frame or greenhouse ready to plant out in late winter. Long-podded types are the most suitable for forcing in this way. Short-podded 'Windsor' beans should be used only for spring plantings.

SITE AND SOIL Deep, heavy soils produce the best crops, but the ground must not be waterlogged. Broad beans do best on a soil that is neutral or very slightly acid (pH 6–6.5). Do not grow them in the same place 2 years running or you run the risk of encouraging a build-up of pea cyst eelworm in the soil (see page 192).

SOWING The seeds are large and can be planted with a trowel or dibber. Set them about 3cm (1½in) deep, at intervals of 23cm (9in), in rows that are also 23cm (9in) apart (see page 170). The beans germinate well at low temperatures, but overwintering crops will succeed better under a floating mulch (see page 166) or cloches. Sow a few extra seeds at the end of the row to fill in any gaps.

ROUTINE CARE This is an easy crop and the plants are so vigorous they deter all but the most pernicious perennial weeds. Support will be necessary, especially for the tall forms. Posts at either end of a row with strings stretched between provide a simple method of keeping the plants on their feet. Dwarf cultivars such as 'The

Sutton' can be propped up with short lengths of twiggy hazel.

YIELD AND HARVESTING
Expect about 9kg (20lb) of beans from a 3m (10ft) row, less if you eat them when they are at their best, before the skins have become leathery and when the scar on the bean's edge is still white or green rather than black. Broad beans can also be picked and eaten whole, pod and all. Pick them when they are no bigger than your little finger.

PESTS AND DISEASES The worst pests are aphids (see page 190), which cluster on the growing tips from midsummer. Nip out the shoot together with its colony of aphids and get rid of it (and them). If you sow in late autumn or early spring, the plant will be well enough advanced by midsummer to take this treatment. Chocolate leaf spot is a rarer problem that is more likely to occur where winter sowings coincide with unusually wet conditions (see page 193).

RECOMMENDED CULTIVARS

LONG-PODDED BEANS
'Aquadulce Claudia': *early, hardy, white-seeded old variety, 1m (3ft) tall.*
'Meteor': *brownish beans, very early, disease-resistant.* **'Red Epicure'**: *red flowers, followed by bronze beans in green pods.*
'The Sutton': *compact, rarely more than 30cm (12in) high, excellent flavour.*
SHORT-PODDED BEANS
'Green Windsor': *one of the best for flavour.*

SPRING			SUMMER			AUTUMN			WINTER		
Early	Mid	Late	Early	Mid	Late	Early	Mid	Late	Early	Mid	Late
							♣				
♣	♣		✂	✂	✂	✂					

LIMA BEANS & SOUTHERN PEAS
Phaseolus lunatus & Vigna unguiculata

THE LIMA BEAN IS AS ANCIENT AS THE BROAD BEAN, cultivated by the Mayans in Yucatan and growing in the wild from Guatemala to Peru. It will not succeed in a cool European climate, although it can be grown in the southern states of North America. So can the southern pea, which goes by many other names, including crowder, blackeye bean and cowpea. This is a decorative vegetable, producing pods that are variously stippled with cream, green, pink and purple. The beans inside are equally diverse: some have pink blotches, crowders are greenish but turn khaki when cooked, and blackeyes are cream with a distinct black notch.

Cultivation

Both lima beans and southern peas can be grown as bushes or climbers, depending on the cultivar, and both can be eaten fresh or dried. Southern peas will mature in 60–70 days from planting, but the seeds need a temperature of about 21°C (70°F) to germinate and grow. They succeed in areas where French beans would frazzle. The climbing varieties of lima bean need a growing season of about 80 days, the bush types a slightly shorter time. The soil needs to reach a temperature of 18°C (65°F) before the seeds will germinate.

SITE AND SOIL In the southern states of the US, southern peas and lima beans are grown in sandy loam, which gives good drainage. On heavier soils, they will do best on raised beds. The soil should have a pH of 6–6.5. More acid soils can be limed (see page 161) but you will need to do this at least 3 months before sowing.

SOWING Sow in late spring, 2 weeks after the last expected frost. Set the seeds about 2cm (1in) deep and 10cm (4in) apart in rows about 1m (3ft) apart (see page 170). Climbing types need canes or some other support. Make successive sowings from early to midsummer.

ROUTINE CARE Watering increases eventual yield, but if water is scarce, save it for the time when the plants are in flower. This is when they will need it most, if the beans are to set well and swell.

YIELD AND HARVESTING For fresh beans, pick the pods when they are bulging, but not showing any signs of drying out. For dried beans, leave the pods on the stem to dry off and then shell the beans into a container. Expect about 2kg (4lb) of beans from a 3m (10ft) row.

PESTS AND DISEASES Insects such as cowpea curculio (see page 191) can be a problem, but breeders are concentrating on producing cultivars that are resistant to this pest. Viruses are quickly transmitted to plants by visiting aphids. Buy only seeds that are certified virus-free.

RECOMMENDED CULTIVARS

LIMA BEANS
'Cliff Dweller': *climbing variety, small pods, seeds speckled purple.*
'King of the Garden': *strong-growing climber, large pods, whitish-green seeds.*
'Fordhook 242': *reliable bush variety, white seeds.*

SOUTHERN PEAS
'Bettergro Blackeye': *tall, upright bush type, disease-resistant.* **'Carolina Crowder'**: *bush type, pods ripen to brilliant red.* **'Early Acre'**: *cream beans in pods flushed pink.* **'Knuckle Purple Hull'**: *old, climbing variety, prone to virus but producing large, brownish beans in purple pods.* **'Texas Pinkeye'**: *compact plant, pink-blotched beans in purple pods.* **'Zipper Cream'**: *bush type, long pale pods.*

SOUTHERN PEAS/ BLACKEYE BEANS

LIMA BEANS

SPRING			SUMMER			AUTUMN			WINTER		
Early	Mid	Late	Early	Mid	Late	Early	Mid	Late	Early	Mid	Late
		⚘	⚘	⚘	✂	✂	✂	✂			

STEM, BULB & ROOT VEGETABLES

THIS GROUP IS LARGELY composed of plants whose important edible parts are hidden underground. What you see is not what you eat. Among these vegetables, your greatest allies in arranging decorative combinations will be onions, leeks, fennel, kohl rabi, carrots, beetroot and parsnips. Asparagus is very ornamental when the spears are allowed to grow up into fine clouds of foliage, but you need a lot of space for a proper asparagus bed and it cannot be moved. Put some plants in the herbaceous border instead, or grow them among roses for an instant buttonhole. Rhubarb is a handsome plant, but it also ties up ground on a permanent basis. Leeks, however, give double value. Any not harvested will produce splendid round heads of pale lilac flowers.

GOURMET ASPARAGUS
A fashionably gaunt scarecrow spreads its protective arms over an asparagus patch that is in danger of being swamped by nasturtiums. Flowers such as this can be sown directly into the ground and soon spread to make a colourful, weed-suppressing carpet.

POTATOES AND ROSES
Potatoes do not have great decorative merit, but they are an important crop in this traditional kitchen garden where they have been surrounded by roses. Low floribundas and hybrid teas grow in the side border, while the central path is swagged with climbers.

CURIOUS KOHL RABI

The swollen stem of a kohl rabi rests on the earth like a strange egg from which a baby dinosaur might suddenly emerge. In themselves kohl rabi are not especially decorative vegetables, but their curious form of construction makes them a good choice for a potager.

BRIGHTER BEETROOT

Marigolds provide bright strokes of colour in a patch of beetroot, but they are useful too. They attract hoverflies, which hoover up aphids faster than any other predator in the garden. Companion planting can be a visual delight as well as having practical advantages.

FEATHERED FENNEL

A thick swathe of cornflowers fences in a patch of feathery Florence fennel, cool as a pool of water. Tall Verbena bonariensis, *with its lean, wiry stems, would be equally at home in this kind of planting scheme, or you could introduce purple-leaved beetroot and aquilegias.*

ONIONS *Allium cepa*

"KITCHEN GARDEN GODS," SAID JUVENAL, the Roman satirist, about the pungent family of onions. It is true. There are few savoury dishes that do not require a hint of onion, although when the onion tribe first swept into the West from the East they were considered luxury items, only useful to flavour a rich man's meat. In the garden, the tubular, blue-green leaves contrast well with the feathery foliage of carrots. There is also a practical reason for combining these two crops. The scent of the onions is said to mask the smell of carrots and so deter the carrot fly from laying its eggs.

Cultivation

The first task is to choose between seed or sets (small, immature bulbs). Sets, although more expensive, have advantages. You skip stage one of the growing process and move swiftly on to stage two. There are disadvantages, however. The range of cultivars is limited and the plants are more likely to bolt (run up to flower). If possible, use "heat-treated" sets, as the flowerbud inside will have been destroyed. If size is important, grow yellow-skinned onions which tend to be larger than the red-skinned varieties.

SITE AND SOIL Well-drained, fertile soil that has been well manured the previous autumn is ideal. The site should be sunny so that bulbs will ripen satisfactorily.

SOWING Sow seed in pots indoors from midwinter and prick the seedlings out into trays to grow on (see page 168). Sets can be planted outdoors in the first half of spring. Push them gently into the soil so that the tops just show above the surface. Set them 10cm (4in) apart in rows 25cm (10in) apart. Spring onions can be sown direct in drills outside every 3 weeks from early spring to midsummer (see page 170).

TRANSPLANTING After hardening off (see page 169), seed-grown onions will be ready to plant out in early spring, spaced as above. Plant them at the same depth as they were set in their growing trays.

ROUTINE CARE Onions hate competition and weeding is essential in the first stages of growth.

YIELD AND HARVESTING Expect 3.5kg (7lb) from a 3m (10ft) row. They will be ready to pull up when the foliage starts to wither. Thorough drying is essential if onions are to be stored through the winter

(see page 186). Lay them on some wire netting in the sun. Use any with thick necks immediately as they will not keep.

PESTS AND DISEASES Onion fly (see page 190) is the worst pest, laying its eggs in the bulbs. The maggots eat them and can quickly destroy a crop. Parsley, planted in rows between the onions, is a traditional deterrent. Downy mildew (see page 193) may be a problem in damp, humid summers and can be controlled with a proprietary fungicide.

RECOMMENDED CULTIVARS

YELLOW-SKINNED
'Buffalo': *fine flavour, crisp, quick to mature.*
'Giant Fen Globe': *mild, high-yielding.*
RED-SKINNED
'Long Red Florence': *traditional, torpedo-shaped onions from Italy.*
'Southport Red Globe': *round bulbs with pink-tinged flesh, strongly flavoured.*
SPRING ONIONS
'White Lisbon': *fine, fresh flavour.*

	SPRING			SUMMER			AUTUMN			WINTER		
	Early	Mid	Late	Early	Mid	Late	Early	Mid	Late	Early	Mid	Late
										🌱	🌱	
	➡				✂	✂	✂					
	🌱	🌱			✂	✂	✂					
	🌱	🌱	🌱	🌱	🌱							
					✂	✂	✂	✂				

☐ Onions from seed ☐ Onion sets ☐ Spring onions

SPRING ONIONS

RED-SKINNED ONION

YELLOW-SKINNED ONION

IN THE KITCHEN

The onion may be the most frequently used vegetable in the kitchen, but it rarely has a chance to star alone. This soup warms the foulest winter day. Treat it as a main course rather than a starter.

FRENCH ONION SOUP
Serves 6

60g (2oz) butter
1 tbsp olive oil
750g (1½ lb) onions, thinly sliced
60g (2oz) flour
2 litres (3½ pints) good beef stock
150ml (¼ pint) dry white wine
salt and black pepper
6 thickish slices bread
1 clove garlic, halved
2 tbsp grated raw onion
175g (6oz) grated Gruyère cheese

1 Heat the butter and oil in a large, heavy-bottomed pan and gently braise the onion for 15 minutes. Stir in the flour and cook for another 2–3 minutes. Add the stock and wine, stirring to prevent lumps, and simmer for 45 minutes. Season to taste.

2 Rub the slices of bread with the garlic and bake them in the oven until crisp and dry.

3 Pour the soup into individual ovenproof bowls or one large bowl. Stir in the raw onion and float the bread on top. Sprinkle the cheese over and brown under the grill or at the top of the oven.

CULINARY NOTES

❧ For less of a meal, omit the bread and cheese and add 2 tablespoons of flamed brandy. (Heat in a ladle and put a lighted match to it to burn off the alcohol quickly.)

❧ For more of a meal, ladle the soup into bowls and add a very lightly poached egg to each. Top with bread and cheese as before.

GARLIC & SHALLOTS
Allium sativum & A. cepa Aggregatum Group

GARLIC HAS LONG BEEN SUPPOSED to have magical properties. A single whiff is considered enough to see off even the most bloodthirsty vampire. Shallots, though, have a more prosaic reputation. Nobody carries them in their pocket on a dark winter's night. In the kitchen, they are invaluable, and in the garden, both are equally easy to grow if given the right conditions. Their upright foliage, like that of onions, provides welcome contrast to the dumpy, rounded shapes of lettuce.

Cultivation

Shallots can be harvested earlier than onions, which is useful in a small plot as the ground can then be used for a catch crop. They also last better in store, especially the golden-skinned type. Garlic only develops a good head if the dormant clove undergoes a period of cold, 0–10°C (32–50°F), for 1–2 months. If you plant in autumn, this occurs naturally during winter. Garlic leaves grow best in cool conditions. When foliage growth stops, the underground bulb begins to swell, usually in early summer.

SITE AND SOIL Light, well-drained soil suits garlic; shallots can cope with something heavier. Both need an open situation and fertile soil, although it need not be heavily manured.

SOWING Heads of garlic should be broken up into individual cloves before planting. Plant both garlic and shallots like onion sets (see opposite) – garlic in mid to late autumn or late winter, shallots from midwinter to early spring. Set both 15cm (6in) apart, in rows 30cm (12in) apart.

ROUTINE CARE As with onions, weeding is the only imperative.

YIELD AND HARVESTING Expect about 20 heads of garlic and 3.5kg (7lb) of shallots from a 3m (10ft) row. Harvest shallots, which grow in small clusters, in the same way as onions. Garlic should be lifted as soon as the foliage turns yellow.

SHALLOTS

GARLIC

PESTS AND DISEASES They are generally trouble-free, but may sometimes suffer the same problems as onions (see opposite).

RECOMMENDED CULTIVARS

GARLIC
Little selection has been carried out.
SHALLOTS
'Atlantic': *gold-brown bulbs, fine flavour.*
'Giant Yellow Improved': *large bulbs that store well.*
'Pikant': *flavoursome red bulbs, high yield.*
'Santé': *large, round, reddish-brown shallots.*

SPRING			SUMMER			AUTUMN			WINTER		
Early	Mid	Late	Early	Mid	Late	Early	Mid	Late	Early	Mid	Late
							☘	☘			☘
				✂	✂						
										☘	☘
☘			✂	✂	✂						

☐ Garlic	☐ Shallots

LEEKS *Allium porrum*

THE ONLY GOOD THING known about the Roman emperor Nero is that he liked a bowl of leek soup as often as he could fit one in. Was vichyssoise born in the steamy cookhouses of first-century Rome? Leeks are easy to grow and the steel-blue ribbons of foliage look surprisingly good set among tall waving heads of purple *Verbena bonariensis*. Leek plants will furnish the ground from midsummer until spring and need little attention. Plant them to pierce a ferny blanket of the yellow daisy *Bidens aurea*, or to paint stripes of blue across a golden patch of marigolds.

Cultivation

If you are lucky, some other grower will take on the responsibility of raising young plants and you can buy bundles to set out in summer. If not, take heart. Leeks are not difficult to raise from seed.

SITE AND SOIL Leeks need rich, well-drained ground that has been liberally fed with manure or compost. Dig thoroughly before planting. In order for long, well-blanched stems to develop, the soil needs to be loose enough for you to be able to make deep holes for the young plants.

SOWING There are early, mid-season and late varieties, the early ones tending to be tall and thin, the late ones squat and fat. For the earliest crops, sow an early variety indoors in late winter (see page 168). Main sowings can be made in drills (see page 170) outside during spring. Sow seed as thinly as possible, 1cm (½in) deep.

TRANSPLANTING Leeks can be thinned and left to grow in drills where they were sown, but the best results come from transplanting (see page 171). Water the seedbed well before lifting young plants in early or midsummer. They should be about 20–23cm (8–9in) tall. Using a dibber, make holes 15cm (6in) deep, 15cm (6in) apart in rows that are 30cm (12in) apart. Drop a leek into each hole and fill it with water to wash soil over the roots. At one time leaves and roots were shortened before transplanting, but this is unnecessary.

ROUTINE CARE Little attention will be needed. Water only in the driest summers.

YIELD AND HARVESTING Expect 5kg (10lb) from a 3m (10ft) row. Leeks can be lifted as needed, although they are extremely difficult to extract when the ground is frozen. The stem snaps, leaving the best part of the vegetable in the earth. Where this is likely to be a problem, lift a supply before the soil freezes and trim the leaves (generally called flags). Wrap the leeks in newspaper and store them in a cool place.

PESTS AND DISEASES Rust is the biggest problem (see page 194) and breeders are now trying to produce cultivars that are resistant to the disease. It shows as orange spots on the leaves, but is disfiguring rather than fatal. Plants overfed on high-nitrogen fertilizers are worst affected. Rotate leeks to prevent a build-up of the disease in any particular spot and burn leaves that are badly affected.

RECOMMENDED CULTIVARS

'Autumn Giant': *matures in mid-autumn, yet will stand in the ground until late spring.* **'Giant Winter'**: *late cultivar, slow to bolt.* **'Bleu de Solaise'**: *beautiful, deep greenish-purple foliage.* **'Verina'**: *strong resistance to rust.*

❀ LEEKS

SPRING			SUMMER			AUTUMN			WINTER		
Early	Mid	Late	Early	Mid	Late	Early	Mid	Late	Early	Mid	Late
										🌱	
🌱	🌱	🌱	➡	➡			✂	✂	✂	✂	
✂											

IN THE KITCHEN

Leeks, gentler in taste than other members of the onion family, make superb soups. Sliced and briefly sautéed in butter, they also combine with bacon to make an excellent filling for a tart. This one can be eaten hot or cold, but is best somewhere between the two.

LEEK TART
Serves 6 as a starter, 4 as a main course

For the shortcrust pastry
90g (3oz) butter
175g (6oz) plain flour
pinch of salt
a little cold water
For the filling
90g (3oz) butter
500g (1lb) leeks, washed, trimmed and finely sliced
black pepper and salt
125g (4oz) smoked streaky bacon
2 eggs
175ml (6fl oz) milk or single cream, or a mixture of the two

1 Make the pastry by rubbing the butter into the flour and salt to form fine crumbs. Bind with a little water to form a dough and leave to rest for 30 minutes.

2 To make the filling, melt the butter and cook the leeks gently for 3–4 minutes. Season with pepper and allow to cool. Grill the bacon and cut into small pieces.

3 Line a 23cm (9in) greased flan dish with the pastry and bake blind in a hot oven (200°C/400°F/gas mark 6) for about 10 minutes, until the pastry is lightly cooked.

4 Mix the bacon with the leeks and tip into the pastry case. Beat the eggs with the milk or cream. Add a little salt and pour over.

5 Bake in a cooler oven (180°C/350°F/gas mark 4) for about 30 minutes, until the egg is just set.

FLORENCE FENNEL
Foeniculum vulgare var. *dulce*

WITH ITS FINE FEATHERY FOLIAGE and neatly interleaved bulb, Florence fennel is an extremely decorative vegetable but, rather like a highly bred horse, it tends to bolt if faced with anything it does not understand. It is widely grown in the warm countries around the Mediterranean, especially Italy, where, well watered, it will grow unchecked to produce a succulent crop. In chillier climates, it may leap into flower before the base has swollen to anything even remotely edible.

Cultivation

The earliest sowings are the most likely to run up to flower where plants are checked by late chills. The best results in cool climates come from seed sown in midsummer. Allow 15 weeks between sowing and harvesting. Fennel withstands light frost, but is not generally hardy.

SITE AND SOIL Light sandy soil is best, although the bulbs must never dry out.

SOWING Do not sow too early. Florence fennel is one of many plants that adapts its behaviour to day length. Sow after the longest day to minimize the possibility of bolting. Scatter the seed thinly in drills outside (see page 170), 1cm (½in) deep in rows 30cm (12in) apart, watering first if the soil is dry.

THINNING Thinning is much better than transplanting, as fennel rarely recovers from the shock and bolts into flower instead of swelling to form a bulb. Thin to leave about 30cm (12in) between plants.

ROUTINE CARE Fennel must never be allowed to become starved or thirsty. Keep the plants growing smoothly by watering and feeding well. Mulch to conserve moisture and to keep down weeds. Once the bulbs start to swell, earth them up to keep plants stable and to blanch the stems (see page 167).

YIELD AND HARVESTING Expect about 9 bulbs of fennel from a 3m (10ft) row. Cut the bulbs just below ground level 3 weeks

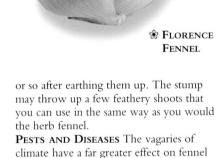

❀ **FLORENCE FENNEL**

or so after earthing them up. The stump may throw up a few feathery shoots that you can use in the same way as you would the herb fennel.

PESTS AND DISEASES The vagaries of climate have a far greater effect on fennel than any pest or disease.

RECOMMENDED CULTIVARS

'Cantino': *developed to resist early bolting.*
'Di Firenze': *authentic aniseed flavour.*
'Perfection': *produces medium-sized bulbs from an early summer sowing.*
'Sirio': *Italian-bred, solid, white bulbs.*
'Zefa Fino': *strong resistance to bolting, ideal for cool climates.*

SPRING			SUMMER			AUTUMN			WINTER		
Early	Mid	Late	Early	Mid	Late	Early	Mid	Late	Early	Mid	Late
			⚘	⚘		✂	✂	✂			

CELERIAC & KOHL RABI

Apium graveolens var. *rapaceum* &
Brassica oleracea Gongylodes Group

GREEN KOHL RABI

PURPLE KOHL RABI

CELERIAC

THE BULBOUS, EDIBLE PARTS of celeriac and kohl rabi are not roots, such as a carrot has, but swollen parts of the lower stem. Although home-grown celeriac rarely swells to the impressive size of shop-bought specimens, it has crisp, cut foliage that can be used to good effect in a potager. It is a rugged vegetable and, after a long growing season, shows a marked reluctance to leave the cradle. Horizontal roots cover the manically uneven surface and lifting requires a crane rather than a fork. Kohl rabi is one of the cabbage family and its smooth globes of purple or whitish-green can look very decorative in the kitchen garden.

Cultivation

The most critical time in raising celeriac is immediately after setting out the plants. Keep them growing as smoothly as possible, watering if necessary. They have a long growing season. Kohl rabi, in contrast, may be ready to pull only 7 or 8 weeks after sowing and is more tolerant of drought than most brassicas. Eat it when it is no larger than a tennis ball, as it can quickly turn woody.

SITE AND SOIL By nature, celeriac is a plant of marshland and likes rich, damp soil. Kohl rabi can take drier conditions and does best in fertile, light, sandy soil.

SOWING Sow celeriac in a pot inside in early spring (see page 168). Germination takes about 3 weeks. When the seedlings are large enough to handle, prick them out into trays, 7cm (3in) apart. You can also sow in modules: set several seeds in each one, thinning out the weakest seedlings. Sow kohl rabi little and often outdoors in its growing position (see page 170), 1cm (½in) deep, in drills 30cm (12in) apart.

TRANSPLANTING By the time of planting out, the celeriac seedlings should be about 7cm (3in) tall and hardened off (see page 169). Set them 30–40cm (12–16in) apart. Do not plant too deep. The point where the leaves join the root should be level with the soil surface. Thin kohl rabi as it develops, leaving the plants about 15–23cm (6–9in) apart.

ROUTINE CARE Water celeriac liberally and mulch to keep the ground moist. Gently pull off any leaves that start to splay out from the globe and do not allow secondary growing points to develop. Kohl rabi needs little attention apart from weeding.

YIELD AND HARVESTING You should get 8–10 celeriac and 15–20 kohl rabi from a 3m (10ft) row. Both can be left in the ground, even in winter, until needed.

PESTS AND DISEASES Celeriac may suffer the same problems as celery (see opposite). Clubroot is the most likely disease to attack kohl rabi (see page 193), but crops may also be spoiled by flea beetle or cabbage root fly (see page 191).

RECOMMENDED CULTIVARS

CELERIAC
'Iram': *modern cultivar with flesh that does not discolour.*
'Monarch': *smooth-skinned, tender flesh.*
KOHL RABI
'Purple Vienna': *purple type with some resistance to frost.* **'Rowel'**: *pale green with juicy, crisp-textured, white flesh.*

SPRING			SUMMER			AUTUMN			WINTER		
Early	Mid	Late	Early	Mid	Late	Early	Mid	Late	Early	Mid	Late
🌱		➡	➡				✂	✂	✂	✂	✂
✂	✂										
	🌿	🌿	🌿	🌿	🌿						
				✂	✂	✂	✂	✂			

☐ Celeriac	☐ Kohl rabi

IN THE KITCHEN

If you grow a modern type of celeriac such as 'Iram', you escape the palaver of using lemon juice to stop the flesh turning brown as you prepare it for cooking.

GRATIN OF CELERIAC
Serves 4

1 large or 2 small celeriac
6 tbsp freshly grated Parmesan cheese
30g (1oz) butter
30g (1oz) breadcrumbs
For the tomato sauce
125g (4oz) streaky bacon or Italian coppa, chopped
1 large onion, finely chopped
3 large cloves garlic, finely chopped
3 tbsp olive oil
1 large carrot, diced
1kg (2lb) tomatoes, skinned and chopped
150ml (¼ pint) dry white wine
salt and black pepper
dried oregano, to taste
about 8 fresh basil leaves, chopped

1 Preheat the oven to 190°C/ 375°F/gas mark 5.

2 Make the tomato sauce by softening the bacon, onion and garlic in the oil. Add the carrot, tomatoes and wine and cook over a high heat for 15 minutes, then add seasoning and herbs to taste.

3 Peel the celeriac, cut it into chunks and cook it in boiling, salted water for about 15 minutes or until just tender.

4 Drain and arrange the celeriac in layers in a shallow gratin dish, adding some grated Parmesan and a few knobs of butter between each of the layers.

5 Pour over the tomato sauce, then top with breadcrumbs and the remaining Parmesan and butter. Bake for about 25–30 minutes until the sauce is bubbling and the top is golden and crunchy.

CELERY *Apium graveolens*

HUNDREDS OF YEARS OF SELECTION have turned pungent wild celery into the succulent kind we now crunch noisily at table. There are three types. The hardiest are the trench varieties, which you need to blanch by earthing up. They mature in midwinter. Self-blanching cultivars require less effort, but need mild winters. American green varieties have long, pale stems and a reasonable flavour. But the best flavour of all – aromatic and nutty – comes from an old-fashioned trench type such as 'Giant Pink'.

Cultivation

Good celery is rated by the size and succulence of its leaf stalks. To achieve this end, plants have to grow fast with an endless supply of water to hand. Self-blanching and green cultivars are ready by late summer, trench celery by midwinter.

SITE AND SOIL Deep, well-drained ground is a necessity. Work plenty of organic matter into the soil. The pH needs to be between 6.5 and 7.5.

SOWING Seed may take a long time to germinate or fail completely if too warm. Aim for 10–15°C (50–60°F) and sow the seed indoors on the surface of a pot of compost (see page 168). Do not cover; it needs light to germinate. Prick out seedlings into trays as soon as possible.

TRANSPLANTING When the seedlings have 5 or 6 proper leaves, harden them off and transplant to their growing quarters (see page 169). Dig a trench 30cm (12in) deep for trench celery, half fill it with manure and top it with 5cm (2in) of soil so that the final level is about 10cm (4in) below the surrounding soil. Leave the soil to settle. Space the plants 30–45cm (12–18in) apart. Self-blanching and green kinds can be planted in a block, 15–30cm (6–12in) apart, depending on the size of plant you want to grow.

ROUTINE CARE Water generously during the whole growing period, and mulch to conserve moisture. On hungry soils, a liquid feed given a month or so after transplanting may be beneficial. Start

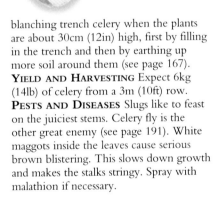

SELF-BLANCHING CELERY

blanching trench celery when the plants are about 30cm (12in) high, first by filling in the trench and then by earthing up more soil around them (see page 167).

YIELD AND HARVESTING Expect 6kg (14lb) of celery from a 3m (10ft) row.

PESTS AND DISEASES Slugs like to feast on the juiciest stems. Celery fly is the other great enemy (see page 191). White maggots inside the leaves cause serious brown blistering. This slows down growth and makes the stalks stringy. Spray with malathion if necessary.

RECOMMENDED CULTIVARS

TRENCH CELERY
'Giant Pink': *superb flavour, pale pink stems.*
SELF-BLANCHING CELERY
'Celebrity': *early and resistant to bolting.*
GREEN CELERY
'Victoria': *early, crunchy and well flavoured.*

SPRING			SUMMER			AUTUMN			WINTER		
Early	Mid	Late	Early	Mid	Late	Early	Mid	Late	Early	Mid	Late
🌱		➡	➡		✂	✂	✂	✂	✂	✂	

ASPARAGUS
Asparagus officinalis

ASPARAGUS TAKES UP A LOT OF SPACE in a decorative kitchen garden. You need at least 30 crowns, or roots, to be able to pick a decent meal at any one time and, once made, the bed should remain undisturbed for 20 years. But on the other hand, there are few vegetables that are so ambrosial, and asparagus is expensive to buy. It also deteriorates fast. The asparagus pan should be steaming on the stove even before you cut the spears. Left to itself, asparagus produces both male and female plants: female ones carry small red berries among the fern that grows up when you finish cutting the spears in early summer. You can now buy "all-male" asparagus that produces fatter spears.

Cultivation

Make a good rich home for your asparagus by digging in plenty of manure. The time spent will be amply rewarded by the crop. Any perennial weeds must be eradicated before you start. Traditional asparagus beds are 1.2m (4ft) wide, giving room for 2 rows of plants and allowing for easy weeding and cutting. Leave 1m (3ft) between beds.

SITE AND SOIL Asparagus grows best in well-drained, sandy soils, but not hungry ones. Incorporate grit as well as manure if the soil is heavy. On really heavy soil, make a deep bed (see page 166) so that water drains away from the crowns. If they are permanently soggy, they rot. Acid soils will need to be limed (see page 161) to achieve a pH of 6.5–7.5.

PLANTING Asparagus can be raised from seed – the cheapest method – but is usually sold ready-grown as crowns, which may be 1–3 years old. The younger crowns transplant more easily, although you will have to wait longer before picking a decent crop. If you plant 1-year-old crowns, you can start cutting in the second year after planting. Plant them in early spring, about 45cm (18in) apart in rows that are also 45cm (18in) apart. Soak the crowns in water for 2 hours before planting.

ROUTINE CARE Asparagus must be kept free of weeds at all times. In some European countries, white asparagus is preferred to green and the shoots are blanched by earthing up (see page 167).

Mulch the beds thickly with manure or compost in late winter. Cut down the fern only when it has turned yellow in the autumn.

YIELD AND HARVESTING Expect 8–10 spears from each crown, once established. Cut just beneath the surface of the soil when the spears are 12–18cm (5–7in) high. The cutting season should last no more than 6–8 weeks, ending in early summer. Cut sparingly in the first year.

PESTS AND DISEASES Moles and slugs can inflict great damage (see page 192). The asparagus beetle overwinters by asparagus beds and lays its black eggs on the emerging shoots. Both larvae and adult beetles feed on the foliage (see page 191). Violet root rot is a soil-borne fungus that infects asparagus roots (see page 193). They become covered with violet strands of mycelium that may even kill the plant. Move the bed and burn infected stock.

RECOMMENDED CULTIVARS

'Connover's Colossal': *early and heavy-cropping.*
'Franklin': *all-male, high-quality spears.*
'Giant Mammoth': *the best for heavy soils.*
'Limbras': *exceptionally thick shoots.*
'Lucullus': *the original all-male variety.*

PLANTING ASPARAGUS CROWNS
Take out a trench 30cm (12in) wide and 20cm (8in) deep with a ridge down the middle. Plant asparagus crowns with roots draped either side of the ridge. Crowns should be 10cm (4in) below the surface when the trench is filled in.

IN THE KITCHEN

Given the shortness of the season, there is little time to tire of asparagus simply steamed and served with butter or, for a special occasion, hollandaise or cream sauce. Steam it by standing the spears upright so that the heads are out of the water. Fix a domed cap of foil over the pan instead of a lid.

HOLLANDAISE SAUCE
Serves 4 as a starter

2 tbsp white wine vinegar
4 tbsp water
4 crushed black peppercorns
4 egg yolks
175g (6oz) butter, melted
salt and black pepper
juice of 1 lemon, or to taste

1 Place the vinegar, water and peppercorns in a pan and boil to reduce by a third. Strain into a basin set on top of a pan of hot water (or into a double saucepan).

2 Over a gentle heat, whisk the egg yolks into the mixture until it begins to thicken. Add the butter in a slow stream, whisking continuously.

3 Season with salt, pepper and lemon juice and serve promptly while the sauce is still warm.

CREAM SAUCE
Serves 4 as a starter

300ml (½ pint) single cream
2 tbsp mixed, chopped fresh herbs
(try tarragon, chives and parsley)
salt, black and cayenne pepper

1 Gently heat the cream, stir in the herbs and season to taste with the salt and the peppers.

2 Serve warm. If you prefer, this sauce is also good served slightly chilled as a dressing for cold spears of asparagus. You need not heat the cream for this.

RHUBARB
Rheum × cultorum

RHUBARB IS A MISFIT. It is the vegetable that wants to be a fruit and nobody quite knows in which category to put it. Unfortunately, it is not so showy as its ornamental cousin *Rheum palmatum*, with its purplish-red, deeply cut leaves. Culinary rhubarb has stalks of greenish-pink that will grow longer if covered with a forcing pot. In terracotta, these are very decorative, but a bucket will do the same job.

Cultivation

Like asparagus, rhubarb, once settled, does not like to be moved and will tie up ground for a long time. But you can pick it from early spring until summer and it will give little trouble if planted in the right place.

SITE AND SOIL Rhubarb will grow on any kind of soil, including an acid one, providing it is well fed and well drained. The site needs to be open, away from shade cast by overhanging trees. Dig plenty of manure or compost into the soil before planting.

PLANTING Rhubarb can be grown from seed, but is usually planted as a dormant "set". Each set should have a plump bud sitting on top of the rootstock with plenty of fibrous root underneath. You must start with certified virus-free stock. Plant in the dormant season between mid-autumn and early spring, setting the plants 1m (3ft) apart. The buds should be covered by no more than 2cm (1in) of soil.

ROUTINE CARE The best plants are those that can be kept damp in summer and dry in winter. Water liberally, if necessary, and mulch around the stems with manure or grass cuttings to retain moisture. Tall stems of cream flowers are produced on mature plants. These are decorative and can be left without harming the plant in any way. About every 5 years, plants need dividing (see page 172). The most vigorous offshoots are generally those that have

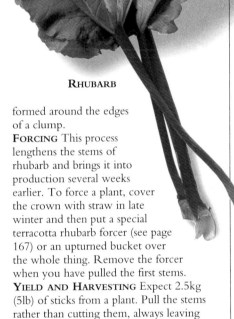

RHUBARB

formed around the edges of a clump.

FORCING This process lengthens the stems of rhubarb and brings it into production several weeks earlier. To force a plant, cover the crown with straw in late winter and then put a special terracotta rhubarb forcer (see page 167) or an upturned bucket over the whole thing. Remove the forcer when you have pulled the first stems.

YIELD AND HARVESTING Expect 2.5kg (5lb) of sticks from a plant. Pull the stems rather than cutting them, always leaving at least 4. Do not pull any stems after midsummer to give the plant a chance to replenish itself.

PESTS AND DISEASES The most likely problems are untreatable: honey fungus, which attacks the roots (see page 193), and various virus problems that either cause stunted growth or an unhealthy mottling on the leaves. Dig up affected sets and burn them.

RECOMMENDED CULTIVARS

'Champagne Early': *produces long, bright red stalks of good flavour.* **'Timperley Early'**: *red-skinned, green-fleshed variety.* **'Victoria'**: *reliable late variety.*

CARROTS *Daucus carota*

MODERN CARROTS ARE ALL DESCENDED from purple and yellow types that came into Europe from Arabia in the 14th century. Selection by 17th-century Dutch growers produced the forerunners of the varieties we grow today. For decades, breeders have been in pursuit of the perfect carrot, but unfortunately the carrot fly, *Psila rosae*, whose larvae greedily attack the roots, has had the same objective. Intercropping carrots with onions or annual flowers such as love-in-a-mist may discourage attack by carrot fly. The ferny, upright foliage also contrasts well with the rounded shapes of lettuce or with strappy garlic leaves.

❀ NANTES CARROTS

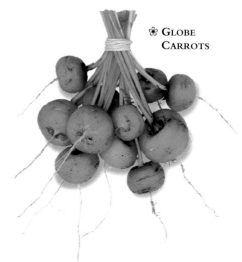

❀ GLOBE CARROTS

Cultivation

By sowing seed of different varieties at regular intervals, you can have fresh carrots for much of the season. The Nantes and globe types mature from mid to late summer; Autumn King types are ready in autumn; Chantenay types crop from late autumn to early winter, and Berlicum from late winter to spring. To limit carrot fly damage, sow a fast-maturing Nantes type in midsummer to avoid the peak egg-laying period.

SITE AND SOIL The ideal soil is light, well drained and deep so that roots can swell without constraint. In heavy soil, leaves tend to grow at the expense of roots, which are sometimes misshapen.

SOWING Sow seed as thinly as possible (see page 170), 1cm (½in) deep, in rows 15cm (6in) apart. Seed germinates poorly below 8°C (45°F), so for early sowings warm up the soil beforehand with cloches or plastic film (see page 166).

THINNING Thinning carrots is bad practice. It releases a smell that the carrot fly finds irresistible and the little crevices left in the soil provide ready-made entry holes for the adults to lay their eggs. Sow sparsely instead.

ROUTINE CARE Weed carefully while the seedlings are small. Do not overwater.

YIELD AND HARVESTING Expect 4–5kg (8–10lb) from a 3m (10ft) row. On light soils, leave carrots in the ground and pull them as required. On heavy soils, lift and store in boxes of sand (see page 187).

PESTS AND DISEASES Carrot fly is the most persistent nuisance as the larvae burrow deep into the roots (see page 190).

Some cultivars have a much greater resistance to it than others. This seems to be associated with the level of phenolic acids contained in the roots. The fly's larvae need the acids to further their own development and stay away from carrots with a low level of this particular fix.

RECOMMENDED CULTIVARS

NANTES
'Nanco': *long, cylindrical roots of exceptional flavour, maturing late summer to early autumn.* **'Nantes Express'**: *ready by midsummer, excellent quality.* **'Panther'**: *early hybrid for summer cropping, resistant to cracking.*

AUTUMN KING
'Campestra': *deep orange-red, wide-topped roots, for use in autumn and early winter.*

CHANTENAY
'Chantenay Royal': *stump-rooted, ready late autumn and winter, excellent flavour.*

BERLICUM
'Camberley': *tapered roots 18–23cm (7–9in) long; overwinters well on heavy soils.* **'Ingot'**: *long stump roots, excellent flavour and high concentrations of carotene and vitamin C.* **'Bangor'**: *(Berlicum/Nantes hybrid) medium-sized, cylindrical, smooth-skinned roots, ready late winter to early spring.*

GLOBE
'Parmex': *tiny, globe-shaped roots, very sweet and ideal for growing in containers.*

SPRING			SUMMER			AUTUMN			WINTER		
Early	Mid	Late	Early	Mid	Late	Early	Mid	Late	Early	Mid	Late
❀	❀	❀	❀	❀							
✄				✄	✄	✄	✄	✄	✄	✄	✄

IN THE KITCHEN

Home-grown carrots have a much sweeter flavour than shop-bought ones. Do not overcook them. If you steam them, you may feel that they need nothing more than to be finished off with some melted butter and finely chopped parsley.

SUMMER CARROTS WITH CREAM SAUCE
Serves 4

375–500g (¾–1lb) summer carrots, scrubbed and cut into chunks
300ml (½ pint) chicken stock
½–1 tsp puréed garlic (see below)
150ml (¼ pint) single cream
to garnish: 1 tbsp chopped chervil

1 Simmer the carrots in the chicken stock for about 8 minutes, or until just tender.
2 Stir in puréed garlic (see below) to taste. The sauce should be quite thick. Add the cream and sprinkle with chervil to serve.

CULINARY NOTES

❧ This recipe calls for puréed garlic. A small supply is very easy to make. Cover several heads of peeled cloves with boiling water, and blanch them for 2–3 minutes. Drain and repeat the blanching process twice more using fresh water, until the cloves are really soft. Then purée them. The purée will keep for several weeks in the refrigerator topped with olive oil.
❧ Hot steamed carrots are delicious sprinkled with grated Stilton cheese and browned under the grill.
❧ If you like them raw, try Madhur Jaffrey's Indian carrot salad: heap some grated carrot on to a large dish and sprinkle it with fresh lemon juice to taste. Heat together in a pan 2 tablespoons of oil and 1 tablespoon of mustard seeds until the seeds start to pop. Pour the mixture over the carrot.

BEETROOT *Beta vulgaris*
subsp. *vulgaris*

YOU CAN USE SHINING beetroot leaves to telling effect among the lacy foliage of carrots or coriander. They also look sumptuous with bright pot marigolds. For the greatest impact, choose a variety like 'Bull's Blood' with dark burgundy-coloured leaves. Beetroot is easy to grow but has had problems shedding its dreary pickled image. Try cooking it fresh with butter and orange juice.

Cultivation

Besides the traditional deep red varieties, there are many "novelty" beetroot that are worth experimenting with: yellow and white forms, and a very pretty old cultivar called 'Chioggia', which has dark flesh marked with concentric white rings. Unfortunately the contrast fades when the beetroot is cooked.
SITE AND SOIL The best soil is rich, light and fertile, but not recently manured.
SOWING Start sowing in mid-spring. Choose a bolt-resistant cultivar for early sowings, to stop plants running to seed, and sow as thinly as possible, 1.5cm (¾in) deep, in rows 20cm (8in) apart, or 30cm (12in) for later sowings (see page 170). Seed contains a natural germination inhibitor and it may help to soak it for half an hour first. The seed is usually gathered in small clusters, but monogerm varieties produce only one plant from each seed and so reduce the need for thinning.
THINNING Thin as soon as the seedlings start to touch each other, leaving them about 15cm (6in) apart (see page 171).
ROUTINE CARE Mulch around the crop to conserve moisture, and keep weeded.
YIELD AND HARVESTING Expect 5–8kg (10–18lb) from a 3m (10ft) row. Use before the roots are too big. Beetroot can be stored in boxes of sand in winter, but twist off the foliage first (see page 187).
PESTS AND DISEASES Beetroot is generally free from pests and diseases.

❀ **LONG BEETROOT** 'Forono'

❀ **ROUND BEETROOT** 'Monogram'

RECOMMENDED CULTIVARS

ROUND BEETROOT
'Action': *ideal for baby beet, pull when golf-ball size.* **'Bikores'**: *the most bolt-resistant.* **'Boltardy'**: *can be sown earlier than other cultivars.* **'Bull's Blood'**: *dark, lustrous leaves.* **'Monogram'**: *monogerm variety.*
LONG BEETROOT
'Cheltenham Green Top': *old variety with excellent flavour.*
'Forono': *slow to go woody, good flavour.*

	SPRING			SUMMER			AUTUMN			WINTER		
	Early	Mid	Late	Early	Mid	Late	Early	Mid	Late	Early	Mid	Late
	⚘	⚘	⚘	⚘								
			✄	✄	✄	✄	✄	✄				

POTATOES *Solanum tuberosum*

DIGGING POTATOES IS ALWAYS AN ADVENTURE. The haulm (stems and leaves) gives no indication of the extent of the treasure buried underneath. Sometimes the potatoes cluster together as neatly as a clutch of goose eggs. At other times you dig wildly down a row to find that slugs or blight have beaten you to the prize. Even their best friends would not call potatoes decorative, but what they lack in looks they make up for in comfort. A baked potato, or thick potato and leek soup, makes even the deepest winter doldrum more bearable. In Britain, thanks to connoisseurs who have rescued old varieties from the edge of oblivion, seed suppliers now offer many more kinds than they did 10 years ago. Try a few different novelties each year. There are three types: first earlies, second earlies and maincrop, which you lift in their appropriate seasons from midsummer until autumn.

Cultivation

Early potatoes mature in about 14–16 weeks, second earlies in 16–17 weeks and maincrop potatoes in 18–20 weeks. The heaviest crops come from the later liftings. Choose a succession of varieties, bearing in mind that, in a small garden, early potatoes are the most valuable. You can grow potatoes in pots, but you should not try to fit more than 2 plants in a container less than 30cm (12in) wide and deep.

SITE AND SOIL Although they prefer slightly acid ground (pH 5–6), potatoes grow in a wide range of soils, doing best in moisture-retentive ground. Dig in plenty of manure or compost the autumn before planting.

SOWING Before planting, potatoes are usually "chitted" or sprouted. Do this by setting them in a single layer in trays or boxes indoors, the end with the most "eyes" uppermost, so that shoots start to grow. This generally takes about 6 weeks. Do not plant early potatoes until a month before the last frost is expected. Set them about 10–12cm (4–5in) deep and 30cm (12in) apart in rows 60cm (24in) apart (see opposite). Plant second earlies and maincrop types from mid-spring, setting them at slightly wider spacings, 38cm (15in) apart in rows 75cm (30in) apart. You can also use a no-dig method, laying the potatoes in shallow depressions on top of the soil and then mulching them thickly with compost, grass cuttings or leaf mould. It sounds lazy, but it works.

ROUTINE CARE Earth up potatoes to prevent the greening of any that push their way up to the soil surface (see opposite). With the no-dig method, top up the mulch as necessary. For high yields, water thoroughly once every 2 weeks.

YIELD AND HARVESTING Expect 6–10kg (14–23lb) from a 3m (10ft) row. The earliest crops can be lifted when the flowers on the haulm begin to open, the latest when the haulm has died down. Store in a frost-free shed in the dark, to stop them turning green (see page 186).

PESTS AND DISEASES Eelworm is the worst pest and rotating crops is one way to dissuade it (see page 192). Blight can be a problem in cool, damp summers (see page 193). Where it is prevalent, choose blight-resistant cultivars.

RECOMMENDED CULTIVARS

FIRST EARLIES
'Concorde': *oval tubers, pale yellow flesh, exceptional flavour.* **'Epicure'**: *very old variety, frost-resistant, but susceptible to blight.*

SECOND EARLIES
'Estima': *resistant to slugs, blight, drought. Yellow, slightly waxy flesh that cooks well.* **'Wilja'**: *blight-resistant, high-yielding, good for potato salads.*

MAINCROP
'Desirée': *oval and red-skinned, good for chips and baking.* **'Navan'**: *floury, firm flesh, resistant to eelworm.* **'Pink Fir Apple'**: *not ready until mid-autumn, but has the flavour of a new potato. Superb in salads.*

IN THE KITCHEN

To taste potatoes at their best, you need to choose the right kind for the right dish. Some, like 'Desirée', mash well; others, like 'Epicure', bake beautifully, while knobbly, old-fashioned 'Pink Fir Apple' is supreme in salads. No one potato does everything equally well.

ONION, BACON AND POTATO HOTPOT
Serves 4

(The proportions of the three main ingredients can be varied to taste.)
a little butter
500g (1lb) onions, finely sliced
250g (8oz) bacon, finely chopped
750g (1½ lb) potatoes, thinly sliced
For the sauce
60g (2oz) butter
60g (2oz) flour
600ml (1 pint) milk
125g (4oz) strong Cheddar cheese, grated
salt and black pepper, optional

1 Preheat the oven to 190°C/ 375°F/gas mark 5. (Use a slightly lower temperature if the dish you are using is shallow and wide rather than deep.)

2 Butter a deep ovenproof dish (with a lid, if possible), and put in the onion, bacon and potato in layers, finishing with a potato layer.

3 Make the sauce by combining the butter and flour in a saucepan over a low heat. Slowly add the milk, stirring all the time to avoid lumps. Stir in the cheese until melted. Season if necessary, then pour the sauce over the layers of potato, onion and bacon.

4 Cover the dish (with foil if there is no lid) and bake for about 1 hour, or until the potatoes are cooked. Uncover the dish for the final 10 minutes so that the top becomes nicely crisp and brown.

PLANTING AND EARTHING UP

1 Make a drill 10–12cm (4–5in) deep and set the potatoes in it so that the ends with the most sprouts are pointing upward. Cover with soil. Do not plant early potatoes too soon (see opposite) as the foliage is easily frosted.

2 Earth up potatoes when the foliage is about 30cm (12in) high by carefully drawing up the soil around the stems with a hoe. This prevents tubers near the surface from turning green. Green potatoes are poisonous.

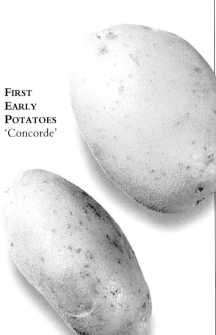

FIRST EARLY POTATOES 'Concorde'

MAINCROP POTATOES 'Navan'

MAINCROP POTATOES 'Pink Fir Apple'

SECOND EARLY POTATOES 'Estima'

TURNIPS & SWEDES
Brassica rapa rapa & B. napus napobrassica

IT HAS USUALLY BEEN THE TURNIP'S MISFORTUNE to be lumped together with the swede, a vegetable of much less charm. The swede began to spread through Europe from Sweden in the 18th century. It is large and yellow-fleshed and however you cook it, it seems to smack more of the farmyard than the dinner table. The turnip, especially since the arrival of the small, summer-maturing Japanese types, is far more succulent, though less hardy. There are two important rules to bear in mind with turnips: never let them get too big and never eat them when they are too old. Neither vegetable is very decorative, but if you grow your own turnips, you can enjoy the bonus of cooking and eating the young green tops.

Cultivation

The early-maturing types of turnip deteriorate quickly. Sow small batches of seed at 3-weekly intervals. A cultivar such as 'Tokyo Cross' may be ready to harvest after only 6 weeks; hardy autumn types take about 12 weeks to mature.

SITE AND SOIL Neither crop will thrive in an acid soil (the ideal pH is about 7). Use ground that has been well manured for a previous crop and is cool and crumbly. Summer sowings of turnip can be made in light shade, if the soil is moist.

SOWING Start sowing turnips in mid-spring for spring and summer crops, and from mid to late summer for autumn and winter crops. Sow seed as thinly as possible in drills about 1.5cm (⅝in) deep in rows 30–38cm (12–15in) apart (see page 170). Start sowing swedes in mid-spring. They can be sown at the same depth, but need a wider spacing of 38–45cm (15–18in) between the rows.

THINNING Turnips grow fast and thinning should be done while the seedlings are still small (see page 171). Thin spring and summer plants to 10cm (4in) apart, autumn and winter plants to 15cm (6in) apart. Swedes need more room to develop. Thin them to 25cm (10in) apart.

ROUTINE CARE If necessary, water during dry periods.

HARVESTING AND YIELD Expect 6kg (14lb) of maincrop turnips and 14kg (30lb) of swedes from a 3m (10ft) row. Early sowings of turnip should be pulled when the roots are no bigger than a golf ball.

Scratch away some soil from the top of the roots if you want to check the size. Summer-sown maincrop varieties can be left in the ground until needed, as can swedes. Any roots not used by midwinter should be lifted and stored in a cool, frost-free place (see page 187).

PESTS AND DISEASES Turnips and swedes are brassicas and, like others in the family, their seedlings may be attacked by flea beetle (see page 191).

RECOMMENDED CULTIVARS

TURNIPS
'Milan Red': *red-topped roots, good for overwintering.* **'Milan White Forcing'**: *early crops of flattish roots.* **'Tokyo Cross'**: *fast-maturing, with small, white-fleshed roots. May bolt if sown before midsummer.* **'Golden Ball'**: *tender, compact, yellow-fleshed roots.*

SWEDES
'Marian': *globe-shaped, yellow-fleshed roots, resistant to mildew.*

SPRING			SUMMER			AUTUMN			WINTER		
Early	Mid	Late	Early	Mid	Late	Early	Mid	Late	Early	Mid	Late
	⚘	⚘		⚘	⚘						
	✂	✂		✂	✂		✂	✂	✂	✂	
⚘	⚘	⚘				✂	✂	✂	✂	✂	

☐ Turnips   ☐ Swedes

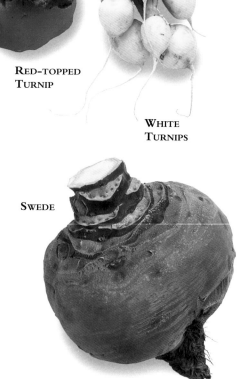

RED-TOPPED TURNIP

WHITE TURNIPS

SWEDE

PARSNIPS *Pastinaca sativa*

NOBODY WRITES POEMS ABOUT PARSNIPS, nor do you find chefs fussing over them in expensive restaurants, as they do with courgettes and fennel. It was the cookery writer Jane Grigson who first pointed out that the Russian for parsnip was *pasternak*. Would we feel the same way about *Dr Zhivago* if we knew it had been written by Boris Parsnip? Yet before the advent of the potato, the unfairly neglected parsnip was highly valued for its sweetness, its hardiness and its ability to overwinter in the ground.

Cultivation

Cold intensifies the flavour of parsnips and converts some of their starch into sugar so that they are sweeter in cold winters than they are in mild ones.

SITE AND SOIL Grow parsnips in an open situation on soil that is deep and light with a pH around 6.5. Acid soils make the roots more prone to canker. Recently manured ground has traditionally been avoided for this crop as it was thought to promote forking in the root, but research has not borne this out. On shallow soil, use a short, bulbous variety such as 'Avonresister'.

SOWING Seed must be fresh. Some vegetable seed can be kept from year to year with no appreciable effect on rates of germination. Not parsnip. Sow seed in spring, about 1cm (½in) deep in rows 30cm (12in) apart (see page 170). If the soil is cold, germination will be slow and erratic. You can warm it up with a floating mulch a month before sowing (see page 166). Crops raised from later sowings seem to be less prone to canker.

THINNING Thin the seedlings once they are well established. For large roots, leave 15cm (6in) between plants; for smaller ones, leave 7cm (3in).

ROUTINE CARE Parsnips are liable to split if watered after a prolonged dry spell. Water regularly, or not at all.

HARVESTING AND YIELD Expect 4kg (8lb) of parsnips from a 3m (10ft) row. Roots can be lifted from mid-autumn if the ground is not frozen. Where winters are severe, laying straw over the crop makes lifting easier.

PESTS AND DISEASES Canker is the main enemy, showing as reddish-brown or black patches (see page 194). There is no effective remedy. Choose a resistant variety and sow later rather than earlier.

PARSNIPS

RECOMMENDED CULTIVARS

'Andover': *long, narrow roots, US-bred, good resistance to canker.* **'Avonresister'**: *short-rooted, good on shallow soil.* **'Cobham Improved Marrow'**: *long shape, smooth skin, good canker-resistance.* **'Javelin'**: *vigorous, giving high yields.* **'Tender and True'**: *traditional cultivar, very long roots with little hard core.*

	SPRING			SUMMER			AUTUMN			WINTER		
	Early	Mid	Late	Early	Mid	Late	Early	Mid	Late	Early	Mid	Late
	🌱	🌱	🌱					✄	✄	✄	✄	✄

IN THE KITCHEN

Traditionally roasted with a joint of meat, parsnips have many other roles to play in the kitchen. They make delicious purées and, having a rich sweetness themselves, combine particularly well with sharp fruit such as apple.

PARSNIP AND APPLE BAKE
Serves 6

1.5kg (3lb) parsnips, peeled and cubed
a little butter, for greasing
2 large cooking apples, peeled, cored and thinly sliced
juice of a lemon
4 tsp soft brown sugar

1 Boil the parsnips for 5–10 minutes or until tender, drain, and then purée in a food processor or blender. Spread half the purée into a buttered gratin dish and cover it with half the apple slices.

2 Repeat with the remaining purée, arranging the second batch of apple slices neatly on top. Sprinkle the lemon juice and sugar over the apples.

3 Bake in a moderate oven (180°C/350°F/gas mark 4) for 30–40 minutes, until the apples have softened.

CULINARY NOTES

❦ Try glazing parsnips with melted butter mixed with a little fresh orange juice to serve as a side dish.

❦ You can make parsnip chips to eat as a snack or a side dish. Parboil them first, cut them up and deep-fry in hot oil.

❦ If you intend to roast parsnips, parboil them for a couple of minutes before putting them in the roasting pan. This will make them succulent and crisp.

❦ Parboiled parsnips are delicious finished off under the grill with a sprinkling of Parmesan cheese.

RADISHES *Raphanus sativus*

THE RADISH IS TAKEN MORE SERIOUSLY in China and Japan than it is in other countries. Chinese chefs carve huge 'China Rose' radishes into intricate flowers, and Japanese gardeners cultivate long white mooli radishes, a single root of which can weigh 15kg (33lb). The typical European red radish is the size of a marble, although there is a bigger, black Spanish radish grown for winter use. None is very decorative when growing, but they are good in salads and the summer varieties are useful as a catch crop.

Cultivation

Different types of radish need different treatment as regards sowing time. Start in early spring with the small red summer types, such as 'French Breakfast'. As these will be ready to harvest within a few weeks, you can grow them between other slower-maturing vegetables such as parsnips. Delay sowing mooli (daikon) types until after the longest day or they will run to seed, as will winter radishes. These are best sown toward late summer.

SITE AND SOIL Radishes grow best in a light, sandy soil in an open situation. Summer crops will tolerate partial shade.

SOWING Little and often is the key with summer radishes. Sow in short rows, 1cm (½in) deep and 15cm (6in) apart, at fortnightly intervals (see page 170). Encourage rapid germination by watering the drills if necessary. Sow mooli and winter types 1cm (½in) deep in rows 20–25cm (8–10in) apart, watering the drills first if the ground is dry.

THINNING Thin summer radishes to leave about 2cm (1in) between plants. Leave at least 15cm (6in) between mooli and winter types.

ROUTINE CARE This is an easy, carefree crop, requiring no feeding but some watering. Excessive watering makes leaves grow at the expense of the roots.

YIELD AND HARVESTING Expect about 30 summer radishes and 1.5kg (3lb) winter radishes from a 1m (3ft) row. Summer radishes should mature within a month and need to be eaten as quickly as possible before they become tough or woolly. If you let them run up to flower, the plants produce small, hot seedpods that can be steamed, stir-fried or made into a spicy pickle. Mooli and winter radishes have a much longer growing season. Expect to wait 3 months for a crop.

PESTS AND DISEASES Flea beetle may leave seedlings peppered with small holes, and roots of winter radishes may suffer from slug damage (see pages 191–92).

RECOMMENDED CULTIVARS

SUMMER RADISHES
'**Fluo**': *smooth, cylindrical roots, bright red with white tips.* '**French Breakfast**': *classic cylindrical root, mild and sweet.* '**Ribella**': *round roots that are slow to become pithy.*

MOOLI RADISHES
'**April Cross**': *roots more than 30cm (12in) long; stands well through winter.*
'**Mino Early**': *popular and mild.*

WINTER RADISHES
'**Black Spanish**': *old variety that can be round or long-rooted.*
'**Cherokee**': *round roots like a cricket ball.*
'**China Rose**': *long red roots, white flesh.*
'**Mantanghong**': *tennis-ball size with greenish-white skin and magenta flesh.*

SEEDPODS
'**Münchner Bier**': *good winter roots and by far the best pods, crunchy and succulent.*

SPRING			SUMMER			AUTUMN			WINTER		
Early	Mid	Late	Early	Mid	Late	Early	Mid	Late	Early	Mid	Late
⚘	⚘	⚘	⚘	⚘	⚘	⚘					
	✂	✂	✂	✂	✂	✂	✂				
				⚘	⚘	⚘	⚘				
							✂	✂	✂	✂	✂
✂											

☐ Summer radishes ☐ Mooli/winter radishes

SUMMER RADISHES

WINTER RADISH

MOOLI RADISH

JERUSALEM ARTICHOKES *Helianthus tuberosus*

MOST PEOPLE KNOW ONE THING about Jerusalem artichokes and that was described by the 17th-century botanist John Goodyer. "In my judgment," he wrote, "which way soever they be drest and eaten they stirre and cause a filthie loathsome wind within the bodie." Being tall, however, they make useful summer screens, and some cultivars bear large, yellow, daisy flowers.

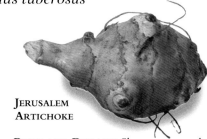

JERUSALEM ARTICHOKE

Cultivation

Jerusalem artichokes can grow to 3m (10ft) high and, as well as making a good screen, will provide shelter on a windy site.
SITE AND SOIL No plant could be less fussy, but the best tubers come from plants grown in rich, cool soil, where they may spread rapidly and become invasive.

PLANTING Plant tubers 10–15cm (4–6in) deep and 30cm (12in) apart in spring.
ROUTINE CARE The top growth dies back in late autumn. Cut the withered stalks to within 7cm (3in) of the ground.
YIELD AND HARVESTING Each plant should yield about 1.5kg (3lb) of tubers. Lift as required during winter, but clear completely by spring and replant as needed.

PESTS AND DISEASES Slugs may munch on the tubers (see page 192). The stems may be attacked by *Sclerotinia*, a fluffy white mould (see page 194). Burn them.

RECOMMENDED CULTIVARS

'Dwarf Sunray': *small and free-flowering.*
'Fuseau': *long, relatively smooth tubers.*

SALSIFY & SCORZONERA
Tragopogon porrifolius & Scorzonera hispanica

THESE TWO VEGETABLES GROW in a similar fashion, producing long, thin, thong-like roots that are fiddly to prepare. It is easiest to skin them after cooking, like new potatoes. Salsify is a biennial and produces conical flowerbuds that are delicious picked just before they open for use in omelettes. Salsify produces a whitish root, but scorzonera's is much darker and the foliage is less glaucous. It is a perennial. Its name comes from the Spanish word for viper, for the root was once used to cure snake bites.

SCORZONERA

SALSIFY

Cultivation

If you can persuade the roots to swell thicker than your little finger, you will be doing well. You also need to prevent the roots from forking, which they will do if the ground has been too recently manured. The flowers of mature plants are very decorative (salsify's are pinkish-purple, scorzonera's are bright yellow). As the plants age, the roots become woody.
SITE AND SOIL Both need deep, light soil and prefer an open, sunny site.
SOWING Sow seed thinly in mid-spring, 1cm (½in) deep, in drills that are at least 15cm (6in) apart (see page 170).
THINNING Thin to 10cm (4in) apart.
ROUTINE CARE Neither is troublesome, provided seed is sown in suitable soil.

YIELD AND HARVESTING You should get about 20 roots (2kg/4lb) from a 3m (10ft) row. They can be left in the ground until needed. If it is likely to freeze, lift the roots, trim the tops, and keep in a cool store, loosely wrapped in paper.
PESTS AND DISEASES White blister may develop on the leaves (see page 193).

RECOMMENDED CULTIVARS

SALSIFY
'Sandwich Island': *long, sweet roots.*
SCORZONERA
'Habil': *long, well-flavoured roots.*
'Russian Giant': *black skin, delicate flavour.*

SPRING			SUMMER			AUTUMN			WINTER		
Early	Mid	Late	Early	Mid	Late	Early	Mid	Late	Early	Mid	Late
🌱						✂	✂	✂	✂		

HERBS & EDIBLE FLOWERS

YOU ARE AS LIKELY TO FIND THYME on a rockery as in a herb garden or to use sage to bolster a herbaceous planting of misty blue as you are to pen it off in a kitchen garden. The decorative possibilities of herbs were recognized long ago: pyramids of bay to flank a front door, feathery stands of fennel to bring variety to a foliage border. Collecting herbs together in one place has an academic kind of charm, but you may find you can create better plant groups by combining them with annual flowers or perennials. Set your chives free to edge a rose bed or let them fraternize in a windowbox with ivy and feverfew. But be careful about liberating rampant herbs; *Mentha × gentilis* 'Variegata' is the only mint that will not try to overrun its neighbours.

TIME FOR BASIL
Basil is one of the most rewarding of herbs to grow, either outside in beds or in pots on a windowsill. Most common is the plain green basil, but there are types with luxuriant purple leaves and others, such as Greek basil, that grow as neatly as topiary.

BORDER OF FENNEL
Both green and bronze-leaved types of fennel have an important part to play in this cleverly thought-out herbaceous border. Seen here in late spring, the fennels' flat heads of yellow flowers will later reinforce the colour of the golden hop climbing the backdrop of the hedge.

INTRICATE SAGE

'Tricolor' is the most complex of all sage cultivars. The green leaves have white edges and the new growth is flushed with pink and purple. It grows more weakly than other types, and is not reliably hardy. Plant it in full sun, where it can make a low, informal hedge.

CHEERFUL CHIVES

Chives, often used as edging, combine here with frilly lettuce to fill the box-edged bed of a potager. The purple flowers echo the tone set by the dark-leaved lettuce. If chives are sheared down when they begin to look scruffy, they will quickly sprout again.

BORAGE BLUES

Although the foliage is somewhat coarse, the fine hairs on the stems and flowerheads give borage a shimmering quality, especially when seen against the light. In mixed plantings use it with foxgloves, or grow it in its own bed in a formal fashion and allow it to self-seed with abandon.

ANNUAL & BIENNIAL HERBS

THESE HERBS NEED TO BE SOWN each spring, so use their relative impermanence to advantage by growing them in different places every year where they can bring variety to the decorative kitchen garden. The plan for a herb garden on page 49 mixes annual with perennial herbs in a formal design, but you can grow annual herbs in rows among vegetables to add colour and contrast to a productive plot. You could also fill an open corner with some of the sun lovers, broadcasting the seed in irregular patches to produce a carefree, random effect.

DILL
Anethum graveolens
Dill is grown for the aniseed flavour of its leaves and seeds, the seeds having the stronger taste. Like fennel, it has thread-like leaves and flat heads of yellow flowers from mid to late summer. 'Dukat' is the best strain for leaves, 'Mammoth' for seed.
CULTIVATION Height 1m (3ft). Sow in drills or broadcast seed in a sunny spot (see page 170), from spring to midsummer. Sow by mid-spring if you want to harvest the seeds, to be sure of them ripening in time. Cut heads as the seeds turn brown and shake them upside down over a sheet of paper. Pick out insects and stray bits of stem before storing in an airtight jar.

ANGELICA
Angelica archangelica
A statuesque biennial, producing umbels of pale green flowers on tall, stout stems. *Angelica gigas* has dramatic purple stems.
CULTIVATION Height 1.8m (6ft). Thrives in moist soil, in sun or partial shade. It will self-seed enthusiastically. Sow outside in mid-spring and thin to 30cm (12in). Lift and plant in permanent positions in late summer.

CHERVIL
Anthriscus cerefolium
Fresh chervil is a revelation to anyone used only to the dried kind. It grows fast, and useful quantities of its ferny leaves can be picked only 6 weeks after sowing.
CULTIVATION Height 30cm (12in). Prefers light shade. Sow in drills or broadcast seed (see page 170) fortnightly in small batches from early spring until late summer. Grown in deep boxes in a greenhouse kept at 8°C (45°F), it will give fresh supplies of leaves all winter.

BORAGE
Borago officinalis
Borage is easy to please and bees love it. The brilliant blue flowers can be sprinkled on salads, while the cucumber-flavoured leaves are traditionally used in Pimms.
CULTIVATION Height 60cm (24in). Prefers a sunny site and well-drained soil. Sow in spring in drills 30cm (12in) apart (see page 170). Thin to 30cm (12in) apart.

MARIGOLD
Calendula officinalis
An enthusiastic self-seeder with bright orange flowers that continue throughout summer. Use the petals instead of saffron to flavour and colour rice, or sprinkle them fresh on top of a green salad.
CULTIVATION Height 45cm (18in). Likes sun. Broadcast seed in early spring (see page 171), covering with 5mm (¼in) of soil. Thin to 15cm (6in) between plants.

CORIANDER
Coriandrum sativum
The first leaves of coriander are like flat French parsley, but as the plant shoots up, the leaves become wispy and develop a different taste. The seeds and the first leaves, which can be difficult to get in sufficient quantity, are what you need for cooking. 'Cilantro' is the best strain for leaves, 'Moroccan' for seeds.
CULTIVATION Height 1m (3ft). Prefers sun. Seed germinates quickly. For a constant supply of leaves, sow in drills or broadcast seed fortnightly in small batches from early spring (see page 170). You can also sow quite thickly in a large pot indoors and snip off foliage as needed. The seeds are ready to harvest in late summer, but you have to be quick since they drop as soon as they are ripe.

BASIL
Ocimum basilicum
One of the most rewarding herbs to grow. It can be raised very successfully on a windowsill indoors (see The City Larder, page 42) and picked until late winter. Grown outside, its season is shorter, for it is tender. For fat, bushy plants, pinch out the tops once they are established. This will force new growth to sprout from the leaf junctions. If you grow Greek basil, the plants will naturally be fat and bushy. 'Dark Opal' is a very decorative variety with large purple leaves. There are many others. All are good.
CULTIVATION Height 30–45cm (12–18in). Needs warmth and sun. Sow seed indoors in pots or trays in early spring and prick out seedlings into individual pots or containers (see page 168) to keep on the windowsill. Outside, sow seed 1cm (½in) deep in drills 38cm (15in) apart in late spring or early summer (see page 170). Thin seedlings to 30cm (12in) apart. Cover with a floating mulch (see page 166) for extra protection in the early stages.

PARSLEY
Petroselinum crispum
One of the most useful of all culinary herbs. You need two types: the curled kind for decorative effect, to grow among marigolds and red lettuce; and the flat-leaved French kind for the finest flavour.
CULTIVATION Height 30–45cm (12–18in). Grow in fertile, well-drained soil in sun or partial shade. Sow seed thinly in drills 25cm (10in) apart from early spring to early summer (see page 170). It may be slow to germinate, but do not give up hope. Thin gradually until plants are 23cm (9in) apart. Cut down in early autumn and water to encourage fresh growth.

NASTURTIUM
Tropaeolum majus
The colourful flowers make pretty edgings in a potager but are edible, too, and can be strewn over salads. The peppery leaves are excellent in salads or sandwiches, while the seeds can be used as a substitute for capers.
CULTIVATION Height 23–30cm (9–12in). Best in sun. Sow in situ in mid-spring, setting seed 1cm (½in) deep (see page 170).

DILL

ANGELICA

CHERVIL

BORAGE

MARIGOLD

BASIL

PURPLE-
LEAVED BASIL

CORIANDER

FLAT-
LEAVED
PARSLEY

CURLED
PARSLEY

NASTURTIUM

PERENNIAL HERBS

ALTHOUGH SOME OF THESE PLANTS reach an impressive height by summer, in winter they disappear from view. In a herb garden, mix them with some of the evergreen herbs overleaf. Several, notably tarragon, fennel, mint and sorrel, are thuggish in behaviour and your problem will be in controlling rather than growing them. Contain mint by planting it in a bottomless bucket sunk in the ground. Fennel spreads by enthusiastic self-seeding. Be prepared to cut off its head before it starts to shed its seed. Chives are blameless and, if space is limited, should be your first choice in this group.

CHIVES
Allium schoenoprasum
Chives make neat edgings for paths, the delicately onion-flavoured foliage topped with small, round heads of purple flowers from early to midsummer. They also do well in windowboxes if well watered. The dramatic giant variety 'Forescate' is twice the normal size. Chinese chives, *Allium tuberosum*, have white star-like flowers in late summer (see page 23) and the leaves taste mildly of garlic.
CULTIVATION Height 15–25cm (6–10in). Chives do best in moist, fertile soil. They can be raised from seed, but it is simpler to buy a clump and divide it with a sharp knife in early autumn to make more plants. Set these about 30cm (12in) apart.

HORSERADISH
Armoracia rusticana
The peppery-flavoured tap root is grated to flavour sauces. Horseradish is difficult to get rid of once established, so grow it in a corner where it can be left undisturbed.
CULTIVATION Height 60cm (24in). Plant the thongs (roots) in spring 30cm (12in) apart in a short row, with the top of the root about 5cm (2in) below the surface of the soil. Dig up roots as required.

FRENCH TARRAGON
Artemisia dracunculus
Tarragon spreads quickly by underground rhizomes, so you are unlikely to need more than one plant. The flavour of the leaves diminishes as plants get older. Renew them every 2–3 years.
CULTIVATION Height 45–60cm (18–24in). Plant in a sunny, sheltered site in light, well-drained soil in spring or autumn. Extend the cropping season by planting a few rhizomes in a cold frame.

FENNEL
Foeniculum vulgare
Fennel gives sculptural height to a herb garden, especially the bronze-leaved variety, *Foeniculum vulgare* 'Purpureum'. The filigree foliage is topped by flat heads of golden flowers in midsummer.
CULTIVATION Height 1.5–2.5m (5–8ft). Buy plants or raise them from seed (see page 170), and set them out in well-drained soil in spring or autumn. Cut down stems in autumn, and be ruthless about discarding unwanted seedlings or you will end up with a fennel forest.

LOVAGE
Levisticum officinale
A luxuriant plant, the leaves tasting of celery with a dash of yeast. These are the most commonly used part, but you can also use the seeds to flavour soup. Lovage takes at least 3 years to reach full size.
CULTIVATION Height 1.8m (6ft). Lovage likes rich, moist soil in sun or partial shade. You can buy plants or raise them from seed, sowing inside in early spring (see page 168) and transplanting seedlings to their final positions in early summer.

MINT
Mentha spp.
Mints are bullies, inclined to engulf their neighbours. Try to grow them together in one bed. *Mentha rotundifolia*, or applemint, with round, hairy leaves, is said to make the best mint sauce. Ginger mint (*Mentha × gentilis* 'Variegata') has gold-variegated leaves and makes excellent ground cover.
CULTIVATION Height 45cm–1m (18in–3ft). Mints like rich, moist soil and will grow happily in shade. If foliage becomes shabby in midsummer, shear it down to encourage fresh growth.

MARJORAM
Origanum spp.
Pot marjoram (*Origanum vulgare*) has purple-pink flowers, bliss for bees, but the flavour of the leaves is not as strong as that of sweet marjoram (*Origanum marjorana*). This has a smaller, neater, bushy habit, with greyish-green leaves and white flowers. Both flower in late summer, but sweet marjoram has a longer season. The herb can be used fresh or dried and brings a Mediterranean tang to the bland flavour of chicken. Like basil, marjoram has a natural affinity with tomato.
CULTIVATION Height 30–45cm (12–18in). Plant in late spring in well-drained soil in full sun. Cut bushes down by two-thirds in late autumn. Both types are reasonably hardy.

SORREL
Rumex spp.
Sorrel (*Rumex acetosa*) is a large-leaved plant, suspiciously like a dock. The leaves are sharp-tasting, becoming more bitter as the season progresses. Use fresh in small quantities in salads, or cook to make a purée. Sorrel also makes good soup. French or buckler-leaved sorrel (*Rumex scutatus*) has prettier leaves, like little shields, that loll around on the ground.
CULTIVATION Height 23–30cm (9–12in). Sorrel succeeds in any well-drained ground in sun or partial shade. Raise it from seed (see page 170) or buy plants to set out in spring or autumn. Pinch out the flowering stems when they appear, to force the plant to produce more leaves.

SWEET VIOLET
Viola odorata
The flowers, in shades of purple and white, are carried from late winter to mid-spring. They are often crystallized and used to decorate cakes, puddings and ice cream. You can also scatter them fresh over salads or use them to garnish a dish of fruit, tied in a little bunch with some of their own heart-shaped leaves.
CULTIVATION Height 7cm (3in). Plants of sweet violet are easy to establish in any fertile, moist soil. They will thrive in sun or partial shade, and clump up quickly by means of overground runners.

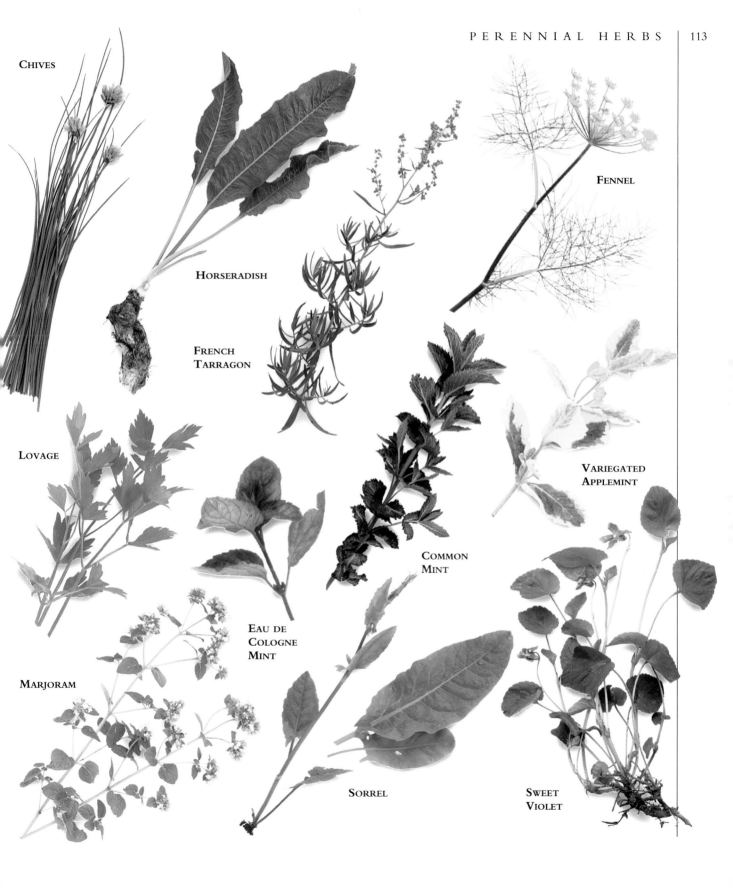

CHIVES

HORSERADISH

FENNEL

FRENCH
TARRAGON

LOVAGE

VARIEGATED
APPLEMINT

COMMON
MINT

EAU DE
COLOGNE
MINT

MARJORAM

SORREL

SWEET
VIOLET

SHRUBBY PERENNIAL HERBS

THIS GROUP INCLUDES herbs with evergreen leaves and woody stems that range in size from miniature bushes to small trees. They are likely to be permanent fixtures in any planting, the built-in furniture of the garden room, so you need to think carefully about where you site them. All are sun lovers and some, such as thyme, rosemary and sage, may rot if planted in wet, badly drained ground. Bay can be clipped into splendid architectural shapes, but rosemary, too, lends itself to topiary treatment. Sage has the most handsome leaves, whether grey, purple or variegated.

BAY
Laurus nobilis

Left to its own devices, the sweet bay makes a handsome tall tree, as broad as it is high, the evergreen leaves joined in mid-spring by knobbly little clusters of pale greenish flowers. Trimmed into a geometric shape or grown as a mop-headed standard, it is the perfect plant for a formal herb garden or potager. The 17th-century herbalist Nicholas Culpeper said that "neither witch nor devil, thunder nor lightning, will hurt a man in the place where a bay tree is". The leaves can be used fresh or dried in cooking; dried, they are an essential ingredient of a *bouquet garni*.

CULTIVATION Height 3–6m (10–20ft). Plant in mid-spring in a sunny, sheltered position. Bay is not dependably hardy, but will grow well in a pot that can be moved inside where winters are harsh. Clip to shape if necessary during the summer. Bay can sometimes become infested with scale insects (see page 191).

ROSEMARY
Rosmarinus officinalis

Most rosemaries have greenish foliage and bluish flowers, both of which drift toward grey. The cultivar 'Miss Jessopp's Upright' is markedly taller and more upright in growth than the common kind, and is useful, clipped as topiary, to give structure and height in a mixed planting. 'Severn Sea', with bright blue flowers, has the opposite habit and can be planted to sprawl over a step or the edge of a raised bed, or hug a sloping bank. Rosemary can also be trained, fan-like, against a wall. If you want to train it into a more idiosyncratic free-standing shape, make a wire frame, tie in the growths and trim regularly. Pillars

and pyramids may need to be tied in, corset-like, with fine nylon line.

CULTIVATION Height 1m (3ft). Plant in spring in a sunny spot in well-drained soil. Some of the cultivars are less hardy than the common type. Overgrown bushes can be cut back hard in mid-spring. This is also the time to trim any unwanted growth from plants that are being trained against a wall, to avoid missing out on the following year's flowers.

SAGE
Salvia officinalis

The variegated varieties of sage are just as useful in the kitchen as the ordinary plain green type. There is virtually no difference in flavour. 'Icterina' has rough-textured leaves of green and gold. 'Tricolor' is even showier, its leaves splashed in pink, white and green. The deep purple leaves of 'Purpurea' look splendid combined with green-leaved herbs or orange pot marigolds. Sage is handsome enough to be used in a herbaceous border, especially when topped by its spikes of bright blue flowers.

CULTIVATION Height 45cm–1m (18in–3ft). Sages hate prolonged winter damp and may rot in heavy soils. Plant in spring in light, well-drained soil in a site that gets plenty of sun. Sages quickly become leggy but are easy to propagate from cuttings taken in summer. Pull off sideshoots about 7cm (3in) long with a "heel" attached, and line them out in a cold frame or poke them into pots of sandy compost. When the cuttings are rooted, nip out the tops to encourage bushy growth. Alternatively, try mound layering (see page 173). Tidy up plants by clipping them over during the summer. You can dry the leaf clippings and store them in airtight jars.

WINTER SAVORY
Satureja montana

Winter savory is a hardy, almost evergreen, dwarf sub-shrub unlike its cousin summer savory, which is an annual. Summer savory has the better flavour of the two, but winter savory has, of course, a much longer season of use. The leaves are peppery in taste, and are often used to flavour salami. Tiny, rather insignificant, whitish-pink flowers appear in summer.

CULTIVATION Height 30cm (12in). Plant winter savory in spring in any fertile, well-drained soil in full sun. It will need replacing every 2–3 years as plants quickly become woody and intractable. Propagate plants by dividing them in spring or autumn. They can also be mound layered (see page 173).

THYME
Thymus spp.

The thyme family contains various species with different habits of growth; some form tiny bushes, others dense, spreading mats of foliage that put down roots as they travel. The creeping kinds, such as *Thymus serpyllum*, are excellent in paths and paving, but more difficult to manage in a mixed herb bed. This is the place for upright varieties such as *Thymus vulgaris*, the common thyme, with grey-green leaves and mauve flowers. The bushy cultivar 'Silver Posie' has pretty silver-variegated leaves and pink flowers. *Thymus × citriodorus* smells of lemons, and there is a variegated form, 'Silver Lemon Queen', with silver-splashed leaves. The cultivar 'Doone Valley' is a creeping thyme with green leaves variegated with gold.

CULTIVATION Height 25–30cm (10–12in). Dry, well-drained chalky soil is best for all the thymes. Plant in spring, incorporating some grit into the soil to improve drainage where necessary. Trim frequently in spring and summer to stop plants getting straggly. The harder they are cut, the more vigorously they grow. New plants are easily propagated by mound layering (see page 173). Like most of these herbs, wet winters and soggy ground are much more likely to cause problems than any pests or diseases.

BAY

ROSEMARY

PURPLE-LEAVED SAGE

COMMON SAGE

COMMON THYME

VARIEGATED THYME
'Silver Lemon Queen'

WINTER SAVORY

IN THE KITCHEN

Some herbs have a long-established partnership with particular fish, flesh or fowl: tarragon with chicken, rosemary with lamb. But the cook with a ready supply of fresh herbs will want to experiment: sprinkle chopped mint over strawberries, add thyme to salads of mixed leaves and flowers. In this dish, French tarragon (see page 112) is the catalyst.

BAKED EGGS WITH TARRAGON
Serves 4

a little butter
4 eggs
4 tbsp double cream
4 tbsp water
2 large sprigs of tarragon
salt and black pepper

1 Butter 4 small ramekins and break an egg into each. Heat the cream gently in a small pan with the water and tarragon. Allow to reduce slightly, pressing the tarragon with a wooden spoon.

2 Take out the tarragon and pour the creamy mixture over the eggs, dividing it equally between the ramekins. Add a tiny pinch of salt and a flourish of freshly ground pepper on top.

3 Lower the ramekins into a pan with 1cm (½in) of boiling water in the bottom and cook the eggs gently (about 4–5 minutes), until the whites are just set. Serve decorated with a few leaves of fresh tarragon sprinkled on top.

CULINARY NOTES
❦ To make a highly flavoured savoury bread, add some finely chopped sage leaves and some sun-dried tomatoes or stoned black olives to the dough when you are preparing it. Prove the shaped bread and bake in the usual way.

FRUIT

WHILE MOST vegetables are temporary
residents in the garden, fruit, once planted,
will be with you for many years. Its presence
gives a comfortable sense of permanence and
continuity. Careful selection and breeding
has brought some fruit, such as apples and
peaches, a long way from their undomesticated
counterparts. Others, such as blackberries,
still have a whiff of the wild about them. Fruit
will only set if flowers have been properly
pollinated. Some trees are self-fertile, others
are not, and you must have different types
within reach to be sure of a crop. The
following pages explain how to achieve the
best results. Stars indicate the most decorative
varieties, especially when the trees or bushes
are trained in a formal style.

TREE FRUIT

These will be the longest-lived elements of your kitchen garden. The type of tree you buy – bush, standard, cordon, fan or espalier – depends on where you want to put it (see pages 174–75 for details of the various styles). Bushes start fruiting when very young and are easy to pick, but they will never have the satisfying shape of a full-blown standard. Cordons trained against wires make an excellent screen. You need to study a pruning handbook to keep them in order and they will not crop as abundantly as a big tree, but this is a good way of growing fruit in a restricted space. Trees trained as fans or espaliers are even more elegant. You can create outdoor rooms, walled around with trained trees. Half-standards have a clear stem of at least 1.2m (4ft), while full standards go up to 1.8m (6ft) before the branches start. Picking is slightly more difficult but the trees are infinitely more pleasing to look at than a dwarfed bush. All trees can be grown as standards or half-standards, although in cold areas, peaches, nectarines, greengages and apricots are most likely to succeed as fans against a warm wall.

SOFT FRUIT

Soft fruit is too rarely trained into decorative shapes, although redcurrants make attractive double cordons, shaped like wine glasses, and gooseberries take on quite a different character when grown on single stems to make round-headed standards. Use the long, exploratory growths of a blackberry to wind in and out of a hedge, or train a loganberry or tayberry to make a summer screen. Strawberries can be planted as neat edgings to beds.

VINE FRUIT

In a decorative kitchen garden, you are as likely to plant a vine for its foliage as its fruit, for the leaves have great style and the wayward, exuberant way that a vine grows gives a sense of generosity in a garden. In cooler climates, serious grape fanciers will probably grow their vines in a greenhouse, training out the rods and assiduously thinning bunches of grapes as they swell. Grown outside, the fruit may not be flawless, but the foliage can be allowed its head to a greater extent. Other vine fruit such as melons, kiwi and passion fruit need warmth to crop successfully.

TREE FRUIT

TRAINED FRUIT TREES give to the kitchen garden what clipped yew hedges and topiary give to a flower garden: good structure. With help, apples and pears can both be trained to make living screens between one part of the garden and another or to provide a fruitful backdrop for a border of old-fashioned flowers. Fruit trees pay rent twice a year, with spring blossom and autumn harvest. Compared with a Japanese flowering cherry, this is rather generous. And trees such as apples and pears grow old gracefully, welcoming lichens and ferns to their capacious branches. In winter, they assume the gnarled, twisted shapes of avant-garde sculptures. In a small garden, a single tree, grown as a half-standard, may be used as a centrepiece in a lawn or splayed in a fan against a warm wall. When the tree itself is well established, use it as a prop for a rose or clematis.

BARE BONES

The supports on which this old espaliered apple were originally trained have long since rotted, but the tree, its structure fixed in youth, makes a strong feature in this kitchen garden. At this stage, it is easy to maintain and needs only a midsummer haircut.

SPRING PLUM

A warm brick wall protects the blossom of this plum tree from frost in spring and will later be equally useful in hastening the ripening of the fruit. This old tree has long since lost any pretension to being a formal fan, but nothing can stem its exuberant display.

WAIT FOR THE PEACH

The whitewashed wall of a greenhouse reflects sparkling light on to a peach tree, the unripe fruit thinned to regular spacings along the branches. A lean-to greenhouse on a sheltered wall provides ideal growing conditions for peaches, apricots and nectarines.

ADD LEMON

Lemons are one of the easiest of the citrus family to grow in pots. Lined in a row, they give a formal air to a garden scheme, but they look equally at ease in an informal courtyard grouped with pots of basil, lavender and other aromatic Mediterranean herbs.

SCREEN OF PEARS

Pears, trained as espaliers, make a formal screen at the back of an asparagus bed, the long branches tied in to sets of parallel wires. Pears are amenable creatures to train, easier in this respect than apples, which generally have a stiffer habit of growth.

APPLES *Malus sylvestris* var. *domestica*

NEXT TIME YOU SINK YOUR TEETH into a crunchy 'Cox's Orange Pippin', spare a thought for Richard Cox, a retired brewer and besotted gardener who grew the first one from the pip of a 'Ribston Pippin' in 1826. The new apple would never have been known outside Mr Cox's two acres in Slough, Buckinghamshire, were it not for the Duke of Devonshire's gardener, Joseph Paxton. When Paxton became the first president of the British Pomological Society in the mid-19th century, he promoted the new apple vigorously and, being a man of even more influence than his employer, sent 'Cox' graft wood all over the country. The type of apple tree you buy will depend on where you want to grow it. In grass, bushes will start fruiting when they are very young, are easy to pick, but difficult to mow under, and will never have the heart-warming profile and character of a full blown tree. Cordons, espaliers or fans can be used to make a decorative screen in the garden.

Cultivation

Apple cultivars are grafted on to rootstocks that largely determine the final size of the tree (see page 175). The question of the best rootstock is bound up with the style of tree that you choose (see page 174). The trend is to graft apples on to extremely dwarfing rootstocks such as M27, but a tree grafted on this is difficult to look after as it needs very good soil and does not like sharing its patch with grass or other plants. MM106 is a good compromise, particularly for bushes and cordons.

SITE AND SOIL Apples like deep, well-drained ground that does not dry out. On hungry soil, dig in plenty of compost. They seldom succeed in coastal sites where they may be damaged by salt-laden spray. Avoid planting on a site exposed to wind, or at the bottom of a slope where trees may be set back by late frosts.

PLANTING Apples are best bought as bare-rooted trees and planted in late autumn. If you do this, the roots will be well established before they have to haul up food and drink for the blossom and new leaves in spring. Make a planting hole in which the roots can spread out, and stake with a short stake (see page 176).

POLLINATION Apple crops will be much improved if trees are cross-pollinated (see page 177). This means that you must have more than one variety in the vicinity. Any cultivar described as a triploid will not be a good pollinator. 'Jupiter', 'Crispin' and 'Bramley's Seedling' are all triploids. Trees must be in blossom at the same time if they are to cross-pollinate. Most good catalogues indicate which trees overlap in this respect, although late frosts can play havoc with the most carefully laid plans.

ROUTINE CARE During the first winter or two, firm the ground around young trees that may have been lifted by frost. Water well if the spring season is dry. Once the soil has warmed up in late spring, mulch thickly around the trees with compost or manure. If the tree is not thriving, try a dressing of sulphate of ammonia at a rate of 30g/sq m (1oz/sq yd). If fruit does not develop well, dress the soil in late winter with sulphate of potash at the same rate. Keep a circle of 1.2m (4ft) in diameter around the base of the trunk clear of grass and weeds. Adjust ties on the stake as the stem swells. Thin fruit if necessary, as shown opposite.

PRUNING Specimen trees growing on their own in grass, or as orchard trees, can, if necessary, be left entirely unpruned. Trees trained as cordons, espaliers or fans need careful summer pruning (see pages 178–79) if they are to retain their geometric charm. Late summer is the time to take off excess growth – anything you cannot train in as part of the basic shape. If you start pruning too early, the trees will start to sprout again and you may have to do the job a second time.

YIELD AND HARVESTING Yield depends on the style and variety of tree. The earliest apples such as 'Discovery' and 'George Cave' should be picked as soon as the stalk parts easily from the tree and eaten immediately. 'Ellison's Orange' and 'James Grieve' will keep for a fortnight or 3 weeks if stored in a cool place. 'Egremont Russet' and 'Sunset', which ripen in mid-autumn, will keep until early winter. Pick 'Ribston Pippin' in mid-autumn. It ripens in late autumn but can be kept until the new year. 'Orleans Reinette' and 'Wagener' should be left on the tree as long as possible before picking and storing. In good conditions they will keep until early spring (see page 187).

PESTS AND DISEASES Avoid disease where possible by choosing varieties that have some resistance. This means doing without 'Cox's Orange Pippin', 'Elstar', 'Fiesta', 'Gala' and 'Spartan' which are all prone to canker. Canker also attacks apples growing in poor, badly drained ground (see page 192). Scab is most likely to be a problem in mild, wet seasons (see page 194). There is no control available. Avoid using the most dwarfing rootstocks, which make a tree fussier about its growing conditions.

RECOMMENDED CULTIVARS

DESSERT (IN ORDER OF RIPENING)
'Discovery': *fruit, flushed scarlet, form on tips of branches and spurs.* **'George Cave'**: *well-flavoured apples, deep red flush.* **'Ellison's Orange'**: *clean, strongly scented fruit.* **'James Grieve'**: *prolific, handsomely striped.* **'Egremont Russet'**: *closely spurred, so makes a good cordon.* **'Sunset'**: *crisp fruit, resistant to scab.* **'Ribston Pippin'**: *superb flavour, prone to canker in poor soil.* **'Orleans Reinette'**: *prolific, hardy, golden fruit.* **'Wagener'**: *prolific, hardy, free from scab.*
COOKING
'Early Victoria': *ready by midsummer, cooks to a pale froth.* **'Bramley's Seedling'**: *classic cooking apple, but a vigorous tree, not suitable for a cordon or fan.*

✿ **DESSERT APPLE**
'Egremont Russet'

✿ **DESSERT APPLE**
'Orleans Reinette'

✿ **DESSERT APPLE**
'George Cave'

✿ **DESSERT APPLE**
'Sunset'

✿ **DESSERT APPLE**
'Ribston Pippin'

APPLE THINNING

1 *If a tree has a very heavy crop, you will need to thin some of the apples. Wait until the tree has shed some fruit itself. This usually happens naturally in midsummer.*

2 *Remove any very small and misshapen fruit, leaving about 10–15cm (4–6in) between the remaining apples. They will then have room to develop and ripen.*

✿ **COOKING APPLE**
'Bramley's Seedling'

PEARS *Pyrus communis* var. *sativa*

THE PEAR'S NATURAL HOME is around the Mediterranean and you need to bear this in mind when planting, for it needs warmth and sunshine if it is to fruit well. Pears are as ornamental as they are useful, but unfortunately it is harder to bring a pear to luscious perfection than it is an apple. The difficulty lies off rather than on the tree. A pear changes radically after it has been picked. Its flesh, still hard when the fruit is gathered, gradually softens in storage until it has the melting texture of butter. But the point of no return is quickly reached and it is difficult to know when you have got there. Pears are like statesmen: their outside appearance gives little indication of what is going on underneath.

Cultivation

The wild pear, *Pyrus communis*, is a deep-rooted tree, able to make the best of poor soils. Most pears that you buy, apart from half-standards, have been grafted on to quince rootstock. This restricts the tree's size and brings it into fruit more quickly, but quince rootstock is shallow-rooting and needs good soil. Pear trees usually grow to about 4.5–6m (15–20ft). Site and style of tree (see page 174) need to be considered hand in hand. Some of the more aristocratic dessert pears such as 'Marie-Louise' and 'Glou Morceau' are best grown as fans or espaliers against a warm wall. Others, such as 'Beurré Hardy' and 'Conference', are not so fussy and can be grown either as bushes or half-standards. Fruiting will also depend on the effort you put into arranging a decent sex life for your pear.

SITE AND SOIL Pears generally flower two weeks earlier than apples, so are more prone to frost damage: choose a sheltered spot. They are tolerant of most soils, but will struggle in shallow chalk.

PLANTING Autumn is the best time to plant (see page 176), when the trees are dormant. Bushes will need 3.5–4.5m (12–15ft) between them, half-standards 6–7.5m (20–25ft), cordons 2–3m (7–10ft) and espaliers 2.5–3m (8–10ft).

POLLINATION Cultivars can be sorted into three pollinating groups, depending on the time of flowering (see page 177). For the most effective cross-pollination, choose pears from the same group, although there is usually enough overlap between the flowering seasons to pair off trees from adjoining groups.

ROUTINE CARE Mulch well in autumn or spring with manure or compost. Add 30g/sq m (1oz/sq yd) sulphate of potash. Keep a 1.2m (4ft) wide circle of clear ground around trees growing in grass.

PRUNING Pears need little pruning in the early years and trees growing as standards can be left alone entirely. Trees growing as cordons and espaliers will need summer pruning (see pages 178–79).

YIELD AND HARVESTING Harvest pears before they are ripe, as soon as they will part from the tree. Summer pears are soon ready to eat. Others, like 'Conference', need to be stored (see page 187), then ripened in the warm, a few at a time.

PESTS AND DISEASES Birds can wreak havoc on flowerbuds. Some varieties, such as 'Conference', are highly susceptible while others, like 'Beurré Hardy', are usually left alone. Diseases are more likely to be due to poor growing conditions than to anything else.

RECOMMENDED CULTIVARS

(IN ORDER OF RIPENING)
'Jargonelle': *small, tapering fruit, cropping freely when established.* '**Marguerite Marillat**': *upright, small tree with enormous golden fruit, flushed scarlet.* '**Beurré Hardy**': *good resistance to scab.* '**Conference**': *self-fertile but tree is susceptible to wind damage.* '**Doyenné du Comice**': *superb flavour, but unreliable in cropping and susceptible to scab.* '**Joséphine de Malines**': *one of the best-flavoured winter pears, but not a vigorous tree.*

IN THE KITCHEN

For this dish, you need pears of firm texture and pleasing shape. Use fruit with slight blemishes that may prevent their being stored successfully.

PEARS IN BURGUNDY
Serves 4

1kg (2lb) small pears
250g (8oz) sugar
¼ tsp ground cinnamon
150ml (¼ pint) water
150ml (¼ pint) red Burgundy wine
double cream, to serve

1 Peel the pears, leaving the stalks intact. Do not core them. Stand them upright, stalk-end up, in a pan just large enough to hold them without crowding. Sprinkle over the sugar and cinnamon and add the water. Simmer, covered, for 10–15 minutes.

2 Add the wine and simmer, uncovered, for a further 10–15 minutes, until tender. Using a slotted spoon, lift the pears into a serving dish and allow to cool.

3 Meanwhile, bring the liquid to the boil and leave it to simmer, uncovered, for 5–7 minutes, until it is reduced to a light syrup.

4 Pour the syrup over the pears and refrigerate the whole dish. Serve chilled with cream.

CULINARY NOTES

❧ The true connoisseur of pears will eat them uncooked, dwelling, as the Edwardian nurseryman and fruit expert Edward Bunyard did, on the texture and aroma of each different variety: "As it is in my view the duty of an apple to be crisp and crunchable," he wrote, "a pear should have such a texture as leads to silent consumption." A perfect 'Doyenné du Comice', he considered, should melt upon the palate "with the facility of an ice".

❀ **PEAR**
'Beurré Hardy'

❀ **PEAR**
'Conference'

❀ **PEAR**
'Doyenné du
Comice'

❀ **PEAR**
'Joséphine de
Malines'

PLUMS, GREENGAGES & DAMSONS *Prunus domestica*

FEAST OR FAMINE SEEMS THE RULE with the plum family, the famines caused chiefly by insatiable birds and badly timed frosts. The scale of the feasts will depend on the varieties you have chosen. With 'Coe's Golden Drop', 15 fruit on a tree is cause for rejoicing. It is what is euphemistically described as a "shy cropper", the meanest of them all. But what a fruit! It has the melting sweet flavour of a perfect greengage, intensified threefold. Once you have tasted it, you have an inkling of what Paradise might be like. Planted as orchard trees, or as fans against a wall, the plum family is decorative in flower and fruit, although the blossom is not so eyecatching as that of apple or pear. Choose half-standards or standards for planting in grass. These will make long-lived features and you can mow under them without catching your hair in the branches.

Cultivation

As with apples and pears, all varieties of plum are grafted on to rootstocks that control their vigour (see page 175). The most common is 'St Julien A'. Grown on this, a 'Victoria' plum will spread at least 4.5m (15ft) after about 10 years. Dwarfing rootstocks are less common with plums, although there is one called 'Pixy'. It reduces the eventual size of the tree by two-thirds or a half, but the tree needs richer soil and more cosseting than the same variety growing on 'St Julien A'. Where there is room for only one tree it should be the self-fertile 'Victoria', which is not too fussy about its position and crops well and regularly. In fact, it has a tendency to overcrop and, if you let it, will then want to rest the following year, like an enervated actor after a particularly stressful run of *Hamlet*.

SITE AND SOIL Plums like hot summers, hard winters and a late, short spring. The Caucasus and the countries around the Caspian Sea are their home and they have not forgotten it. They also need shelter from the wind and as much protection as possible from late frosts. Late-flowering cultivars such as the dual-purpose 'Ouillins Gage' have a better chance of escaping frost than the early-flowering 'Jefferson'. The most succulent fruit comes from fan-trained trees planted against sheltered walls. Plums are too prolific in growth to make cordons or espaliers. Damsons, which in appearance are more like the wild plum, are generally hardier.

PLANTING Plant in late autumn (see page 176) when the trees are dormant but the ground is still warm enough to promote fresh root growth. If you are planting in grass, keep a circle at least 1.2m (4ft) in diameter clear around the base. Fans will need securing. If you buy them ready-trained, they will probably already have 6 or 8 long arms. Fix the corresponding number of bamboo canes to the wall or support so that they fan out to match the branches. Tie the branches to the canes and keep tying them in as they grow.

POLLINATION Some cultivars, such as 'Victoria' and 'Denniston's Superb', are self-fertile and do not need pollinators to set a crop, but even self-fertile plums crop more liberally if they are cross-pollinated by a different variety. To pollinate each other, plums obviously need to flower at the same time, and this is the most important thing to bear in mind when you are choosing cultivars (see page 177). Most good suppliers mark the season of flowering – early, mid or late – so that you can choose suitable companions. Flowering seasons overlap to some extent.

ROUTINE CARE Firm down any trees that have been lifted by frost in the first winter after planting. Mulch trees heavily every year with manure. If this is not available, top dress established trees with sulphate of ammonia, at a rate of 60g/sq m (2oz/sq yd). Thin fruit if a tree overcrops, leaving no more than one plum or gage every 7–10cm (3–4in). The tree may shed some fruit itself, usually in early summer.

PRUNING Free-standing trees require very little pruning. Just take out dead wood and thin out overcrowded growth. Any cutting should be done in late spring or summer. This reduces the risk of spores of silver leaf getting into the system. Fans require more attention to keep them in shape (see page 179). Shoots sprouting from the main framework should be nipped out in two stages. In midsummer, pinch back all sideshoots to leave about 6 leaves. These will be the shoots that bear fruit in the subsequent summer. When they have fruited, cut back these sideshoots by half, to about 3 leaves. Take out entirely any shoots that are pointing forward or backward into the wall.

YIELD AND HARVESTING Expect about 14kg (30lb) of fruit from a 10-year-old fan-trained tree and 23kg (50lb) from a free-standing tree. Harvest when fully ripe.

PESTS AND DISEASES Silver leaf is the most serious problem (see page 193) and there is no cure. You can cut out infected branches and hope, but if more than a third of the tree is blighted, you will be lucky to see it recover.

RECOMMENDED CULTIVARS

PLUMS (IN ORDER OF RIPENING)
'Czar': *heavy-cropping, purple-black cooking plum.* 'Early Laxton': *small, golden, well-flavoured fruit on rather a weak tree.* 'Ouillins Gage': *dual-purpose plum, good dessert fruit when fully ripe; excellent for jam.* 'Marjorie's Seedling': *vigorous tree bearing large, black cooking plums.* 'Victoria': *most famous of all, juicy when ripe; useful for cooking when under-ripe.* 'Jefferson': *excellent hardy dessert plum, greengage-like flavour.* 'Coe's Golden Drop': *finest flavour but meagre crops.*

GREENGAGES (IN ORDER OF RIPENING)
'Denniston's Superb': *hardy and self-fertile.* 'Cambridge Gage': *vigorous tree with round, green fruit.* 'Reine Claude de Bavay': *large, well-flavoured gage; self-fertile.*

DAMSONS (IN ORDER OF RIPENING)
'Farleigh Damson': *small, fine-flavoured fruit.* 'Merryweather': *large, self-fertile, spreading tree bearing big, blue-black damsons.*

IN THE KITCHEN

PLUM CHUTNEY
Makes 2.25kg (4½lb)

*1kg (2lb) plums, washed, quartered
and stoned
500g (1lb) apples, peeled, cored, chopped
500g (1lb) shallots, peeled and chopped
500g (1lb) raisins
175g (6oz) brown sugar
1 tsp ground ginger
1 tsp ground allspice
¼ tsp each of cayenne pepper, ground
cloves, dry mustard, ground nutmeg
30g (1oz) salt
600ml (1 pint) vinegar*

1 Bring all the ingredients slowly to the boil in a preserving pan. Simmer for 1–2 hours, or until the mixture has thickened considerably.

2 Ladle the chutney into warm, sterilized jars. Cover with waxed discs while warm and seal with paper covers.

PICKLED DAMSONS
Makes 4kg (8lb)

*2kg (4lb) sugar
1.25 litres (2 pints) vinegar
1 tsp cloves, crushed
1 tsp ground allspice
2cm (1in) root ginger, crushed
2cm (1in) cinnamon stick, crushed
zest of half a lemon
4kg (8lb) damsons, washed*

1 Dissolve the sugar in the vinegar in a preserving pan over a low heat. Tie the spices and zest in a muslin bag, add to the pan, then add the fruit. Simmer until tender.

2 Remove the spices, lift out the damsons with a slotted spoon and pack into warm, sterilized jars.

3 Bring the liquid to the boil and simmer until it becomes slightly thick and syrupy. Pour over the damsons, so that they are well covered, and seal the jars securely.

❀ **PLUM**
'Marjorie's Seedling'

❀ **PLUM**
'Victoria'

❀ **GREENGAGE**
'Cambridge
Gage'

DAMSON
'Merryweather'

❀ **PLUM**
'Coe's
Golden
Drop'

PEACHES & NECTARINES

Prunus persica & P. p. var. *nectarina*

MOST ACCOUNTS OF GROWING PEACHES AND NECTARINES in cool climates concentrate on the disasters, not the delights. By the time you have read through gloomy predictions of leaf curl, canker, red spider mite and peach mildew, you may want to give up all idea of growing your own and let the growers of California and Spain take the strain instead. Forget peach mildew, it may never happen. Remember instead Mme Recamier, siren, muse and toast of the salons of 19th-century Paris. When she and all those around her thought she was on her death bed, when for days she had refused all food however cunningly prepared, it was the smell and taste of a freshly picked peach that persuaded her she would, after all, prefer to live.

Cultivation

Peaches and nectarines are only likely to succeed outdoors when they have a sunny spring to ensure pollination, a hot summer to ripen the fruit, a dry autumn so that new shoots can mature ready for the next year's crops, and a short, cold resting season during the winter.

SITE AND SOIL Only in regions with a Mediterranean or Californian climate will peaches and nectarines succeed as free-standing trees. Elsewhere, grow them as fans against a sunny, sheltered wall, where they may spread to 4.5m (15ft) wide. In cold areas, plant under glass.

PLANTING This is best done in late autumn (see page 176). For fans outside, plant trees about 30cm (12in) away from a wall, slanting the trunk back toward the wall. In a greenhouse, they can be grown in big pots, but they do better set in a border against a wall.

POLLINATION Peaches and nectarines are self-fertile, so you do not have to plant different varieties to ensure pollination. But under glass, and where cultivars flower very early before there are any insects on the wing, you must do the pollinating yourself (see page 177).

ROUTINE CARE Mulch around outdoor trees each spring with a thick layer of manure. Replace the top layer of soil around greenhouse trees in late winter with good garden soil mixed with bonemeal and sulphate of potash. Thin the shoots and fruit in spring and early summer as shown opposite.

PRUNING Fruit is borne on shoots produced the previous season, so cut out a proportion of old wood each spring to encourage new growth. If you want to grow a fan, make life easy for yourself by buying a ready-trained tree. Pinch out unwanted shoots (including those pointing forward or back) in spring, leaving the foliage shoots on each lateral branch spaced as shown opposite. In early summer, prune back each of these shoots to 6 leaves. When you have picked the fruit, cut out the growth that bore it and tie in the replacement shoots (see page 179).

YIELD AND HARVESTING Expect about 9kg (20lb) of peaches or nectarines from a mature trained fan; free-standing trees will give much heavier crops. Pick the fruit when the flesh around the stalk feels soft.

PESTS AND DISEASES Pests are most troublesome under glass. Damping down will deter red spider mite (see page 191). Peach leaf curl is the most likely problem for trees growing outside (see page 194).

RECOMMENDED CULTIVARS

PEACHES (IN ORDER OF RIPENING)
'Duke of York': *heavy crops of juicy, yellow fruit.* **'Early Rivers'**: *tender, well-flavoured flesh.* **'Peregrine'**: *one of the easiest in cool areas, well flavoured and juicy.* **'Rochester'**: *late-flowering, an advantage in cooler areas; juicy fruit, not so well flavoured as* 'Peregrine'.
NECTARINES (IN ORDER OF RIPENING)
'Lord Napier': *regular, heavy crops of white-fleshed, aromatic fruit.* **'Pineapple'**: *yellow-fleshed fruit with a distinct pineapple flavour.*

IN THE KITCHEN

Only when there is a glut of fruit will you want to cook a peach or nectarine, or do anything other than sink your teeth straight into its luscious, melting flesh. This recipe combines peaches with a piquant raspberry sauce.

POACHED PEACHES WITH A RASPBERRY SAUCE
Serves 4

4 ripe peaches
125g (4oz) caster sugar
150ml (¼ pint) water
250g (8oz) raspberries

1 Skin the peaches by immersing them in boiling water for 1 minute. Drain, then carefully peel off the skin and cut the fruit in half.

2 Combine the sugar and water in a saucepan over a low heat and stir continuously until the sugar has dissolved. Bring the syrup to the boil, add the peaches and simmer gently for 5 minutes, until tender.

3 Using a slotted spoon, transfer the peaches to a serving dish. Return the syrup to the boil and simmer until it is reduced by half.

4 Purée the raspberries by rubbing them through a sieve with a wooden spoon, gradually adding the syrup to the raspberry pulp to ease the process. You should be left with a fairly thin sauce. Spoon this over the peach halves and chill before serving.

CULINARY NOTES

❧ Over the years we have been bludgeoned into believing that "fresh" can apply to any produce not pickled or canned. But the day you pick your first fresh peach or nectarine from your own tree and carry it, pulsating with ripeness, inside for breakfast, is the day you break faith with supermarket fruit in their cold, plastic beds.

❀ PEACHES

❀ NECTARINES

THINNING SHOOTS

1 *This branch, with its shoots closely grouped together, has yet to be thinned. In spring, it may be worth removing some of the foliage shoots on both peaches and nectarines to give enough room for the fruit to swell and ripen.*

2 *Leaving 1 or 2 good shoots near the base of each branch to form the stems that will bear next year's crop, nip out all the others to give a shoot every 12–15cm (5–6in). Leave one shoot at the end to draw the sap along the branch.*

THINNING FRUIT

When the fruit is no bigger than a hazelnut, thin again. Remove any fruit that is awkwardly placed or facing into the wall, leaving a final gap of about 23cm (9in) between each one.

APRICOTS *Prunus armeniaca*

THE PERFECT APRICOT IS NOT EASY TO FIND. Often you sink your teeth into the fruit to discover nothing better than a mouthful of cotton-wool. When they are good, apricots are very, very good, but in cool climates they need the help of a warm wall if they are to ripen to perfection. Although they are not subject to leaf curl, apricot trees have a distressing habit of suddenly dying back. The strongest branches are often the first to go. This problem has been known in Britain ever since apricots were introduced in the reign of Henry VIII. The knowledgeable gardeners of Edwardian times suggested that they should be root pruned, to curb the speed at which they grow. The famous old variety 'Moor Park', brought to England in 1760 by Lord Anson, is more susceptible to this problem than modern cultivars.

Cultivation

The apricot, which was carried by silk merchants westward from China into Armenia, needs cold winters and early springs to perform well. Then it must have a long, warm summer to ripen the fruit. It copes, just, with a north European summer, but is more reliable outdoors in warmer climates.

SITE AND SOIL The soil needs to be well drained, but not too well fed. Choose a sunny, warm wall against which to train a fan-shaped tree.

PLANTING Plant in late autumn (see page 176). A full-grown fan is likely to spread 3.5m (12ft). If planting more than one tree, allow 4.5m (15ft) between them. Set the tree about 30cm (12in) from the wall with the stem leaning back toward it. Tie the branches to canes or wires stretched between vine eyes.

POLLINATION Apricots are self-fertile, but flower very early, often in late winter. Protect trees outside from frost with fine-meshed net. If no insects are about, hand-pollinate the flowers with a fine camel-hair brush (see page 177).

ROUTINE CARE Water copiously in dry summers to help the fruit swell. Keep the soil around trees free of weeds, but do not disturb the roots by cultivating deeply. Thin the fruit at intervals during mid and late spring, so that it is spaced roughly every 10cm (4in) along the branches.

PRUNING Aim to build up a series of fruiting spurs about 15cm (6in) apart all the way along the branches of a fan tree. Do this by pinching back the lateral growths (sideshoots from the main branches) in early summer, leaving about 7cm (3in) of each growth in place. Any shoots springing from these laterals should be pinched back to leave just one leaf. Keep tying in new growth on the ends of the main branches to maintain the fan shape (see page 179). Because fruit is borne on stems formed the previous season, on mature free-standing trees cut back a proportion of old wood in early spring to encourage new growth each year.

YIELD AND HARVESTING Expect about 9kg (20lb) of fruit from a good fan, twice as much from a free-standing tree. Pick apricots carefully (they bruise easily) when the stem parts readily from the branch. They will keep for 2 weeks or more in a cool place.

PESTS AND DISEASES Die-back is the main problem; there is no cure. Choose resistant types and do not overfeed. Rust may attack in late summer (see page 194).

RECOMMENDED CULTIVARS

(IN ORDER OF RIPENING)
'New Large Early': *larger and earlier than* 'Moor Park' *with better resistance to die-back.* **'Moor Park'**: *popular variety with superb flavour but prone to die-back.* **'Alfred'**: *resistant to die-back but prone to biennial cropping; juicy, orange-fleshed fruit.*

❦ APRICOTS

CHERRIES *Prunus avium & P. cerasus*

A CHERRY LEFT TO ITS OWN DEVICES will quickly make a large tree, and is best in an orchard where it can spread its wings up to 9m (27ft) or more. Allow grass and wild flowers to grow uncut beneath it for the kind of scene that drove the French Impressionists to their paintboxes. Cherries are extremely decorative when covered with blossom, and often perform well again in autumn when the foliage may turn fiery shades of red and orange. Sweet cherries can be trained as fans, but you will need a big wall and you will have to fight to keep the tree under control. The best type for a wall, especially if it is north-facing, is the acid 'Morello', superb in pies and tarts. You can also drown them in brandy. Fished out months later they make suitably drunken toppings for home-made ice cream.

SWEET CHERRIES

SWEET CHERRIES

ACID CHERRIES

Cultivation

Most cherries need to be cross-pollinated if they are to bear fruit. If there is not enough room for two cherry trees in your garden, plant the sweet cherry 'Stella' or the acid 'Morello' as both are self-fertile.

SITE AND SOIL Cherries fruit best where the climate is dry and reasonably warm, although acid cherries can cope with a cooler site. They are not worth planting where late frosts may ruin the blossom. The soil should be rich but well drained.

PLANTING Plant in late autumn (see page 176), setting half-standards or standards 12m (40ft) apart and fan-trained trees 6m (20ft) apart.

POLLINATION The self-fertile, acid 'Morello' cherry will pollinate sweet cherries, such as 'Napoleon Bigarreau', that flower at the same time. 'Governor Wood' and 'Merton Bigarreau' will pollinate each other, and 'Early Rivers' will pollinate all the 'Merton' varieties (see page 177).

ROUTINE CARE Mulch with compost or manure in spring and fix scarers if birds attack the flowerbuds. Keep wall-trained trees well watered during summer.

PRUNING Sweet cherries growing as standards or half-standards do not need pruning. Simply cut out any dead wood and remove branches that cross over each other. 'Morello' cherries only fruit on new wood, so you must prune to force the tree to produce new growth by cutting out some old stems each year (see page 179).

When a wall-trained tree has fruited, cut out the long growths at its extremities so that it will make new shoots in the centre. Without this "sides to middle" treatment, the tree will bear fruit only at the tips of its branches. Tie in as many new shoots as you can fit in.

YIELD AND HARVESTING A mature free-standing cherry may provide 32kg (70lb) of fruit, and a fan-trained 'Morello' about 9kg (20lb). Sweet cherries are ready to pick in midsummer, 'Morello' cherries slightly later.

PESTS AND DISEASES Bacterial canker is the most troublesome disease (see page 192) and is most likely when trees grow too fast due to overfeeding. Spores enter through wounds, so avoid damaging the bark and prune late in summer. Aphids can distort new growth (see page 190). Cut off the worst-affected shoots and burn them. Spray trees with a tar oil wash to kill overwintering pests. Wall-trained trees can be netted to protect fruit from birds.

RECOMMENDED CULTIVARS

SWEET CHERRIES (IN ORDER OF RIPENING)
'Early Rivers': *shiny, juicy, black-fleshed fruit.* **'Governor Wood'**: *large, pale yellow fruit with red cheek.* **'Merton Bigarreau'**: *extremely vigorous, bearing large black fruit.* **'Napoleon Bigarreau'**: *firm, sweet white flesh.* **'Bigarreau Gaucher'**: *black-fleshed variety.* **'Stella'**: *dark red fruit, self-fertile.*
ACID CHERRIES
'Morello': *self-fertile, wide-spreading tree.*

CITRUS FRUIT *Citrus* spp.

CITRUS TREES, GROWING IN swagged terracotta pots or square wooden boxes, can be used like statues to decorate a garden, however small. As a centrepiece for a potager, or set like guardsmen at the side of a series of steps, they look grand and faintly unreal. The leaves are glossily evergreen and the fruit hangs on the branches like decorations on a Christmas tree. They are not hardy and, wherever frost strikes, will need to be brought inside a conservatory for the winter. But here, too, they are immensely decorative and the flowers, which begin to open in spring, scent the air for weeks. The fruit takes a year to develop, so while the present season's flowers are opening, the previous season's fruit is maturing on the tree.

Cultivation

Growing in containers will be the only option for gardeners who do not share the balmy climate of the Mediterranean or west coast of America. Fortunately, citrus trees adapt well to pot culture, particularly the lemon-mandarin hybrid *Citrus* × *meyeri* 'Meyeri' (often referred to as Meyer's lemon) and the calamondin, a mandarin-kumquat hybrid.

SITE AND SOIL All citrus need to be kept frost-free in winter. Fruiting is more likely to occur if the plants can be kept at about 10°C (50°F) during this time. Use an acid, ericaceous, compost (pH 6–6.5, slightly lower for lemons) and make sure that the container has adequate drainage. Coarse grit mixed with the compost will help.

PLANTING Trees may start their lives in small containers but must eventually be potted on into larger tubs. Winter is the best time for this job. When the trees are in their final homes, scrape off the top 5cm (2in) of compost each year in mid-spring and replace it with fresh compost.

POLLINATION Citrus trees are parthenocarpic, which means they set fruit even when the flowers do not contain viable pollen. In other words, you need only one plant to be assured of a crop.

ROUTINE CARE Watering and feeding are of prime importance. Feeding should continue throughout the year, with a high-nitrogen formula used during summer to maintain growth. Winter feed should contain trace elements, particularly iron, magnesium, manganese and zinc. Without these, trees will have yellowish foliage, growth will be stunted and the fruit liable to drop in winter. Never allow the compost in pots to dry out.

PRUNING Citrus trees do not need regular pruning. Trim new growth in early spring, if necessary, to keep the plants shapely.

YIELD AND HARVESTING Yield depends on the size and maturity of the tree. Expect 20 or 30 fruit from a well-grown specimen. Fruit can be harvested from late autumn through until early spring.

PESTS AND DISEASES In a conservatory plants may suffer from red spider mite, aphids, sooty mould, scale and mealy bug (see pages 190–93).

RECOMMENDED CULTIVARS

SEVILLE ORANGES
Citrus aurantium **'Bouquet'**: *bitter fruit on a spiny tree with slender, pointed leaves.*
SWEET ORANGES
Citrus sinensis **'Navelina'**: *distinctive navel orange, first introduced to America in 1870.*
MANDARINS AND MANDARIN HYBRIDS
Citrus reticulata **'Clementine'**: *vigorous, large bushy tree with rounded mandarin fruit.*
× *Citrofortunella microcarpa,* syn. **C. mitis**, *or calamondin: mandarin-kumquat hybrid that flowers and fruits while still small.*
Citrus × *meyeri* **'Meyeri'**: *lemon-mandarin hybrid, slow-growing and ideal in containers.*
GRAPEFRUIT
Citrus × *paradisi* **'Golden Special'**: *well-branched tree with glossy, ovate leaves.*
LEMONS
Citrus limon **'Garey's Eureka'**: *open, spreading habit, excellent juicy fruit.*
LIMES
Citrus aurantiifolia **'Bearss'**: *compact tree, with seedless, exceptionally juicy fruit.*

IN THE KITCHEN

Many citrus recipes include the peel in some way, for the zest of the skin gives an extra-sharp kick to the taste of the dish. This orange salad is enhanced by the flavour and appearance of a sprinkling of finely cut strips of caramelized peel.

CARAMELIZED ORANGES
Serves 6

6 large oranges
300ml (½ pint) water
125g (4oz) sugar

1 Finely peel away the zest of 1 orange with a vegetable peeler and cut into very fine strips, each about 2cm (1in) long.
2 Put the peel in a small pan with the water and sugar, bring to the boil and simmer gently for about 30 minutes, until the liquid is thick and syrupy.
3 Peel the remaining oranges, then cut all 6 fruit into thin rounds, taking out any pips. Arrange the slices in a dish and pour over the syrup, with the strips of peel. Chill before serving.

CULINARY NOTES
❧ The arrival of bitter Seville oranges in the new year is the signal in Britain for a brief orgy of marmalade-making, for nothing else gives marmalade such a tang. But you can experiment with mixes of other citrus fruit to make conserves that, if not so sharp, are no less good to eat.
❧ Lime, one of the best marmalades, is also the most difficult to make as the skins are tough to cut. Easier to prepare is grapefruit marmalade. With each 1kg (2lb) grapefruit, include 300g (10oz) lemons, to provide the necessary pectin. A three-fruit preserve of 2 grapefruit, 2 sweet oranges and 4 lemons also makes an excellent breakfast treat.

✿ MANDARIN

✿ SWEET ORANGE

✿ SEVILLE ORANGE

✿ LEMON

✿ GRAPEFRUIT

✿ LIME

✿ **THE CALAMONDIN**
This cross between a mandarin and a kumquat (✕ Citrofortunella microcarpa, *syn.* C. mitis*) is one of the best to grow in pots or tubs.*

FIGS & MULBERRIES
Ficus carica & Morus nigra

THESE TREES ARE BOTH GREAT SURVIVORS, hanging on in old gardens long after the lawns and walls on which they were displayed have disappeared. Both give an air of distinction to a garden, for they are fruit with an ancient lineage and make splendid specimen trees, although they need protection from chilly winds and are unlikely to succeed in very cold areas. Figs can be grown successfully in cool greenhouses or splayed out as fans on a warm wall, but the mulberry, which makes a big, bushy, round-headed tree, needs an expanse of lawn to set it off properly. Although both lose their leaves in winter, the trees, starkly stripped, still contribute to the garden scene. They have the attribute of all true aristocrats: good bones.

❀ MULBERRIES

❀ BROWN FIGS

❀ GREEN FIGS

Cultivation

Where space is limited, a fig can be grown in a large pot to stand in a sheltered corner, but a mulberry needs space. It will gradually develop into a tree at least 6m (20ft) high and 4.5m (15ft) wide. You sometimes see veteran trees leaning on their elbows in a relaxed way, which makes them spread even further.

SITE AND SOIL Figs are forgiving trees, as you might guess from the way they grow outside the National Gallery in London's Trafalgar Square, drenched by the fumes of a thousand buses. There, they were planted for their architectural foliage. If you want them to fruit, they need sun and shelter, which may mean a sheltered wall or cool greenhouse. A mulberry needs deep, well-drained, rich soil that does not dry out in summer.

PLANTING Both figs and mulberries are best planted in spring (see page 176). Figs, which are inclined to make too much growth in a north European climate, fruit more freely if the roots are restricted. Dig a hole about 1m (3ft) deep and wide and line it with brick or concrete slabs. Plant the fig inside this box, mixing in plenty of bonemeal with the soil.

ROUTINE CARE Mulch trees thickly with manure in late spring. Water mulberries if necessary in summer. Water fig trees in dry weather while the fruit is swelling, but do not overwater while the figs are ripening or they may split.

PRUNING Mulberries bleed badly if cut, so should not be pruned on a regular basis.

On mature trees it may be necessary in winter to cut out dead wood or branches that cross over each other. Remove frost-damaged shoots and overcrowded young growth from fig trees in mid-spring and tie in growth on fan-trained specimens. If necessary, you can thin out branches again in midsummer. By taking out one of the oldest branches every year, you can persuade the tree to throw up more productive young growth from the base.

YIELD AND HARVESTING Yields depend on winter weather and the age of the tree. Figs are usually ready to pick by late summer or early autumn. Wait until the fruit droops on its stem, with the skin just beginning to split, and a drop of nectar hangs from the eye. The easiest way to gather mulberries is to spread sheets out under the tree and shake the branches.

PESTS AND DISEASES Neither is usually troubled by pests, but grey mould/*Botrytis* may attack the young shoots of figs (see page 193). It may also make the fruit rot.

RECOMMENDED CULTIVARS

FIGS
'Brown Turkey': *the hardiest, producing chocolate-coloured fruit with deep red flesh.*
'White Marseilles': *pale green fruit with opalescent flesh.*
MULBERRIES
'Chelsea': *comes into fruit early.*
'Wellington': *abundant, extremely fine fruit.*

PRODUCING MORE FIGS
In summer, you can encourage a fig tree to produce more fruit by pinching back new shoots to 5 or 6 leaves. This prevents the tree putting its energy into making unwanted fresh growth.

MEDLARS & QUINCES

Mespilus germanica & Cydonia oblonga

MEDLARS AND QUINCES are as attractive in bloom as any purely ornamental tree, and by planting one or the other you have the added advantage of an autumn crop. Both fruit make excellent jellies. The quince was popular before the upstart apple ever appeared in south-east Europe and is still a favourite in Turkey, although elsewhere it is seldom grown as a commercial crop. Like figs and mulberries, medlars and quinces bring an air of ancient peace to a garden. The medlar, with its angular branches, makes a tree wider than it is high, casting a dense shade. Where soil and weather conditions suit it, the leaves flame into an orange, yellow and red blaze before falling in autumn. Quince trees turn clear butter-yellow.

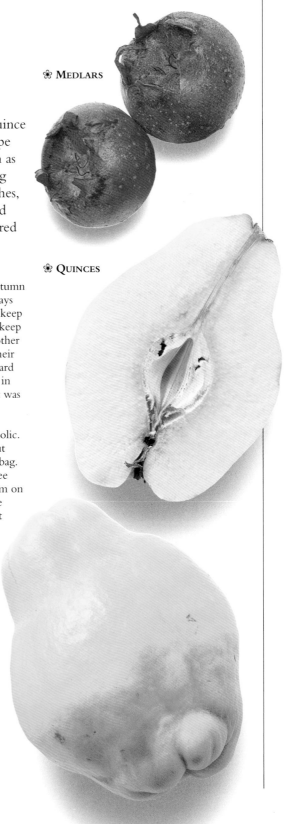

❧ MEDLARS

❧ QUINCES

Cultivation

Quinces usually make round-headed trees not more than 3.5m (12ft) tall, but where they are happy they can reach 6m (20ft). Allow them room for expansion. All cultivars are self-fertile and should start to crop by the time they are 6 years old, although 'Meech's Prolific' is more precocious. The medlar is an anciently cultivated tree, with fruit that looks like large, bronze rosehips. Watch out for suckers, as the trees are often grafted on to hawthorn rootstock.

SITE AND SOIL Quinces like warmth and a deep, rich soil that is not too limy. They love moisture and you sometimes see old specimens planted by the side of ponds. A damp corner of the garden will suit them just as well. Medlars are hardier than quinces and will succeed in any ordinary, well-drained garden soil.

PLANTING Plant any time after leaf fall, digging a hole large enough to accommodate the roots easily, and stake the trees to provide support for their first year (see page 176). Keep the ground around the trunk clear of grass or weeds.

ROUTINE CARE Mulch around the trees every spring with compost or manure.

PRUNING Thin out crowded branches of quince trees if necessary during winter. Treat medlars in the same way, removing branches that are weak or crossing over each other.

YIELD AND HARVESTING Expect about 23kg (50lb) of quinces and perhaps 14kg (30lb) of medlars from a mature half-

standard tree. Pick quinces in mid-autumn before the first frost. Store them in trays in a cool, dark place where they will keep for up to a month. It is important to keep quinces as far away as possible from other fruit, which will otherwise pick up their strong aroma. Medlars are still very hard when you gather them from the tree in late autumn. In Tudor times the fruit was stored in damp bran or sawdust until "bletted", that is until the flesh had become soft, brown and faintly alcoholic. Then the pulp was sucked straight out from the skin, like wine from a winebag.

PESTS AND DISEASES Leaf blotch (see page 194) can sometimes be a problem on quinces. Spray with a fungicide as the leafbuds burst and again after the fruit has set. Medlars are usually free of any trouble.

RECOMMENDED CULTIVARS

MEDLARS
'Dutch': *very large fruit on a small weeping tree.*
'Nottingham': *prolific, often bearing fruit when only 3 years old.*
QUINCES
'Bereczki' ('Vranja'): *large, pear-shaped fruit.* **'Champion'**: *large, apple-shaped fruit.* **'Meech's Prolific'**: *slow-growing, but often bears its pear-shaped fruit when only 3 years old.* **'Portugal'**: *vigorous, slow to crop, bearing large, oblong-shaped fruit with exceptionally woolly skins.*

NUTS

THE MOST USEFUL NUTS FOR THE GARDENER are cobnuts and filberts, both types of hazel. The trees make a good informal hedge and are very decorative in winter, hung with long, soft catkins. Where squirrels allow, they produce heavy crops of nuts in the autumn. Left to themselves they make useful thickets, which you can plunder for pea-sticks, bean poles and twiggy stems to weave into decorative supportive lattices for your French beans. Other nuts, such as almonds and walnuts, are better used as specimen trees. Almonds are breathtaking in spring, iced all over with pale blossom. Walnuts are grander, more restrained – and slow. You may have to wait 20 years for a crop but you will have, meanwhile, the pleasure of anticipation.

Cultivation

Country of origin is the best guide to the conditions these nuts need in order to bear good crops. Hazelnuts – cobnuts (*Corylus avellana*) and filberts (*C. maxima*) – do well in temperate northern Europe. The cobnut is a rounded nut, only partly covered by its husk. A filbert is longer and enclosed completely by the husk. Walnuts (*Juglans regia*) also generally do better in cool climates, but almonds (*Prunus dulcis*) are natives of north Africa and fruit most successfully in Mediterranean areas.

SITE AND SOIL Hazels will grow in sun or partial shade, doing best in deep, damp limestone soils. Almonds are not as fussy about soil as they are about having a warm climate. A walnut is long-lived, so you need to think carefully about its planting position. It may inhabit it for 200 years, spreading eventually to make a tree 30m (100ft) high and at least 15m (50ft) wide.

PLANTING Mid-autumn is the best time to plant (see page 176). Choose only young walnut trees as they resent being moved when they are older.

POLLINATION Hazels are wind-pollinated, with male and female flowers borne on the same bushes, but for the best crops, plant several different kinds together. New walnut cultivars are reliably self-fertile. Almonds are not, and cross-pollinating varieties may have to be planted to produce a crop.

ROUTINE CARE Water until trees are well established and mulch well.

PRUNING When hazels are 4–5 years old, cut out some of the oldest stems in late

winter at ground level to encourage new shoots. Walnuts bleed horribly when cut and fortunately require no regular pruning. It may sometimes be necessary to remove a crossing branch. Do this in mid-spring or late summer. Do not let the tree develop a forked trunk. Almonds need no regular pruning, but cut out any dead wood.

YIELD AND HARVESTING Yield varies enormously according to age and climatic conditions. Expect about 11kg (25lb) of nuts from a hazel, 9kg (20lb) from an established almond, and 23kg (50lb) from a full-grown walnut. Hazelnuts fall to the ground when they are ripe, but almonds can be harvested from the tree when the shells split. Husks still cling around the shell of walnuts when they are ready to harvest in autumn and must be removed before you store the nuts. Use gloves: the juice stains skin a startling dark brown.

PESTS AND DISEASES Squirrels are the chief pest of all nut trees. No other pests compare with their depredations.

RECOMMENDED CULTIVARS

COBNUTS
'Cosford Cob': *vigorous, upright bush with large, thin-shelled nuts.* **'Pearson's Prolific'**: *compact bush producing abundant small nuts.*
FILBERTS
'Kentish Cob': *prolific bearer of well-flavoured nuts.* **'Purpurea'**: *small, well-flavoured nuts on decorative, purple-leaved tree.*
ALMONDS
'Macrocarpa': *best fruiting variety.*
WALNUTS
'Broadview', **'Buccaneer'**: *both self-fertile.*

IN THE KITCHEN

Nuts store beautifully in their shells, and were once highly valued as a winter food. We still associate them with Christmas fare: ground almonds make marzipan for the cake and roast chestnuts are served with the turkey. This compote of dried fruit and nuts is popular in Muslim countries. It is traditionally made with seven fruits and seven passages from the Koran are read out before it is eaten.

AFGHAN COMPOTE
Serves 4–6

125g (4oz) each of small dried apricots and dark seedless raisins
60g (2oz) each of sultanas, shelled almonds, pistachios and walnuts (unsalted)
6 cherries (fresh or preserved)
double or single cream, to serve

1 Wash the dried fruit, put it in a serving bowl with just enough cold water to cover and set aside, in a cool place, for a couple of days.
2 Put the almonds and pistachios in a bowl and cover them with boiling water. Cool, then slip the skins off the nuts.
3 Add the walnuts, almonds and pistachios to the soaked fruit. Decorate with cherries. Put the bowl in the refrigerator for a day or two before serving with cream.

CULINARY NOTES
❧ A fresh, home-grown walnut is worth the years of waiting. Its soft, creamy texture bears no relation to that of the dry, slightly rancid, shop-bought nuts that masquerade under the name around Christmas.
❧ Ground hazelnuts can be used successfully to thicken soups. They combine particularly well with delicately flavoured vegetables such as cauliflower and celery.

❀ FILBERTS

ALMOND DELIGHT
An almond, its branches covered with fragile blossom, makes an enchanting sight on a clear spring day. To produce a good harvest of nuts, however, it must have a warm site.

❀ HAZELNUTS

ALMONDS

WALNUTS

UNRIPE
WALNUTS
WITH HUSK

SOFT FRUIT & VINES

THE MOST SPECTACULAR VINES are not those with the best grapes, so you will have to decide which of the two is more important, appearance or taste. All vines, however, have handsome foliage that can be used to good effect on arbours, trellises and pergolas. *Vitis vinifera* 'Purpurea' provides a fine contrast for a scrambler such as *Clematis flammula,* or you could combine its purple leaves with pale blue clematis and deep red climbing roses. Soft fruit such as redcurrants and gooseberries are no less decorative when carefully trained. Grow gooseberries as mop-headed standards to mark the corners of a herb garden. Train redcurrants on wires as U-shaped cordons to make an unusual, airy screen. Strawberries, particularly the alpine kinds, are pretty enough to grow as groundcover, with woodruff and hostas. They will succeed in any moist, rich soil.

BLAZING BLUEBERRY
Blueberries will only be happy in acid soil, where they can be used to good effect as groundcover under other lime-haters such as azaleas and rhododendrons. The late summer crop of berries is followed by a brilliant blaze of orange from the leaves before they fall.

REFRESHING GRAPES
This vine is planted outside the greenhouse, but the rods, or stems, are trained up inside against the ribs of the roof. The handsome foliage makes a dappled pattern against the light and provides useful natural shading for crops growing underneath.

PERFECT MELON

The fruit of a musk melon is kept clean by an underlying sheet of plastic. Musk melons are generally smaller than cantaloupes or winter melons, and in warm climates the vines can be trained over an arbour. Elsewhere, all melons need protecting under glass.

BLISSFUL HARVEST

Autumn-fruiting raspberries, such as this cultivar 'Autumn Bliss', are not attacked by birds in the way that summer-fruiting ones are. This is a great advantage, as it saves the trouble of netting the crop. Use them to make a hedge-like screen in the garden.

STRAWBERRY COVER

Cloches like these old-fashioned hand-lights are both practical and decorative. They will protect fruit and help it to ripen a little faster. Large-fruited strawberries such as these need fresh ground every few years, but alpine strawberries can be left to wander at will.

RASPBERRIES *Rubus idaeus*

ALTHOUGH NOT PARTICULARLY ORNAMENTAL in themselves, raspberries, trained tidily on wires, make useful summer screens in a garden or can be used to divide a fruit patch into different areas. Plant them corner to corner in a square plot to make four triangular spaces for gooseberry bushes, currants and strawberries (see the plan for a soft fruit garden on page 25). Potentially, this is a more decorative way of using them than simply planting them in traditional parallel rows. Autumn-fruiting raspberries grow much more densely than summer-fruiting cultivars and make great thickets of canes. Apart from providing a delicious crop at an unexpected time of year, autumn raspberries have the added advantage of not attracting birds for a free meal. Do not plant other fruit too close to the rows, for it is likely to be overwhelmed.

RASPBERRIES

Cultivation

Raspberries need moisture and a relatively acid soil if they are to thrive. They also need support. You can fence them in between two sets of parallel wires, or grow a single row tied to wires stretched between 1.8m (6ft) posts (see page 180).

SITE AND SOIL Raspberries like a deeply dug, light, moist soil and are often disappointing in heavy soils that may bake or crack in summer, disturbing the fine surface roots that feed the canes. They grow best in slightly acid soils (pH 6.5–6.7) and will succeed in light shade.

PLANTING Plant canes in late autumn, setting them so that the fibrous mat of roots is no more than 7cm (3in) below the surface of the soil. They will not grow if they are planted too deeply. Set the canes 38–60cm (15–24in) apart, the more vigorous cultivars at the wider spacing. If you are planting more than one row, allow at least 1.2–1.8m (4–6ft) between the rows. Cut down the canes to about 23cm (9in) after planting to encourage new growth to shoot from the base.

ROUTINE CARE Mulch the rows in early spring with manure, compost or any other non-limy mulch (not mushroom compost, for example, which is alkaline). Keep the ground weed-free, but do not dig deeply around the raspberries as they resent any disturbance to their shallow roots. Water well, if necessary, during the summer.

PRUNING After summer cultivars have fruited, cut out the old canes close to the ground and thin out new canes, leaving no more than 5 or 6 strong stems growing from each original plant. Tie in new canes to their wires, if growing them in a single row. In late winter, cut off the top of each cane just above the top wire. Autumn-fruiting raspberries need different treatment as they carry fruit on canes formed earlier in the same season. Cut the old, fruited canes to the ground in late winter and thin out the thicket of new growth gradually as it grows during the season.

YIELD AND HARVESTING Summer-fruiting varieties may be early, mid or late season, bearing crops from mid to late summer. Autumn-fruiting raspberries can be gathered from early to mid-autumn. Expect about 5.5kg (12lb) of summer raspberries from a 3m (10ft) row and half that amount from autumn types.

PESTS AND DISEASES In limy soils, raspberries may show signs of chlorosis, yellowing of the leaves (see page 192). Spread green sulphur on the soil, use sequestrene, or fertilize with sulphate of ammonia. Plant virus-resistant varieties to minimize the risk of disease spread by the raspberry aphid. Cane spot (see page 193) is a fungus appearing as small purplish spots on the stems in late spring or early summer. Cut out affected canes and spray fortnightly with a systemic fungicide from when the flowerbuds begin to open until the end of flowering. Protect fruit from birds and squirrels with netting (see right). Maggots of the raspberry beetle may damage the fruit (see page 191).

RECOMMENDED CULTIVARS

SUMMER-FRUITING
'Glen Moy': *thornless, with large, firm, early fruit.* **'Leo'**: *useful late-cropper, sparse growth.* **'Malling Admiral'**: *vigorous, resistant to* Botrytis *and some viruses.* **'Malling Jewel'**: *excellent flavour but shy in producing canes.*
AUTUMN-FRUITING
'Autumn Bliss': *high yield of bright red fruit with a firm texture.*

FRAME THE FRUIT
Summer raspberries often need protecting from birds and squirrels. Make a frame, perhaps in a decorative shape as on page 24, and attach netting to it before the fruit starts to ripen.

LOGANBERRIES & TAYBERRIES

PROMISCUITY GENERALLY GETS A BAD PRESS, but in the plant world there is much to be said for it. The wantonness of raspberries and blackberries has produced some fine hybrids. The first was the loganberry, bred over 100 years ago by Judge Logan of California who crossed a raspberry with a blackberry. The same cross produced the tayberry, whose parents were a blackberry called 'Aurora' and an unnamed tetraploid raspberry known tersely as No 626/67.

LOGANBERRIES

Cultivation

Both plants are very vigorous and their long canes need tying to wires or against fences. They do not like cold winters and, if frosted, the canes may die back, although the plant itself usually recovers.

SITE AND SOIL All the hybrid berries like roughly the same treatment. They hate waterlogged soil and are unlikely to do well where there is only a thin skim of earth over chalk.

PLANTING The best time is late autumn, but hybrid berries can be planted until early spring. Set them quite shallowly in the soil to encourage plenty of suckers. Leave 3–3.5m (10–12ft) between plants.

TRAINING If you are training hybrid berries on wires to make a screen, put in posts that stand at least 1.8m (6ft) high, at convenient intervals. Stretch the first wire between them just under 1m (3ft) from the ground with several parallel wires fixed above. Tie the growths securely along the wires, keeping the new canes bunched in a fountain in the middle and the older, fruiting growths trained horizontally away from the centre (see page 180). When you have finished picking the fruit, cut out the old canes, unbundle the new ones and tie them in where the old ones were.

ROUTINE CARE A spring mulch of manure or compost will conserve moisture and help feed the plants. In really cold areas, you may find it best to leave the bundle of new canes lying on the ground

TAYBERRIES

all winter and tie them up in spring. Research has shown that canes treated like this suffer less from die-back.

YIELD AND HARVESTING Expect about 2.5kg (5lb) of fruit per plant after the first year, and 6kg (14lb) when mature. The fruiting season is from mid to late summer.

PESTS AND DISEASES Maggots of the raspberry beetle may tunnel into the fruit. If you must, spray plants at petal fall with a contact insecticide (see page 191).

RECOMMENDED CULTIVARS

LOGANBERRIES
'LY59': *long fruit with a sharp taste.*
'LY654': *a thornless type that is easy to handle but not as vigorous.*

TAYBERRIES
Larger and sweeter than the loganberry, but there are no specific cultivars. The best strain is the Medana type, which is resistant to virus.

BLACKBERRIES *Rubus fruticosus*

IN SOME AREAS, BLACKBERRIES are so prolific in the wild that gardeners may wonder whether they should give them space in the garden. But modern cultivars bear bigger fruit than wild brambles and, carefully trained, will make useful, windproof screens. The most vigorous types, such as 'Himalaya Giant', have spiny canes up to 3m (10ft) long. This is the one to use where a prickly barrier is needed against marauding animals. Other cultivars, such as 'Oregon Thornless', have no prickles. Its leaves are deeply cut like parsley, very decorative and, in some areas, turn rich shades of orange and red in autumn. Blackberries crop well in shade so think, perhaps, of training one on a cool wall.

WILD BLACK-BERRIES

CULTIVATED BLACKBERRIES

Cultivation

Even the less vigorous varieties need plenty of space, so bear this in mind before planting. Train blackberries against a fence or wall or along parallel wires stretched between posts (see page 180). You can also grow blackberries in a hedge (see the plan on page 27), as they grow in the wild. If you are planting a new hedge, let the trees get well established before putting in the blackberries, otherwise they may be smothered in the blackberries' prickly embrace.

SITE AND SOIL Blackberries grow best in ground that retains moisture and is not too limy. You can improve the soil by digging in plenty of manure or compost before planting. As they do not flower until early summer, blackberries can be grown in frost pockets and seem to do well in sun or shade, provided the ground is not dry.

PLANTING Plant in late autumn or at any time up until early spring. Cut the canes (stems) down to about 23cm (9in) immediately after planting. If you are growing two or more plants, set them at least 3.5m (12ft) apart. If you are using a vigorous variety such as 'Himalaya Giant', increase the spacing to 4.5m (15ft). Train the new canes against a wall or fence, or along parallel wires. If planted in a hedge, blackberries need no formal training.

ROUTINE CARE Water, if necessary, in dry spells during summer. Mulch each spring with manure or compost.

PRUNING As with raspberries and loganberries, the fruited canes should be cut out each year after the crop has been gathered. With a late-fruiting variety such as 'Himalaya Giant' this may not be until mid-autumn. Tie in the new canes to replace the old (see page 180). With 'Himalaya Giant', which does not produce canes very freely, a proportion of the old wood may be left in each season.

YIELD AND HARVESTING Expect about 5–9kg (10–20lb) of berries from one plant, depending on variety, from late summer to early autumn. 'Himalaya Giant', the latest to crop, fruits until mid-autumn.

PESTS AND DISEASES Grey mould/ *Botrytis* may attack the berries, especially in wet summers (see page 193). Pick off the worst affected fruit or spray at flowering time with a systemic fungicide. Spraying will need to continue every 2 weeks through the summer.

RECOMMENDED CULTIVARS

'Ashton Cross': *heavy crops, with an authentic taste of the wild.* **'Fantasia'**: *fruit of outstanding size, discovered on an English allotment at Kingston upon Thames, Surrey.* **'Himalaya Giant'**: *largest and thorniest, with decidedly acid fruit.* **'Oregon Thornless'**: *one of the most decorative, excellent foliage and mild-flavoured fruit.*

❀ OREGON THORNLESS

Trained as a screen or against a boundary wall, fence or trellis, 'Oregon Thornless', with its intricately cut leaves, makes a decorative feature in any part of the garden.

IN THE KITCHEN

Wild berries like blackberries make excellent jellies. Since the fruit is free you do not worry that the yield is lower than for jam. If you cannot find enough blackberries, combine them with apple to give a good jelly, less intense in flavour.

BRAMBLE JELLY
Makes about 750g (1½lb) for every 500g (1lb) sugar used

4kg (8lb) blackberries
juice of 3 large or 4 small lemons (or 2 tsp citric acid)
900ml (1½ pints) water
sugar (see below)

1 Wash the fruit and put in a preserving pan with the lemon juice (or citric acid). Add the water and simmer until the fruit is tender and has been gently broken down.

2 Strain the resulting pulp through a scalded jelly bag. For sparkling, clear jelly, do not squeeze the bag.

3 Measure the juice into the cleaned preserving pan, bring to the boil, then add the sugar, using 500g (1lb) for each 600ml (1 pint) of juice. Stir well.

4 Boil rapidly for up to 10 minutes, without stirring, until the setting point has been reached (a drop of jelly on a cold plate should part if you run a teaspoon through it). Skim any froth from the surface and pour into warm, sterilized jars as quickly as possible. When the jars are filled, put waxed circles on top of the hot jelly and secure with lids or cellophane circles and elastic bands.

CULINARY NOTES
❧ To make a good jelly you need pectin (the natural setting agent present in fruit), acid and sugar in the right proportions. Try a mixture of apples and damsons, apples and sloes, or redcurrants and raspberries.

BLUEBERRIES *Vaccinium* spp.

BLUEBERRIES WILL ONLY SUCCEED in the kind of moist, peaty soil in which rhododendrons flourish, and the best way to grow them is in an informal border or woodland setting among other lime-hating shrubs. White flowers, tinged pink, appear in little tassels during late spring and early summer. In autumn, the whole bush often turns into a fiery blaze of orange and copper.

Cultivation

The modern cultivated blueberry is a mixture of several wild American species including *Vaccinium corymbosum*, the swamp or highbush blueberry, which is a shrubby, woody plant common in the eastern United States. The blue-black fruits, covered in a greyish, silvery bloom, are ready in late summer and early autumn. It is not worth bothering with blueberries unless you can supply the very specific growing conditions that they need. They will not survive in ordinary loams and certainly not in limy or heavy clay soil. You can grow them in large pots or tubs filled with ericaceous compost, but they must be watered with water that is free of lime.

SITE AND SOIL Blueberries should be planted in damp, peaty soil with a pH lower than 5.5. They like well-drained ground and the position should be relatively open, although they will grow in sun or partial shade.

PLANTING Plant between mid-autumn and early spring (see page 176), using 2 or 3-year-old plants and setting them about 1.5m (5ft) apart.

POLLINATION To ensure good pollination, two different cultivars should be planted together.

ROUTINE CARE The plants should be netted against birds as soon as the fruit begins to ripen. Work a little bonemeal into the soil around plants in spring and mulch with an acid compost. Water regularly in dry summers.

PRUNING Start pruning the plants in winter by cutting out dead or damaged

BLUEBERRIES

branches together with a proportion of the old, darker-coloured wood. In spring, shear over the tops of the bushes to keep them compact.

YIELD AND HARVESTING Expect about 3kg (6lb) of fruit from a fully established, mature bush. You will need to pick over the bushes several times as the berries ripen over a relatively long period during late summer and early autumn.

PESTS AND DISEASES Blueberries do not generally get attacked by pests or diseases, but they will show signs of chlorosis if the soil is not sufficiently acid (see page 192).

RECOMMENDED CULTIVARS

'Berkeley': *large, prolific, pale blue berries on a vigorous spreading bush.* **'Bluecrop'**: *firm, good-quality berries among leaves that colour well in autumn.* **'Earliblue'**: *one of the earliest to mature, producing a crop in late summer.* **'Herbert'**: *said by connoisseurs to have the best flavoured fruit.*

STRAWBERRIES *Fragaria* × *ananassa*

NOTHING SPEAKS OF SUMMER so eloquently as a dish of strawberries, eaten warm and richly glowing, straight from the garden. Recent breeding has concentrated on producing fruit that travels well. Gardeners can happily ignore this criterion and choose cultivars purely on the basis of taste. The strawberry is the only fruit that, like the Pompidou Centre in Paris, carries its vital working parts on the outside. The seeds dotted in the flesh are the true fruit – the berry is just the carrier. When choosing cultivars, get both early and late-fruiting types, and do not forget the alpine strawberry, which makes an excellent edging for potager or path. The berries are small but there are plenty of them and they do not seem to be attacked by birds.

Cultivation

The strawberry season is short, although the plants tie up the ground for 12 months of the year. In a small garden you may feel that pick-your-own is a better solution, but commercial growers may not put taste at the top of their list. Bear in mind, too, that even if you do grow your own, children, birds and slugs will always find ripe berries before you do.

SITE AND SOIL To grow good crops you must have ground that is in good heart, deep, porous and well fed. Prepare beds in summer, digging in plenty of manure. Old gardening books recommend trenching 1m (3ft) deep. That is pure sadism.

PLANTING You must buy certified virus-free stock as early as possible in summer and practise a 3-year rotation of the strawberry patch so that you keep renewing the plants in fresh ground (see propagating by runners, opposite). This can be difficult to arrange in a small space: the plan on page 25 shows one way, combining strawberries with other soft fruit. Plant rooted runners in late summer so that the plants can settle in before winter. Strawberry plants should be set 45cm (18in) apart in rows 1m (3ft) apart. Set alpine types at 30cm (12in) intervals.

ROUTINE CARE A dressing of sulphate of potash in late winter will help develop flavour. Spread straw around plants as the fruit forms (see opposite). Plastic is sometimes used, but seems to encourage grey mould/*Botrytis*. Nip off runners as they form, unless you need to raise fresh plants. After cropping, cut off the old

leaves (see opposite) and dress the ground lightly with a general fertilizer. Discard old plants after 3 years, starting a new bed with freshly rooted runners. Alpine strawberries are longer lived.

YIELD AND HARVESTING Some cultivars yield much more heavily than others, but flavour tends to decrease as productivity rises. Expect about 250g (8oz) of fruit from each plant. Alpine strawberries crop intermittently from midsummer to autumn. "Perpetual" strawberries are not in fact perpetual but carry a second, lighter crop in the autumn. The summer-fruiting strawberry can be early or late, depending on the cultivar.

PESTS AND DISEASES You will need to net crops against birds, and slugs can be a problem. Grey mould/*Botrytis* is the worst disease (see page 193) as it rots the berries, covering them with a fluffy, brownish-grey fungus. It is worst in wet summers. If prevalent, spray with fungicide as the first flowers open and repeat every 2 weeks until the fruit starts to ripen. Water plants in the morning rather than the evening so that flowers and fruit dry off quickly.

RECOMMENDED CULTIVARS

'Aromel': *medium to large fruit with excellent flavour (perpetual).* **'Cambridge Favourite'**: *reliable, heavy cropper with moderately flavoured fruit.* **'Cambridge Late Pine'**: *dark crimson fruit, perhaps the best-flavoured of all (late).* **'Honeoye'**: *early variety that crops heavily.* **'Baron Solemacher'**: *has the useful habit of growing in neat clumps without runners (alpine).*

IN THE KITCHEN

The advantage of growing your own strawberries is that you can pick them when they are properly ripened. A squeeze of lemon juice on a bowl of fresh fruit intensifies the flavour.

STRAWBERRY SHORTCAKE
Serves 6

For the shortcake
250g (8oz) flour
2 tsp baking powder
½ tsp salt
1 tbsp caster sugar
125g (4oz) butter, cubed
2–3 tbsp milk
For the filling
500g (1lb) strawberries
1 tbsp caster sugar, or to taste
300ml (½ pint) double cream

1 Grease two 23cm (9in) flan tins and preheat the oven to 230°C/450°F/gas mark 8.

2 Sift flour, baking powder and salt into a bowl and sprinkle in the sugar. Rub in the butter with your fingers until the texture resembles breadcrumbs. Add just enough milk to bind the mixture, working it in with a knife.

3 On a floured surface, divide the dough in half and, with the palm of your hand, press out each half into a circle about 15cm (6in) across. Put each circle of dough into a flan tin and press it out gently to fill the whole tin. Bake until the shortcake colours slightly, about 15 minutes. Leave to cool.

4 Halve the strawberries, reserving some to use whole to decorate the top, and sprinkle with sugar.

5 Whip the cream until thick and spread half over one shortcake circle. Put halved fruit on top and sandwich with the second circle. Spread the rest of the cream on top. Decorate with whole strawberries.

❀ ALPINE STRAWBERRIES

EARLY-FRUITING
STRAWBERRIES

STANDARD
STRAWBERRIES

PROPAGATING BY RUNNERS

1 To keep strawberries fruiting well, you will need to renew them every 3 years. Select some of the runners that develop on the plants and let them take root in the surrounding soil.

2 Once they are growing well, carefully lift the rooted runners with a hand fork and sever them from the parent plant. Transplant these new plants to a fresh bed that has been well dug and manured.

PROTECTING FRUIT

Spread a generous layer of straw under and around the plants as soon as the berries begin to form. This will keep them free from soil and well aired.

CLEARING FOLIAGE

After the fruit has finished cropping, chop off all the leaves to within 10cm (4in) of the crown, and remove the old straw to help prevent pests and diseases.

BLACK, RED & WHITECURRANTS
Ribes nigrum & R. rubrum

FOR THE GARDENER, there are three different kinds of currant: black, red and white. For the botanist, there are only two, for the whitecurrant is nothing more than a variant of the red, *Ribes rubrum*. For translucent, luminous beauty, nothing can match the redcurrant, which you often see glowing in the still-life paintings of Dutch artists. Although they are most often grown as ordinary bushes, red and whitecurrants can be trained into extremely decorative cordons to make screens around a vegetable patch. Blackcurrant bushes are living medicine chests. Half a dozen of these tiny fruit contain more Vitamin C than the biggest lemon. Choose compact varieties such as 'Ben Sarek' if you are gardening in a small space.

BLACKCURRANTS

❀ **REDCURRANTS**

WHITECURRANTS

Cultivation

Currants grown in bush form need no support, but if you decide to grow red or whitecurrants as one or two-stem cordons (see page 174), they will need to be trained on a wall or fence, or tied into wires between posts. The eventual height of bushes depends on the cultivar, but is usually about 1.2–1.5m (4–5ft). Blackcurrants tend to make large, spreading bushes, red and whitecurrants more upright shapes. As cordons, red and whitecurrants will reach 1.5–1.8m (5–6ft).
SITE AND SOIL All currants do best in open situations but will tolerate some shade. Blackcurrants are greedier feeders than red and whitecurrants. Dig in plenty of manure or compost before planting.
PLANTING Plant from late autumn until early spring (see page 176). Leave 1.5–1.8m (5–6ft) between bushes. Blackcurrants should be set more deeply than they were in their growing containers. Cut down all stems of blackcurrants to within 7–10cm (3–4in) of the ground immediately after planting to promote fresh growth.
ROUTINE CARE Mulch in spring with a thick layer of manure or compost and top-dress red and whitecurrants with sulphate of potash, about 30g (1oz) for each bush, to improve fruiting. Do not disturb the roots by digging around bushes, but keep the ground well weeded.
PRUNING Blackcurrants are treated differently from red and whitecurrants as they fruit on young, 1-year-old wood and the other two fruit on spurs made on old

wood. When blackcurrants have fruited, cut out the old wood, as shown below, leaving the pale stems that will produce the next season's fruit. As red and whitecurrants bear fruit on old wood, pruning is less drastic. After fruiting, or during autumn and winter, shorten branches by about a third to keep the bushes shapely and compact. On red and whitecurrants grown as cordons, cut the lateral branches back to within 3cm (1½in) or so of the main stem (see page 180).
YIELD AND HARVESTING Currants are ready to pick in mid and late summer. Expect about 5kg (10lb) of fruit from each bush when they are fully established.
PESTS AND DISEASES Protect fruit from birds (see page 189). Aphids may infect plants, causing blisters on the leaves (see page 190). If blackcurrants lose vigour and crop poorly, they may be suffering from reversion disease (see page 194). There is no cure. Destroy the bushes.

RECOMMENDED CULTIVARS

BLACKCURRANTS
'Ben Lomond': *medium-sized bush bearing heavy crops of large fruit.* **'Ben Sarek'**: *compact bush, with good crops of large fruit.*
REDCURRANTS
'Jonkheer van Tets': *large fruit on early-cropping, upright bush.* **'Red Lake'**: *popular variety, upright bush bearing very large fruit.* **'Stanza'**: *small, dark fruit on upright bush.*
WHITECURRANTS
'White Grape': *best for flavour, with large fruit on an upright bush.*

PRUNING BLACKCURRANTS
After fruiting, cut out at least a third of the old, dark wood, leaving the new, pale stems that will bear fruit the following season. This does not apply to red and whitecurrants.

GOOSEBERRIES *Ribes uva-crispa*

"THE FREEDOM OF THE BUSH should be given to all visitors," wrote the Edwardian epicure and fruit grower Edward Bunyard. He was thinking of the gooseberry in its dessert state – squidgy, sweet, highly scented – an almost forgotten delight, for gooseberries are usually gathered hard and green for cooking. Plants can be grown as pretty, metre-high standards, but they need strong stakes as the stems are spindly in relation to the topknot.

❀ **GREEN GOOSEBERRIES**

❀ **RED GOOSEBERRIES**

Cultivation

Gooseberries are found wild in most northern, temperate zones and seem to flourish in cool, moist, high places. They can be grown as bushes, cordons or standards. Eventual height varies with the cultivar. Bushes generally grow to about 1.2–1.5m (4–5ft) and cordons to 1.5–1.8m (5–6ft).

SITE AND SOIL The soil should be well drained but moisture-retentive. On dry ground, the fruit will not swell properly. Gooseberries thrive in sun or partial shade.

PLANTING Plant late autumn until early spring (see page 176). Bushes are best grown on a short stem to prevent suckering at ground level. Set them about 1.5m (5ft) apart and do not plant too deeply. Cordons can be set just 30cm (12in) apart.

ROUTINE CARE Mulch with manure or compost in early spring. Water newly planted bushes in summer, if necessary. Feed plants each winter with sulphate of potash, using 30g (1oz) for each bush. Remove any suckers that sprout from around the base.

PRUNING Gooseberries do not need regular pruning, but it is easier to pick the fruit if you remove some growth each winter to keep the centre of the bush open (see page 181). On cordons, shorten the side growths to 3 buds, and cut back the branches of standards by at least a third.

YIELD AND HARVESTING For cooking, green fruit can be picked in late spring and early summer. Dessert fruit should be left to ripen on the bush. Expect 3–5kg (6–10lb) of fruit from a bush, 1–1.5kg (2–3lb) from a cordon.

PESTS AND DISEASES American gooseberry mildew, a form of powdery mildew, is the most debilitating disease (see page 194). Prune to keep bushes open and let air through. Spray if necessary with a systemic fungicide or plant the resistant variety 'Invicta'. Net bushes if birds attack the flowerbuds in winter and spring.

RECOMMENDED CULTIVARS

'Careless': *popular variety, bearing pale green fruit on a spreading bush.* **'Invicta'**: *vigorous, spreading bush, immune to mildew.*
'Leveller': *ripens into an excellent dessert gooseberry, greenish-yellow and extra large.*
'Whinham's Industry': *upright bush with dark red fruit, good cooked or eaten as dessert.*

IN THE KITCHEN

Gooseberries (and whitecurrants) make a refreshing white wine. To make wine, you need large sterilized containers that can be corked with an air lock. Gases can then escape while the wine is fermenting.

GOOSEBERRY WINE
Makes 4.5 litres (1 gallon)

1 kg (2lb) green gooseberries
3 Campden tablets
3.5 litres (6 pints) cold water
15g (½oz) pectin-destroying enzyme
1.1kg (2¼lb) sugar
1 level tsp yeast nutrient
1 heaped tsp wine yeast

1 Crush the uncooked gooseberries in a clean plastic bucket. Dissolve 2 Campden tablets in the water and add to the fruit. Then add the enzyme and stir.

2 Seal the bucket with polythene film or lid and leave the mixture to steep for 48 hours in a warm place. Strain through a jelly bag or a muslin cloth into a fresh plastic bucket. Squeeze out all the liquid.

3 Dissolve the sugar in 600ml (1 pint) of boiling water. Let this syrup cool, then add it, with the yeast nutrient, to the liquid. Make up the volume to 4.5 litres (1 gallon) with more water if needed.

4 Pour the liquid into its fermenting container (4.5 litre or 1 gallon) and add the wine yeast. Keep under air lock at about 15°C (60°F) until it stops fermenting (bubbling). This may take 12 weeks.

5 Siphon the wine into a container of the same volume, taking care not to siphon off any sediment from the bottom of the original container. Add another Campden tablet and fit a new air lock. Leave to stand until clear: this will take a few weeks rather than days. Decant into sterilized bottles, cork, and store the wine in a cool place.

GRAPES *Vitis labrusca & V. vinifera*

GRAPES MAKE UP THE BIGGEST single fruit crop in the world. Given the amount of liquid that finds its way down the throats of wine buffs each year, this is not surprising, although gardeners may not be growing grapes primarily for their alcoholic potential. Vines are blessed with an elegant, venerable habit of growth and excellent shading foliage. Trained over a seat or arbour, they give just the right air of productive ease in a garden. Combined with clematis, vines are ideal plants for a pergola. In hot climates, they will make a shaded roof over a terrace, where you can sit in dappled light (see the plan on page 45). In a conservatory, a vine will provide useful summer shading for the plants inside. Some varieties of vine are more tolerant of cold than others. One of the most widely grown in the US is 'Concord', a cultivated form of the native species *Vitis labrusca*. Vines grown in Europe are generally derived from a different species, *Vitis vinifera*.

Cultivation

Correct pruning and training are essential, whether you are growing grapes inside or out. In cool, wet areas, vines make far too much growth, which must be restricted if the plants are to be persuaded to fruit.

SITE AND SOIL Although they are hardy, vines will ripen their crop most successfully in areas where summers are long and warm. 'Concord' is the hardiest and may survive outside in areas where more tender *Vitis vinifera* types such as 'Müller-Thurgau' and 'Siegerrebe' will shiver and sulk. In Britain, outdoor grapes rarely succeed north of a line drawn from Gloucester to the Wash. Give them a sheltered, sunny wall and fertile, well-drained soil.

PLANTING Greenhouse and conservatory beds should be filled with a rich mixture of loam and manure. Alternatively, vines can be planted outside in the autumn with the main stem fed through to the inside of the greenhouse, so that subsequent growth is sheltered by the glass. Plant vines from mid-autumn to late winter, setting them 1.2–1.5m (4–5ft) apart.

ROUTINE CARE Keep the atmosphere in greenhouses humid by damping down the floor regularly, and ventilate well as soon as the vines begin to flower (see page 182). Pollinate the flowers by hand with a soft brush (see page 177). Thin the bunches of grapes, leaving one for every 30cm (12in) of stem. As the grapes begin to swell, cut out the smallest and most overcrowded fruit in the centre of the bunch. Give a liquid feed every 10 days until the grapes have fully ripened. As they are ripening, make sure the greenhouse is well ventilated and keep it less damp. Rest the vines in winter by reducing the temperature, untying the rods (branches) from the wires and laying them on the ground. In this way, when the sap begins to rise in early spring it will run right to the end of the stems. If the vines are not dropped, there is a tendency for just the lower buds to break into growth. Tie the rods back into place in spring. Varieties such as 'Muscat of Alexandria' may need extra heat in spring and do best if growing temperatures can be maintained at 10–13°C (50–56°F). Mulch outdoor vines annually in early spring with manure.

PRUNING AND TRAINING When grown under glass, vines should be trained on wires set about 30cm (12in) apart and at least 15cm (6in) away from the glass. The leading shoot should be trained vertically, the laterals horizontally, along the wires. When the vines have flowered, prune the laterals back, leaving just 2 leaves beyond the clusters of fruit. Any subsequent shoots breaking from the laterals should be pinched out, leaving 1 or 2 leaves at most. In the autumn after fruiting, cut the leading stem back to firm, well-ripened wood and cut the laterals back to 2 buds. Train vines outside on walls by allowing, at most, 3–4 main stems to develop from a single rootstock. After the first season, cut back the growth by two-thirds and repeat this in early autumn each year until all the available space is filled. On young plants, tie in the laterals and let them grow to about 60cm (24in) before pinching them out. On mature plants, the laterals should be stopped just beyond the clusters of flowers, leaving no more than 2 leaves. Sub-laterals (shoots springing from the laterals) should be stopped at 1 leaf. (See page 181 for more about pruning.)

YIELD AND HARVESTING A mature vine will yield about 7kg (15lb) of fruit. When harvesting, cut the bunches so that they have a T-shaped piece of stem attached. If you want to keep them for any length of time, put one end of the stem in water.

PESTS AND DISEASES Powdery mildew is the most serious disease (see page 194), whether vines are grown under cover or outside. The disease is most likely to strike where plants are under-watered. Spraying with a systemic fungicide will control powdery mildew and also grey mould/*Botrytis* (see page 193), which is usually worst on outdoor vines in wet seasons. Red spider mite (see page 191) may infect plants in hot, dry greenhouses. Regular damping down helps to keep this particular pest at bay.

RECOMMENDED CULTIVARS

OUTDOOR WHITE GRAPES
'Madeleine Silvaner': *good in cool conditions, yield not high.* **'Müller-Thurgau'**: *one of the best for wine, dessert quality only fair.* **'Siegerrebe'**: *dual-purpose, producing sweet, muscat-like fruit.*

OUTDOOR BLACK GRAPES
'Brant': *one of the best – prolific crops and beautiful autumn foliage.* **'Concord'**: *fruits well, tolerates cool summers.*

INDOOR WHITE GRAPES
'Foster's Seedling': *heavy crops of well-flavoured fruit.* **'Muscat of Alexandria'**: *old variety unparalleled for taste, needs heat.*

INDOOR BLACK GRAPES
'Black Hamburgh': *one of the best dessert grapes, sets freely and ripens well.*

IN THE KITCHEN

Grapes add texture to the smooth, bland, creamy mix of a pudding like *Crème brûlée*. Large grapes should be halved and their seeds taken out. Smaller seedless grapes can simply be washed and used as they are.

CRÈME BRULEE
Serves 4

500g (1lb) grapes
4 egg yolks
600ml (1 pint) single cream
90g (3oz) brown sugar

1 Deseed the grapes if necessary and arrange them in a thick layer on the bottom of a flameproof dish.

2 Beat the egg yolks in the top of a double saucepan. Heat the cream gently and pour it over the yolks. Mix well.

3 Heat some water in the lower part of the double saucepan, set the mixture over it in the top part of the pan and keep stirring until it begins to thicken. It is important that the mixture does not boil. When it has thickened, pour it over the grapes and leave overnight in the refrigerator.

4 Next day, cover the cream with an even layer of brown sugar, and put the dish under a very hot grill until the sugar has caramelized. Let it cool and chill before serving.

CULINARY NOTES

❧ Home-grown black grapes have a beautiful bloom on the skin that is very easily rubbed off and spoiled. Handle bunches with care and bring them to the table displayed on a few of their own handsome leaves.

❧ Grapes also look beautiful divided into small bunches and piled in a glass bowl, together with sparkling ice cubes and a scatter of small flowers such as blue borage.

❀ **BLACK GRAPES**

❀ **WHITE MUSCAT GRAPES**

TYING IN SHOOTS
In spring, tie the rods (branches) back on to the wires using strong twine. They should spend the winter lying on the ground so that as the sap rises, buds break evenly all the way along the stems.

MELONS *Cucumis melo*

ONLY IN COUNTRIES with a Mediterranean climate can melons be grown in open ground, trailing perhaps between tall sheaves of sweet corn, or sitting proudly like kings on little heaped thrones of manure and compost. You may also be able to train melons over a trellis, but you will need to support the fruit with a sling as it gets heavier. In growth, they look like squash, but you need to thin the fruit so that no more than four melons are allowed to develop on each plant. In cool climates, melons will only ripen if they are grown with some protection such as a cold frame, cloche or cool greenhouse. The most successful type for growing in cool areas is a cantaloupe such as 'Ogen'.

❀ CANTALOUPE MELON 'Ogen'

❀ HONEYDEW MELON

Cultivation

To produce the best fruit, melons need a long, warm growing season. Fruit will ripen more quickly if you train vines over a hard surface, such as concrete or paving stones, that stores and reflects heat.

SITE AND SOIL The site will depend on climate. In cold areas, only a greenhouse will provide the necessary summer warmth. Melons grow well in grow bags, or can be planted in greenhouse borders, well enriched with manure. The soil in a cold frame needs to be similarly enhanced.

SOWING Sow seeds in spring, setting each on edge, 1cm (½in) deep in a 7cm (3in) pot of compost (see page 168). Water, and cover with polythene. Keep at about 18°C (65°F) until they have germinated. Plant out when seedlings have 4 proper leaves.

TRANSPLANTING Set plants in their final quarters from late spring (see page 169). In a cold frame or in open ground, melons grow best on a slight mound with a wall of compost built up around the edge to retain water. In a greenhouse border, set the plants at least 1m (3ft) apart.

ROUTINE CARE The main stem will produce laterals (side stems), which you should stop when they have made 5 leaves. From these laterals will come sub-laterals, which you should pinch out at 3 leaves. The flowers that will eventually become fruit form on these sub-laterals, so pinch out growing tips to force the plant to concentrate on producing fruit rather than foliage. Keep the soil moist and the

air as well ventilated as possible. Pollinate the flowers by stripping the petals from a male flower and pushing it into a female flower (female flowers have slight swellings just underneath the flowerheads). One male flower will pollinate at least 4 females. Pollination is best done at midday. Thin the fruit, if necessary, leaving no more than one melon per sub-lateral. Place tiles underneath to keep the fruit off the earth.

YIELD AND HARVESTING Expect 4 fruit from each plant. Do not pick melons until absolutely ripe. The all-enveloping smell will tell you when to pounce.

PESTS AND DISEASES Because melons, like cucumbers, are cucurbits, they may suffer from cucumber mosaic virus (see page 194). The leaves crumple and become flecked with yellow spots. There is no cure.

RECOMMENDED CULTIVARS

CANTALOUPE MELONS
'Minnesota Midget': *small, sweet, fast-ripening fruit.* **'Ogen'**: *small, round, yellow fruit with green ribs.* **'Sweetheart'**: *one of the best for growing in cool conditions.*

MUSK (OR NETTED) MELONS
'Blenheim Orange': *excellent flavour.*
'Tiger': *boldly striped yellow and green skin.*
HONEYDEW (OR CASSABA) MELONS
'Oliver's Pearl Cluster': *grows on a compact plant.*

KIWI FRUIT & PASSION FRUIT
Actinidia deliciosa & *Passiflora* spp.

BOTH THESE FRUIT GROW ON EXTENSIVE twining vines, neither of which is fully hardy. The kiwi, or Chinese gooseberry, has big, round leaves covered with a gingery fuzz when young. The fruit has a brown, furry coat and, where it gets sufficient heat and a long enough growing season, will ripen outside to be harvested in autumn. The passion fruit, a cousin of the common passion flower, *Passiflora caerulea*, has showy white flowers with purple centres in midsummer, set off against handsome, three-lobed leaves. Outdoors in cool climates, the plant is likely to be cut down each year by frost so that growth has to start from the base again in spring. This makes the flowers late and the fruit then has insufficient time to ripen.

❀ **KIWI FRUIT**

Cultivation

Give these plants the hottest spots you can find in the garden, trained on a sunny wall. Alternatively, grow them in the protected environment of a greenhouse or conservatory. If the growing conditions suit them, they can both be rampageous. In order for kiwi fruit to ripen, the vine needs an 8-month growing season. And to get any kiwi fruit at all, you will need two vines: a male and a female. Passion fruit is even more tender and is only likely to succeed outside where the winter temperature rarely falls below 8–10°C (45–50°F). Even though crops might be capricious, both plants have handsome foliage and can be planted to grow over an arbour or shed to provide a leafy background for a scattering of clematis or some other flowery climber.

SITE AND SOIL Both these vines do best in rich, well-drained ground.

PLANTING Set out plants in late spring when all danger of frost has passed. They both need to be trained and tied in to supports. These should be strong for a kiwi vine, which can be up to 9m (27ft) long, and heavy with it. Plant male and female plants next to each other, but leave 4m (14ft) between each pair.

POLLINATION Female kiwi plants will only set fruit when there is a male vine near by. The passion fruit is self-fertile.

ROUTINE CARE Both plants are greedy for food and water. Mulch liberally in spring with manure or compost and water regularly throughout the growing season.

PRUNING Growth is rampant in the right conditions and may need curbing to persuade the plants to concentrate on the job in hand. For the gardener, this means the production of fruit rather than foliage. Kiwi vines fruit on the shoots that break from the first 3–6 buds of the current year's growth. Treat them like vines (see page 181), summer pruning new growth to a point just beyond the setting fruit. Winter pruning can be more drastic. If necessary, remove whole stems. Prune passion fruit in early spring, thinning out overgrown plants and pinching back the lateral (side) shoots to about 15cm (6in).

YIELD AND HARVESTING Expect about 9kg (20lb) of fruit from both kiwi and passion fruit vines, but only once the plants have become well established. This may take up to 7 years. Pick the fruit when, like a peach, it gives slightly under thumb pressure.

PESTS AND DISEASES These crops are generally trouble-free.

❀ **PASSION FRUIT**

RECOMMENDED CULTIVARS

KIWI FRUIT
'Haywood': *the most reliable female kiwi fruit available.* **'Tomuri'**: *a good male.*
PASSION FRUIT
Little selection of passion fruit has taken place and there are few cultivars to recommend.
'Ruby Gold': *red-skinned cultivar, sometimes available from the National Collection of* Passiflora *in Clevedon, Avon, England.*

3

PLANNING & CULTIVATION TECHNIQUES

IN THIS FINAL SECTION are some ground rules you may find useful. Humus and hardening off, intercropping and insects, pricking out and pollination, they are all here, explained in a way that makes them simple to follow. Garden rules, however, exist only to be broken. Your own ability to tune in to the ebb and flow of the seasons and your plants' reactions to those changes will, in the end, be much more useful than any other source of knowledge. Learn, too, to be sanguine. Even if you follow all the rules you may still have disasters. Do not worry. There is always another spring.

SIZING UP THE OPTIONS

THE OPTIONS AVAILABLE to new kitchen gardeners will depend entirely on the space available. You can grow vegetables on a balcony, but you would not expect to make an asparagus bed there. If all you have is a windowsill, you may become the world's expert on growing basil or rocket but you are unlikely to be able to pull a decent carrot. Finding the right place for the right plant is the secret of success in gardening, and it is as true for fruit and vegetables as it is for flowers. Some vegetables will grow in partial shade. Some demand sun. Some want lashings of food and drink. Others will spin a crop out of little more than thin air. When planning what you want to grow, you must consider the plant's needs as well as your own.

LETTUCE ALL THE WAY
Lettuce make fine foliage plants, and their green and red frills and flounces can be used to stunning effect in the flower border, or mixed with orange marigolds or red-hot zinnias.

THE ALTERNATIVES

Once you grasp the notion that fruit and vegetables do not necessarily have to be grown in purdah, away from the rest of the plants in the garden, all kinds of possibilities arise. Instead of planting a rose on a sheltered wall of your house, you may put a pear there instead and train its malleable branches into a fan. Instead of raising a dividing screen of larchlap fencing, you may think of planting a loganberry or tayberry and training it on parallel wires to make an extremely productive partition. You may think of bringing an artichoke into the flower border to give height and architectural substance to flowers that are lacking in both. Or you may edge a path with crinkled parsley, perhaps planting it alternately with groups of chubby violas. And you may decide to do without the petunias in the hanging basket and fill it with bush tomatoes.

All these crops look beautiful as well as providing food. There is no pleasure to equal that of picking your own supper on a summer evening. The pleasure is more muted if you are hacking a winter parsnip out of frozen ground, but even that may have a masochistic charm. And you can dream of the mouth-watering parsnip purée (see page 105) that will be the reward for your labours.

TUNNEL VISION
Use structures like tunnels to create more growing space. Here, roses, at their height in midsummer, have been imaginatively interplanted with vines of kiwi fruit and grapes that will reach their peak later in the season.

SCREEN PLAY
This cottage garden is just beginning to burst into growth with its neat rows of vegetable seedlings. The wigwam and woven willow screen that acts as a partition — and will later support a fast-growing hop — make good focal points when there is less greenery about.

PLUMMY TONES
No garden is so small that vegetables cannot be used in a dramatic way. Here, a ring of young cabbage plants makes a bold swathe of leaves around a potted shrub. The midnight-coloured flowers of the iris, once they open, will underline the cabbages' dusky tones.

ACCENT ON COLOUR AND SHAPE
Although they all have their role in the kitchen, the herbs and vegetables here have been chosen just as much for their colours and shapes. The round flowerheads of leeks add a sculptural touch to a colourful arrangement of fennel, flowering chicory, nasturtiums, chard and sage.

FRUITFUL FEATURES

When sizing up the options, think hardest about the features that will be the most permanent. These are likely to be fruit trees. Could you fit an apple on to the lawn? The answer is probably yes, but your life will be made easier if you choose a half-standard with at least 1.2m (4ft) of clear stem before the branches start to arch out. This will grow into a fine tree, will be easy to mow under, to sling a hammock from and be infinitely more beautiful to look at than a squat bush reined in by a dwarfing rootstock.

Could you make better use of the paths by turning one of them into a tunnel dripping with grapes from a vine (if you are a romantic) or runner beans (if you take a more pragmatic view)? Tunnels for the vine can be permanent structures –

hoops of iron joined by crosspieces – or temporary. For the runner beans you could make a simple tunnel from hazel poles bent and lashed together over the path and joined at the sides with horizontal poles (see page 10). This would suit a cottage garden where you might have courgettes and round-headed alliums bobbing around under the beans.

PICK OF THE PLANTS

Deciding what to grow has to come after sizing up the options. You might not have enough space to do all that you want, nor enough sunny sites to grow your chosen crops. Taste matters too. However many decorative schemes you dream up for a leek bed, it will be a waste of ground if your family is resolutely anti-leek. With some vegetables, such as tomatoes, there is

no such thing as too much. Tomatoes are attractive, can be trained to grow in vertical rather than horizontal space (which is always at a premium) and they make good centrepieces for a potager. They crop well on balconies, too, where you could train them up canes in a grow bag, surrounded by pots of cut-and-come-again lettuce, endive and rocket.

If the way things look is as important as the process of producing food, you will choose vegetables for appearance as well as for taste. You will plant the parsley-leaved blackberry, 'Oregon Thornless', and not mind that it crops more lightly than the standard kind. You will want yellow courgettes and tiger-striped tomatoes, red-stemmed chard and purple-podded beans. If you choose carefully, you can have the best of both worlds: bounty and beauty combined.

SORTING OUT THE SPACE

THE SIZE OF A GARDEN need not limit your ambition. Indeed, the smaller it is, the greater the need for the gardener to feel that every square centimetre is earning its keep. There are several ways you can bring this about. One is to consider the way the garden is laid out. You need bold, simple lines, with paths wider than you ever thought necessary and beds bigger than you ever thought possible. Introducing key plants, or highlighting existing ones, is another way to pull together a scheme that somehow always seems to have something missing. There is no strict formula for sorting out the space: each individual gardener finds his or her own solution. We may start working from the same set of principles, but we should finish with completely different results that reflect what we want from our own particular patches.

INTERNAL DIVISIONS

Imagine an average back garden where there is a small paved area with a central lawn beyond and narrow flower beds running up either side. At the end there may be a shed, or a play area with a climbing frame. How would it be if, for a start, you did away with the lawn and divided up the space in a more engaging way? If you have children, this may not be an option, but for the moment, forget the children and concentrate on the space – the former lawn space – and its potential. If you are sitting on the paved area immediately outside the house, or looking out from the windows, you will want something there to catch the eye. The garden itself should appear as luxuriant as possible. We are not talking about fearful gardening here.

Faced with a plot of ground that needs dividing up, many gardeners turn first to the edges and work their way around the boundaries, digging borders that are usually too narrow to be useful and leaving a void at the centre. If, instead, you think out from the centre of the space, quite different patterns will emerge.

DIAGONAL PLAN If the squarish space in front of you were divided with a giant X to mark the lines of two new diagonal paths, as in Plan 1, several advantages immediately become clear. Space is apportioned in a clean, simple way, creating the maximum area for growing flowers, fruit and vegetables in the four triangles formed by the X. It becomes possible to create an eyecatching display

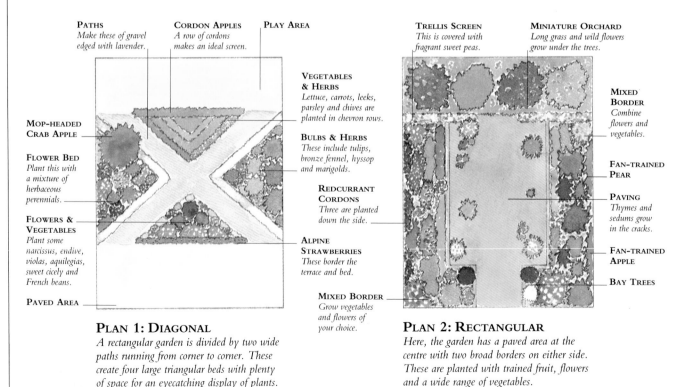

PATHS
Make these of gravel edged with lavender.

CORDON APPLES
A row of cordons makes an ideal screen.

PLAY AREA

MOP-HEADED CRAB APPLE

FLOWER BED
Plant this with a mixture of herbaceous perennials.

FLOWERS & VEGETABLES
Plant some narcissus, endive, violas, aquilegias, sweet cicely and French beans.

PAVED AREA

VEGETABLES & HERBS
Lettuce, carrots, leeks, parsley and chives are planted in chevron rows.

BULBS & HERBS
These include tulips, bronze fennel, hyssop and marigolds.

REDCURRANT CORDONS
Three are planted down the side.

ALPINE STRAWBERRIES
These border the terrace and bed.

MIXED BORDER
Grow vegetables and flowers of your choice.

TRELLIS SCREEN
This is covered with fragrant sweet peas.

MINIATURE ORCHARD
Long grass and wild flowers grow under the trees.

MIXED BORDER
Combine flowers and vegetables.

FAN-TRAINED PEAR

PAVING
Thymes and sedums grow in the cracks.

FAN-TRAINED APPLE

BAY TREES

PLAN 1: DIAGONAL
A rectangular garden is divided by two wide paths running from corner to corner. These create four large triangular beds with plenty of space for an eyecatching display of plants.

PLAN 2: RECTANGULAR
Here, the garden has a paved area at the centre with two broad borders on either side. These are planted with trained fruit, flowers and a wide range of vegetables.

alongside the paved area outside the house, where you most need something to admire. And the crossing of the paths in the middle creates a pivot for the design. The two diagonal paths need to be wide. This is possible as there is untrammelled planting space in between. Be generous.

The style of planting in the four triangles can be formal or not, depending on taste. Each of the four segments should have one big, outstanding specimen: a giant fennel, perhaps, or a neat, mop-headed crab apple tree. Depending on the size of the garden, the far side of the X-shape may mark the back boundary, or you may be able to keep the climbing frame or shed area. Hide this from view with a bold semi-screen. You do not want anything solid or your eye will bounce off it like a rubber ball. Nor do you want anything fussy. This is where fruit trees, planted in rows of slanting cordons or splayed out as fans or espaliers, make an ideal screen.

RECTANGULAR PLAN You might like the idea of a rectangular paved area in the middle of the plot, as in Plan 2, with wide borders of mixed vegetables and flowers on either side, and a miniature orchard at the end. A trelliswork screen covered with

sweet peas divides the orchard from the rest of the garden, and cracks between the paving stones are planted with mats of thyme and fleshy-leaved sedums.

WINDING PATH PLAN This divides the garden with a path that curves up through the centre. The thick planting of lobelia makes the flagstones look like stepping stones in a river of blue. Stepover apples (like a long, low, one-tier espalier, see page 175) have been planted along its edge. Other fruit trees and bushes include plums, a quince and a mixture of currants. Vegetables share the beds with flowers, while marrows and squash have room to roam under the fruit trees.

SYMMETRICAL PLAN A fourth option, shown in Plan 4, has rectangles of grass either side of a central path, with plants in raised beds built at the sides. The path could be made of bricks or stone, to suit the surroundings. Bush tomatoes tumble over the edges of one raised bed, with tall stands of sunflowers and sweet corn behind. The other raised bed combines vegetables, herbs and flowers. Three wigwams at the end add height, and are used to support runner beans, clematis and the cup-and-saucer vine, *Cobaea scandens*.

GETTING STARTED

New gardeners are usually told that they must draw out a plan on paper before they start flailing around with spades and wheelbarrows. Because this is the way professional designers work, it is assumed that it is also best for amateurs. The problem with paper designs is that they tend to get over-complicated. The obvious is avoided at all costs. Another difficulty with paper is that it cannot contain all the information you need to make the right decisions. You will only get this as you prowl around your patch, taking in slight rises and falls in the ground and the consequences these will have on your design. Then you become aware of things beyond your boundary that you would rather not see, things that a well-placed plum tree may be able to conceal. You see where the sun falls and which patches are permanently in shade, and the problems the wind might cause for a too hastily erected wigwam of peas. Above all, working on the ground you develop a proper sense of proportion. Think simple is the best advice. And think big, however small your plot.

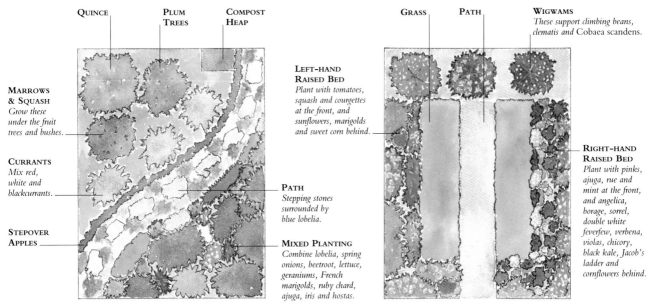

QUINCE   PLUM TREES   COMPOST HEAP

GRASS   PATH   WIGWAMS
These support climbing beans, clematis and Cobaea scandens.

MARROWS & SQUASH
Grow these under the fruit trees and bushes.

CURRANTS
Mix red, white and blackcurrants.

STEPOVER APPLES

LEFT-HAND RAISED BED
Plant with tomatoes, squash and courgettes at the front, and sunflowers, marigolds and sweet corn behind.

PATH
Stepping stones surrounded by blue lobelia.

MIXED PLANTING
Combine lobelia, spring onions, beetroot, lettuce, geraniums, French marigolds, ruby chard, ajuga, iris and hostas.

RIGHT-HAND RAISED BED
Plant with pinks, ajuga, rue and mint at the front, and angelica, borage, sorrel, double white feverfew, verbena, violas, chicory, black kale, Jacob's ladder and cornflowers behind.

PLAN 3: WINDING PATH
Stepping stones, surrounded by masses of blue lobelia, meander through the garden, dividing it into two large planting areas filled with fruit, vegetables and flowers.

PLAN 4: SYMMETRICAL
This very symmetrical design has raised beds around its sides, two patches of grass, and three wigwams of climbing plants that act as a focal point as well as a screen.

CHOOSING PATHS

PATHS DEFINE THE MAIN LINES OF THE DESIGN in a garden. They do not all need to be of equal importance. The main thoroughfares may be wide and hard-surfaced, but there may be an interconnecting web of narrow paths between beds that are no more than beaten earth. You need to get these lines of communication sorted out before you proceed with the rest of the plan for your plot. You need also to think of the kind of surface you want on your paths. The most sympathetic coverings in terms of looks and texture will probably also be the ones that need most care and maintenance. If you do not like weeds, but have an equal antipathy to weedkiller, then you had better start learning to love concrete.

SIMPLE SURFACES

The way you treat the paths in your garden will be dictated by cost as well as taste. The simplest and cheapest method is to leave them as beaten earth, but your design will have lost contrasts of colour and texture between paths and vegetable beds. They will also be muddy after rain. The advantage of trodden earth paths is that they cost nothing and are easily re-routed if you feel like a change in layout.

Straw has a rustic look and is, in country areas at least, easy to get hold of. It quickly sops up dampness in the soil and treads down to make friendly paths in vegetable gardens, especially those made in the cottage style.

Another cheap treatment is to cover them with ground or chipped bark, although, like straw, it will need regular topping up. It is not a good idea if you already use a good deal of the stuff as a mulch on your borders. If bark is used on both, your garden will begin to look like a demonstration plot for the waste products of the timber industry. Lay the bark over black polythene if you want to cut down on weeding, but not if you like the idea of the bark itself slowly transmuting to soil. Ground, composted bark disappears faster but gives a smooth, sleek finish. Chipped bark is coarse and rustic in effect. Both are dark treacle-coloured.

GRAVEL AND HOGGIN

Gravel, if you have not used it elsewhere, makes a good path, although it sticks to the bottom of your shoes and then magically unsticks as soon as you walk into the house. The noise that it makes when you walk on it is very satisfying, so crunchy and distinctive that police forces now recommend it as a useful deterrent to burglars. Plants will seed themselves into it, bulbs (and weeds) will grow through it. This may be the effect that you want. If you like the idea of gravel but want to retain it as a formal, clean, unplanted area, put a plastic membrane down first.

Different gravels give different colours and textures. Stick to one kind and make sure that it tones with the colour and texture of the brick or stone of the buildings around you. For a serene, calming finish, rake the gravel in parallel lines with a wide-tined rake. Gravel can be used in combination with other materials – perhaps a few York paving stones set at regular intervals down the length of the path.

Hoggin is the term for a mixture of sand, gravel and pebbles often used in traditional kitchen gardens to provide a firm surface for heavily used work routes. It must be properly rolled, so that the constituents bind together to make a hard, durable crust. The best hoggin paths are made with a "batter", a slightly humped profile, so that water is shed from the centre to run along gutters on either side.

EDGINGS

If you use bark or gravel, both of which kick about easily, you will probably need an edging to the beds, to prevent the one straying into the other. Lengths of board, about 7cm (3in) deep, are simple to hold

STRAW PATH
Straw makes a good surface over a path of beaten earth, especially in a cottage garden. It feels pleasant under foot and soaks up moisture.

GRAVEL PATH
Gravel is easy to lay and has an attractive, crunchy texture but it does have a tendency to wander, especially if the path is on a slope.

STRAW
A good choice in country areas, but it needs regular topping up.

CHIPPED BARK
This makes a natural-looking path and is comfortable to walk on.

GRAVEL
Choose a colour and type that will blend in well with the surrounding buildings.

in place by bashing a few wooden pegs into the ground and fixing the boards to the pegs. Avoid rolls of corrugated plastic edging. It draws attention to itself without having the looks to warrant it.

If you use more permanent forms of paving for the paths, you can dispense with fixed edgings, relying on borders of parsley, alpine strawberries and the like to keep the earth vaguely in place. There will always be some sweeping up to do. Birds do not understand the pleasures of clean paths, and some have beaks that excavate as efficiently as a mechanical digger. In an ornamental kitchen garden, the paths will always tend to be on a lower level than the beds. The mulching that should be an annual routine gradually builds up the level of the soil, which is then more likely to topple on to the paths. In this respect, plants create better nets for catching the earth than narrow planks of wood.

PERMANENT PATHS

Old bricks make good paths. DIY experts will suck their teeth knowingly if you use indoor bricks outside. Yes, they do flake in bad frosts, but they do not disintegrate entirely, and the texture and colour of ordinary bricks is infinitely more pleasant than the unvarying liverish look of what is called engineering brick. Stableyard bricks are equally good, shallower and cross-hatched with a regular diamond pattern.

To do the job properly, you need to excavate the soil to a level of about 18cm (7in) plus the thickness of the brick. Lay down hardcore 15cm (6in) deep along the path and top it with a layer of cement, about 2cm (1in) thick. Lay the bricks on

HERRINGBONE BRICK PATH
A pattern like this can be used to add a further decorative dimension to a potager and give it a pleasantly unhurried air. Plainer patterns tend to give a path a rather more purposeful look.

the cement, leaving narrow gaps between them. Fill the gaps with more cement, mixed very dry. Press the mixture down between the bricks with a trowel or stick, running the top of a stick along the joints to take away any surplus. Wipe the bricks clean before any spare cement sets hard and is impossible to remove. Cobbles are also best laid on hardcore and cement.

Some of the best paths, such as those at Sissinghurst, the famous garden in Kent, are made from a random selection of bricks, cobbles and rubble. Some patterning of the materials – using bricks in threes, incorporating roundels made from bits of blue and white china, making parallel lines of cobbles down the sides – gives a better effect than total anarchy.

COBBLESTONE PATH
Although they can be a little hard on the feet, cobbles are extremely pleasing to the eye and make another attractive option, particularly when mixed with single rows of brick.

The advantage of this sort of path is that it gives a home to all kinds of bits and pieces that you do not want to throw away. Gertrude Jekyll used to sink families of clay flowerpots, one inside the other, to fill the open centres of the millstones that were such a feature in Edwardian gardens designed in the Arts and Crafts style.

Asphalt is perhaps the most unpleasant surface in the garden, although concrete runs it a close second. Laid on an uneven surface, it cracks and becomes as lethal as it is unsightly. If you have such a path, abandon all thoughts of repairing it. Invite around a couple of aggrieved friends and get them to work out their spleen by smashing up the concrete. You can then cart it off to the tip.

PAVING PATTERNS
Bricks, being relatively small paving units and very regular in shape, can be laid in a variety of patterns. Stretcher bond may mirror the pattern of a house wall. Herringbone is much more decorative, but leaves you with the interesting problem of what to do with the triangular spaces that it produces at the edges. Basketweave is equally comfortable, and less problematic to lay. When working with large, irregular slabs of stone, patterning is not so easy. Artificial stone does not have quite the same appeal, but it is cheap and comes in even shapes.

STRETCHER BOND

BASKETWEAVE

ARTIFICIAL STONE

SCREENS & STRUCTURES

THE NEED FOR A FOCAL POINT in a planting scheme dawns on you gradually. If you want your garden to be comfortable and unselfconscious, you tend not to use words like focal point. But in certain places, the eye needs something to fix on to bring the area into focus. A good focal point should seem inevitable, avoiding any sense of manipulation. It should show that it is important, without divorcing itself from the rest of the garden. A seat might do the trick, particularly if you signal its significance by giving it pots as outriders, or by surrounding it with an arbour swathed in vines. Use hazel or willow hurdles if you want to screen one part of the garden from another, and tailor-made wigwams to bring height and consequence to a low planting of vegetables and herbs. The structure itself is appealing, but it is practical, too, and can support crops of climbing beans and peas.

RURAL RETREAT
A seat at the end of a path, inviting you to sit down, is bound to attract attention. Choose a style in keeping with the garden. The woven willow seat above is perfect in a country setting.

USING SCREENS

Hazel and willow are the materials traditionally used to make structures such as wigwams and hurdles for the garden. Both are pliable, and easy to get hold of in country areas, and both grow quickly from clumps that are regularly "stooled" (cut down in rotation) to provide a non-stop supply of stems.

Boundaries made from willow or hazel hurdles will not be long lasting and these materials are best used for internal divisions. They blend sympathetically with plants around them and can be used, like wigwams, to support climbers or trained fruit. You might think of stretching willow hurdles end to end to divide a fruit plot from a flower plot. Use them to support a blackberry, whose stems can stretch out along the structure. The loose, woven pattern of these supports makes it easy to find spots to tie the stems in place. Plant golden hops to twine over a hazel hurdle. Hops die right down in winter and allow you to get in and repair the hurdles where necessary.

The criss-cross, open lattice made from lengths of softwood also makes a decorative structure in the garden and

would be suitable for a light boundary fence. A screen such as this would be strong enough to support the weight of a colonizing pumpkin or an assortment of squash. Alternatively, you could use it to provide the background for a row of slanting cordon apples.

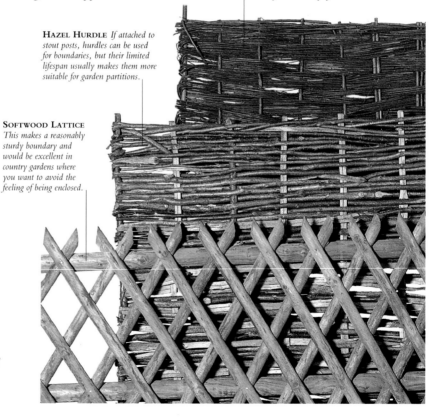

WILLOW HURDLE *The fine stems of willow make a dense yet elegant screen. Choose from a variety of natural colours.*

HAZEL HURDLE *If attached to stout posts, hurdles can be used for boundaries, but their limited lifespan usually makes them more suitable for garden partitions.*

SOFTWOOD LATTICE *This makes a reasonably sturdy boundary and would be excellent in country gardens where you want to avoid the feeling of being enclosed.*

SCREEN ASSORTMENT
Hazel and willow hurdles and lattice fencing can all be used in decorative ways in the garden, adding a soft, rustic air. Grow a blackberry or loganberry against a hurdle, and festoon the lattice with the eccentric shapes and brilliant colours of squash.

WIGWAMS TO SCARECROWS

You can buy wigwams ready-made from metal or wood, but, with a little practice, you can also make your own. Professional basketmakers usually work sitting down. They would start a wigwam, such as the one shown below, with the bunch of hazel sticks clasped between their knees. As they progress, working further and further down the spiral of the wigwam, the whole structure is pushed under and between their knees. You might find it easier to start off by sticking the uprights in the ground, using a dustbin lid or the wheel of a bicycle to mark out the size and shape of the base. Hazel, sweet chestnut or willow can be used for the uprights, and willow, old man's beard or prunings of clematis stems for the woven spiral that holds the whole thing in place. Freshly cut stems do not need to be soaked, but you would need to soften up material that has been cut and stored by soaking it in water for a few hours. You can make the thin wands of willow that you use for the weaving even more supple by swinging them around against your finger and thumb, rather like a cowboy in a Western about to lasso a steer.

In the wigwam shown below there are 18 uprights, which makes a very stable structure. You could use fewer, but there should not be too much space between the uprights, if the wigwam is to make a bold feature in your planting. Structures such as this do not last for ever. Eventually the bottoms of the uprights will begin to rot and, as the wood ages, it will become more brittle and more likely to snap under the weight of the growth it is supporting. If you have the necessary space, bring wooden structures such as this under cover in the winter after you have gathered in all your crops.

Once you have grasped the potential of materials such as willow and hazel, all kinds of possibilities open up. You may even feel you could tackle something similar to the basketwork seat opposite. You may start dreaming about a futuristic scarecrow, with a body made from bowed lengths of hazel and chestnut crosspieces for its arms. Dream on. Then get weaving.

WIGWAM STYLES
Wigwams can be as simple or elaborate as you choose to make them. This one has only two woven bands. More, as right, make a stronger structure.

HOW TO MAKE YOUR OWN WIGWAM

1 *Take 9 uprights, 2–3m (7–10ft) high, and bind them at the top with fine willow wands. This number will make a stable structure. You may find it easiest to work with the uprights stuck in the ground. Soak the wands first only if they have been stored.*

2 *Tie 2 long, thin, flexible wands into the top. Start to weave them into bands around the wigwam, taking one under and the other over each upright. Keep the weaving under tension as you go.*

3 *When you have woven 2 bands, take another 9 stakes, with one end sharpened, and push the sharp end into the second band between each upright, to give 18 uprights altogether.*

4 *Continue weaving the wands in a spiral down the wigwam. Keep the uprights evenly spaced. Slot in new wands as needed, tying them in at the bottom.*

FINISHED WIGWAM

UNDERSTANDING THE SOIL

VEGETABLE HEAVEN IS A SOIL that is well-drained, fertile, open, and neither too acid nor too alkaline. If you have an old garden, someone else might have already converted the underlying sand or clay into a workable tilth. If not, grit your teeth and prepare to mulch, mulch, mulch. Soil is a mixture of bits of rock, water and organic matter such as rotted leaves. Sandy soils (ideal for carrots, which swell easily in this open, free-draining medium) are made from relatively large bits of rock, clay soils (good for brassicas, which prefer a solid soil) from small particles. One is called light, the other heavy. Adding bulky manures is the only way to improve soil structure. The extra organic matter closes up the big spaces in sandy soils, making them capable of holding more water. In clay soils, it adds extra air spaces between the too closely packed particles and so improves drainage.

LIMING
Acid soils can be limed to make them a little more alkaline. Spread ordinary lime (calcium carbonate) thinly and evenly, then rake it in. Wait three months before sowing or planting.

HOW SOIL WORKS

No amount of chemical fertilizer will change the structure of your soil. Before plants can take up food, they need roots that can find it. Plant roots need passages along which they can run and from which they can then absorb the nutrients necessary for healthy growth. Humus – decayed vegetable matter – helps to create these vital passages. In town gardens it may be difficult to acquire bulky manures, the best source of humus, but make a

resolution to haul in a sack of some nourishing mulch once a week until the whole plot has been covered. It will pay enormous dividends in improved growth. If you have space, you can make your own compost (see page 163) and add that to the soil. Home-made compost should have the texture of rich fruit cake.

The minerals that plants need for healthy growth are generally lumped together under the heading "trace elements" and include boron, copper, iron, manganese and zinc. In fertile soils they are present naturally; lack of them shows up in plant deficiency diseases. Organic animal manures are rich in trace elements and if you use these regularly, you are unlikely to have problems. Magnesium deficiency (which makes leaves turn

brown and wither) is more prevalent on acid soils. Chlorosis is more likely on limy soils: leaves that should be bright, pulsating green turn a pallid, sickly yellow. It occurs because the plant cannot absorb the minerals it needs from the soil as they are locked up by too much lime. Correct the imbalance by watering with a solution of chelated iron, or sequestrene.

ACID OR ALKALINE?

Acid and alkaline are terms that apply to the pH (the potential of hydrogen) in the soil. The scale runs from 1 to 14, with neutral around 7. Most vegetables and fruit do best in this middle range.

TYPES OF SOIL
What you grow and how you grow it is to some extent determined by type of soil. The five main kinds each display characteristics that make them reasonably easy to recognize.

SILT
Silt is fertile and retains moisture well but is easily compacted. It has a rather silky feel if you squeeze it.

CHALK
A pale, shallow, stony topsoil indicates chalk. It is free-draining and moderately fertile.

SANDY SOIL
Light, gritty-textured and free-draining, sandy soil is easy to work, but it needs lots of humus to make it fertile.

PEAT
Rich in organic matter, peat looks very dark and crumbly. It retains moisture well and makes an acid soil.

CLAY
Clay is heavy, slow-draining and often quite sticky. It can be hard to work but is full of nutrients.

Asparagus is not happy on very acid soils, whereas blueberries demand it. Generally though, good fertility and drainage have a greater effect on growth than the precise nature of the pH level. There are simple kits available with which you can gauge the pH level of your soil, but remember to take readings from more than one part of the garden.

You can tinker with acid soils by adding extra lime if you want to make them more amenable to the growing of vegetables, especially brassicas. Do not add it at the same time as manure or the chemical reaction with the nitrogen in the manure that is produced may harm plants. The nitrogen will also be wasted. It is far more difficult to convert an alkaline soil to a comfortable home for lime-hating plants. Raspberries, for instance, always look happier in slightly acid soils than they do in alkaline ground.

CULTIVATION METHODS

Prepare ground for planting during autumn, winter and early spring, working only when the soil is dry enough not to stick to the bottom of your boots. Only masochists make digging loom large in the gardening calendar.

On heavy ground, you dig to expose clods of earth so that they can be broken up by frost. You dig to get air into compacted soil, to bury weeds or other organic material and to give birds a decent breakfast. Digging no longer has the

heroic status it once had, along with bastard trenching and double digging, which was twice as back-breaking. On light soils, forking over will often be enough. Mushroom compost or any other weed-free compost that you can spread thickly on top of the ground will eventually be pulled down into the earth by worms. That is a lot less trouble than doing it yourself.

If you are making a new bed, it may not be necessary to dig the earth at all. If you garden on light, sandy soil, weedkill it thoroughly, mulch heavily and plant direct into the ground. Heavy ground, or areas that have been well-trodden or compacted, need more attention.

Digging improves drainage and introduces air into earth that has been packed hard by feet. Heavy clay soils should be dug at the beginning of winter, light soils as late as possible in spring. Light soils do not need to be broken down by frost. The main problem here is hanging on to water and nutrients. By leaving the soil firm over winter, you will be helping it to hold as much water as possible.

THE NO-DIG METHOD

If you have a light, well-drained, fertile soil, the sort of soil that everyone dreams of, then you may well be able to run a fruit and vegetable garden without ever having to dig at all. Some light forking and hoeing to get rid of weeds will be all that is necessary. To maintain fertility you

will have to mulch heavily. The no-dig method works well in areas of the garden where you have permanent crops such as fruit bushes or asparagus. You can use it successfully on ground where you grow transplanted crops such as tomatoes, courgettes and leeks, and also for potatoes (see page 102). It is more difficult, however, to produce the fine tilth needed for seedbeds without doing any digging. A mulch in these circumstances is a hindrance rather than a help.

FORKING
Light soils, which are usually best prepared in spring, will probably only need forking over. Work when the ground is moist but not too sticky, inserting the fork and then turning it over to break up the soil and aerate it.

DIGGING THE KITCHEN GARDEN

1 *If the soil is heavy, or if you are making beds in new ground, you will probably have to dig. To make it less hard work, keep the spade upright as it goes into the soil.*

2 *Do not try to load too much on to the blade, especially if the ground is heavy, and bend your knees as you lift the spade. This makes the task much less back-breaking.*

3 *Turn over the soil to introduce air. This also helps to bury annual weeds and incorporate organic matter. On heavy ground, leave clods for the winter frost to break up.*

MULCHING, FEEDING & WATERING

IF YOU TAKE CARE OF THE MULCHING, the feeding and watering will mostly take care of themselves. A mulch works like a biodegradable blanket – by putting a layer of rotted leaves, farmyard manure, grass cuttings or compost on top of the soil, you can control weeds, retain moisture, improve soil structure, add nutrients (slowly) and keep plants and crops clean. Thick and regular mulches will make watering and feeding far less imperative. Mulches made of materials that have once been plants themselves add a complex cocktail of nutrients to the soil. They also improve its condition, as earthworms gradually pull the mulch underground and aerate the soil. Without these air pockets roots cannot penetrate the soil. By mulching, you feed the soil, which can then feed the plants, and soil that is in good heart is essential for successful gardening.

MULCHING

Spread mulches thickly over the soil to keep down annual weeds – no mulch will stop the growth of perennials such as bindweed. If they are to conserve moisture, do not apply mulches when the ground is dry. The following materials are ideal.
LEAFMOULD Making leafmould is a useful way of exploiting nature's own mulch. It improves soil structure and also, over time, releases valuable nutrients. The easiest method is to pile leaves up inside a cage made of chicken wire where they will gradually rot down. You will need a space about 1.2m (4ft) square. If you do not have room for this, pack leaves into

dustbin liners instead. The best leaves to use are those of beech and oak. Leaves with thick midribs, such as ash and horse chestnut, take much longer to disintegrate.
MANURE A valuable source of organic matter, manure is best used when well rotted. In towns, pigeon lofts are a good source. Droppings are high in nitrogen and dry and light to handle.
GRASS CUTTINGS These are usually available in quantity and are excellent around soft fruit bushes.
GARDEN COMPOST If you have room to make a compost heap (see opposite), you need never be short of mulch. Any organic material – vegetable peelings, weeds, leaves, hair – can be added. Nettles are useful as they speed up decomposition. Covering the heap with old carpet also hurries things along. The hotter you can make your compost, the better. Heat destroys weed seeds, which are the only disadvantage of home-made compost.
MUSHROOM COMPOST Where it is available, this makes one of the best mulches, but it is slightly limed so do not use it around crops such as blueberries that need an acid soil.

FEEDING

Fertilizers are compounds that you use to replace nutrients taken from the soil. They can be organic or inorganic, and a fierce debate rages as to the benefits of one against the other. Organic fertilizers supply nutrients of plant or animal origin; extract

HOW TO MULCH
Mulches need to be spread at least 5–10cm (2–4in) deep in order to keep down annual weeds and conserve moisture in the soil.

TYPES OF MULCH
Use whatever organic materials you can get hold of. The five suggested below are easy to make or buy, but you could also try straw, shredded bark or spent hops, if available. All are excellent but react in slightly different ways.

LEAFMOULD
A fine, crumbly substance made by stacking fallen leaves in a heap and leaving them gradually to rot down.

MANURE
Few mulches benefit the soil as much as manure, but it needs to be well rotted.

GRASS CUTTINGS
These are satisfactory as long as herbicides are not used on the lawn.

GARDEN COMPOST
Any organic material can go on the compost heap. It will rot down finally to resemble earth.

MUSHROOM COMPOST
Easy to use and sterile, but it is alkaline so should not be used around plants that need an acid soil.

of seaweed, hoof and horn, and bonemeal are typical. These are broken down by bacteria in the soil and then drawn in by the plants' roots. Inorganic fertilizers are either manufactured or are of mineral origin, such as ground chalk or ammonium sulphate. Organic fertilizers are cheaper, but tend to work more slowly than inorganic ones.

Using high-octane inorganic fertilizers is like using drugs. Instant benefit is cancelled out by long-term problems. Only plants growing in unnatural circumstances (usually confined in pots or hanging baskets) are likely to need manufactured fertilizers. They work fast. That is one of the reasons they are popular. But they feed the plant rather than the soil. This upsets the delicate balance of the soil's own life which includes important, invisible micro-organisms. Nitrates promote rapid growth, but plants fed in this way grow artificially fast, which may have a detrimental effect on taste. They often have too high a water content and, being sappy, are more open to attack by pest and disease. Which leads you to reach for a different bottle . . . Neither inorganic nor organic fertilizers are enough on their own. You need to add organic matter to the soil to enhance fertility and structure. Back to the mulch.

WATERING

Watering gardens is a luxury, not a prerogative. Plants growing in restricted spaces, such as pots, need frequent drinks; the rest of the garden should not if you use organic manures to enhance the water-retaining capacity of the soil. The crops that respond best to watering are leafy ones, such as lettuce, cabbages and spinach. Crops that bear seeds and fruit, such as beans, peas and tomatoes, are best watered while the plants are in flower and the fruits are swelling. Transplants of brassicas, celery and leeks need frequent watering until established. Overwatering of root crops such as carrots after a long, dry spell tends to make the roots split. Once again, mulching is the long-term solution.

COMPOST CORNER
The frame for the compost heap can be made from any suitable materials you have to hand, from wire netting to old floorboards. You can also buy purpose-built frames, as shown above.

MAKING A COMPOST HEAP
For the best results, build up the heap in layers of about 15cm (6in). Scatter manure, or another material rich in nitrogen, between the layers to help speed the rotting.

Grass cuttings form a dense layer on their own, and stop air circulating. Mix them with other garden waste.

Add any kind of organic garden or kitchen waste, but do not include diseased plants or perennial weeds.

Twiggy material makes a good base layer as it allows air to circulate in the heap.

CROP ROTATION

THE FIRST THING that novice vegetable gardeners need to know about crop rotation is that vegetables will not necessarily crumple up and die if they are not moved to new homes each year. For many years, crop rotation, along with double digging and bastard trenching, was one of the great shibboleths of vegetable growing. Yet the best gardeners are not those who rely on rules but those who use their eyes, take the trouble to learn the vagaries of their own plot, work with the weather and have respect for their soil. Good gardening depends on finding the balance between what you want the plants to do and what they want you to do. Plants are successful because each has managed to adapt, over the years, to a particular set of conditions. Learn to recognize each plant's needs. Crop rotation should reflect those needs, not become an end in itself.

THE REASON WHY

The most persuasive argument for the practice of some form of crop rotation has to do with the soil. Each different type of vegetable crop – brassicas, onions, legumes (podded vegetables) or root crops such as potatoes – needs a slightly different cocktail of nutrients and trace elements from the soil. If you always grow your cauliflowers in the same place, it is likely that the soil there will eventually become drained of the ingredients that cauliflowers most want. By moving them on to a different part of the garden, you give the soil in the first plot a chance to recover and replenish itself from the liberal supplies of compost and manure that you will, of course, be giving it.

The case for avoiding disease by rotating crops is less clear cut. If your brassicas are struck by clubroot, they will do better if you plant them in fresh ground the following season. But the spores of clubroot, which causes distorted roots in members of the brassica family, can live for more than 20 years in the soil. Even if you practise a five-year rotation, those spores will still be lurking when the brassicas eventually return to their original plot. The spores of the fungus that causes white rot in onions are equally long lived. Also, in a small garden, it is unlikely that any of your plots will be distant enough from each other to prevent pests and diseases drifting over the unmarked boundary lines. Your best defence against disease, in plants as with people, is to take every possible step to prevent it breaking out in the first place. And to be sanguine in those seasons when aphids outnumber predators and the noise of flea beetles jumping off cabbage leaves is louder than the crunch of your foot on the snails that are eating the lettuce.

THE MAIN GROUPS

Traditional crop rotations revolve around three main groups of vegetables. First are the legumes, or podded vegetables, the peas and beans. Their group also includes vegetables such as sweet corn, courgettes and tomatoes that do not fit tidily into any other compartment. Legumes are followed by the brassicas, which include swedes, turnips, kohl rabi and radishes as well as

LEGUMES (PODDED VEGETABLES)
The roots of legumes – all the peas and beans – form nodules that are packed with nitrogen and will help enrich the soil. At the end of the season, cut the plants at the base of the stems leaving the roots to break down in the ground.

BRASSICAS
Leafy brassicas such as cabbages, cauliflowers, broccoli and kale are all hungry for nitrogen. If possible, plant them in a patch of ground that was used the previous season for growing legumes and that has also been well-manured.

ROOT VEGETABLES
Beetroot, carrots and the like do not demand much nitrogen, so usually follow brassicas in a rotation. Potatoes and Jerusalem artichokes, which produce a mass of tubers and roots, are ideal for breaking up newly cultivated ground.

more obviously cabbage-like vegetables such as cauliflowers, Brussels sprouts and broccoli. Finally, there are the roots and tubers: beetroot, carrots, Jerusalem artichokes, parsnips and potatoes. In a 3-bed rotation, onions will be included with the legumes. In a 4-bed rotation, the onion tribe has a section of its own.

An inflexible attitude is not likely to help your vegetables as much as a common-sense appraisal of their needs. If you have only one sheltered, sunny plot, it would be a waste to use it for peas or cabbages, neither of which need that kind of protection. Tomatoes and sweet corn, on the other hand, will be unlikely to crop well without it. If one area of your garden soil is markedly lighter and more free-draining than another, then carrots will do better there than in the stiff ground that seems to suit cabbages. In drawing up a plan, you also have to be realistic about what you like to eat and have the skill to grow. If you are not fond of cabbages and are unsuccessful in raising cauliflowers, it will be a waste of space to include them in a rotation.

How a 3-Bed Plan Works

Most gardeners will only need to use a simple 3-year, 3-bed rotation. The easiest way is to list the vegetables you want to grow and split them into the 3 main groups (in rotation terms, beds really means groups, not actual growing beds). Draw a rough plan of the garden and mark which crops can go where, using a different colour for each group. The following year, move on the crops accordingly. Fit fast-growing vegetables (catch crops) into any convenient gaps.

YEAR 1

YEAR 2

YEAR 3

3-Bed Rotation

Peas	Brussels sprouts	Beetroot
Beans	Cabbages	Carrots
Celery	Cauliflowers	Chicory
Onions	Broccoli	Jerusalem artichokes
Leeks	Kohl rabi	Parsnips
Lettuce	Swedes	Potatoes
Spinach	Turnips	
Sweet corn	Radishes	
Tomatoes		
Courgettes		

4-Bed Plan

In a 4-bed rotation, onions can be hived off into a separate group along with leeks, garlic and shallots. Lettuce and other fast-growing salad leaves can be fitted in as catch crops wherever there is a spare patch of ground.

YEAR 1

YEAR 2

YEAR 3

YEAR 4

4-Bed Rotation

Runner beans	Brussels sprouts	Onions	Peppers
French beans	Cabbages	Shallots	Tomatoes
Peas	Cauliflowers	Leeks	Celery
Broad beans	Broccoli	Garlic	Celeriac
Sweet corn	Oriental vegetables	Courgettes	Beetroot
	Swedes	Lettuce	Carrots
	Turnips		Parsnips
	Radishes		Potatoes

5-Bed Plan

A 5-bed rotation is for gardeners with lots of space, who like to lie awake at night dreaming up ever more complex ways of utilizing it. Here, the onion family has a section of its own, as do potatoes and other root vegetables.

YEAR 1

YEAR 2

YEAR 3

YEAR 4

YEAR 5

5-Bed Rotation

Broad beans	Cauliflowers	Courgettes	Onions	Potatoes
Runner beans	Broccoli	Sweet corn	Garlic	Parsnips
Peas	Cabbages	Tomatoes	Leeks	Carrots
French beans	Turnips	Celery	Lettuce	Beetroot
	Radishes	Celeriac	Shallots	Swedes
	Brussels sprouts			Jerusalem artichokes
	Oriental brassicas			

GROWING METHODS

THE WAY THAT YOU GROW is necessarily influenced by the kind of soil that you have. If you garden on heavy ground, the idea of creating deep beds that will need little attention once made may be more compelling than if you have light, free-draining soil. On this type of easy-to-work ground, some gentle hoeing, weeding and mulching may be all that is needed. If you live in a frost hollow, where winter comes early and spring late, you have more reason to try out a floating mulch to extend the growing season. Some cultivation methods relate to particular crops. You will need to earth up potatoes to prevent tubers developing poisonous green patches, and force chicory if you are to produce fat, white buds.

DEEP BEDS

The deep bed system is not as luxuriously sybaritic as it sounds. It is a way of growing plants in a series of beds, no more than 1.5m (5ft) wide, that are divided by narrow paths about 30cm (12in) wide. This sort of layout means you can do all the planting, weeding and general cultivation from the paths without ever treading on the soil. This stops it from becoming compacted, and helps drainage and soil structure. To make the beds, it is essential to dig the ground thoroughly and clear it of all perennial weeds. After that, heavy mulches of bulky organic matter must be applied regularly, making the beds higher than the paths. That is why they are called deep beds. What you lose on the paths you gain by more intensive cropping in the beds. Plant in short, fairly close rows running across the beds. Because you are planting closely, you must feed the soil well. The best way is with a bulky organic mulch of well-rotted manure or compost. The initial labour of making the beds is perhaps daunting but, once made, they are easy to maintain.

FLOATING MULCHES

Plastic films have been used for many years by professional growers to protect crops and accelerate growth. Various types of special film – including perforated or fleecy ones – are now available to the amateur grower. They do not guard against frost, but you can use them to warm the soil or to give extra protection to early crops. Brassicas, lettuce, early potatoes, radishes and onions may all benefit from being covered for the first 4–5 weeks of the growing period. The film must be well anchored at the edges, either by being buried in the soil or weighted down with stones or timber. If the edges are well sealed, it will also give protection against pests such as cabbage root fly, carrot fly, flea beetle and cabbage white butterfly. Soft, fleecy films may be left in place over crops such as lettuce for the whole of its growing period. The term "floating mulch" is confusing, as these films do not do what mulches do (keep down weeds, retain moisture, feed soil), but help to raise the soil temperature and guard against weather and pests.

FLOATING MULCHES
An early crop of lettuce will grow faster under a fleecy film that keeps in warmth. The film will also give some protection against insect pests as well as predatory birds or rabbits.

DEEP BEDS
This system is ideal for heavy ground as it cuts down on digging and relies on replenishing the soil's fertility by heavy mulching. The layout of narrow beds and paths also makes organizing the rotation of crops quite straightforward.

FORCING RHUBARB

Put tall, chimney-shaped terracotta pots over rhubarb plants for an early, succulent crop. Stretching for the light at the top, the stems grow much longer than they would otherwise do.

INTERCROPPING

On fertile soil you can increase yields by intercropping, a way of squeezing more produce from less ground. It only works if plants are well fed and watered. You need to combine complementary crops – two that grow in different directions or one that grows faster than the other. Radishes are a classic example, sown between rows of slow-maturing parsnips. You will have harvested the radishes before the parsnips need the space. Sweet corn mostly needs vertical space. Intercrop by planting bush tomatoes or marrows beneath. Small cos lettuce can be grown between garlic; or try quick, cut-and-come-again saladini between newly planted out brassicas.

EARTHING UP

This gives heavy plants such as Brussels sprouts extra stability, especially in exposed areas. Draw up the soil around the stem with a spade or hoe. Earthing up potatoes prevents the tubers developing poisonous green patches, which they will if exposed to light. Start when plants are about 30cm (12in) high, drawing up the soil around the stems. You can bury the lower leaves, but leave the tops uncovered. Celery is earthed up to blanch the stems.

FORCING AND BLANCHING

These two processes involve keeping light from stems or leaves. Forcing hurries vegetables into growth; blanching makes them more tender or less bitter. Crops such as rhubarb can be forced with special terracotta pots, or an upturned bucket. Celery is usually blanched by placing a paper collar around it as well as earthing up. The hearts of endive can be blanched with a saucer upturned over the centre of the plant. Belgian chicory needs both forcing and blanching. Outside, if the soil is not too heavy or cold, cut any leaves to 2cm (1in) above the neck of the plant and cover the stumps with at least 15cm (6in) of soil. Then fix cloches over the top. The process is faster inside, see right.

FORCING AND BLANCHING CHICORY

After blanching

1 *Take the plants that have been lifted, trimmed and stored in boxes of sand (see pages 66–67), and shorten the roots to 15cm (6in). Fit 3–6 plants upright in a 23cm (9in) pot of moist compost, leaving the tops exposed.*

2 *Invert a similar-sized pot over the top to keep out light and store at 10–18°C (50–65°F) while the blanched chicons develop. This will take about 3 weeks in the warmth of an airing cupboard, longer in a cooler cellar.*

SOWING INSIDE

TO THE UNINITIATED, SEED SOWING is the impenetrable rite of passage that separates the novice from the seasoned gardener. It is not usually half as difficult, however, as experts try to make it, and you do not need batteries of equipment. When you are sowing indoors, propagator heat will make seeds germinate more quickly and plants grow faster than they would otherwise do, but at some stage they must learn to live without it and take on the weather as it really is, and the tougher plants have been raised, the better they will cope. The more sparsely you sow, the stronger plants will be for later transplanting. Greenhouses provide ideal sowing conditions, but there is much you can raise on a light, warm windowsill.

SOWING LARGE SEEDS
Large seeds, such as those of courgettes, are best sown one or two seeds to a pot. If you sow two seeds, pinch out the weaker of the seedlings.

SOWING IN A CONTAINER

Make your initial sowing in a clean plastic pot about 12cm (5in) across. It is better to save your seed trays for pricking out later. Fill the pot with compost and firm it down gently. Scatter the seed as thinly and evenly as you can over the surface of the compost. Every gardener devises their own favourite way of doing this. Some like to tip it into the palm of one hand, then take pinches of seed between the thumb and forefinger of the other and sprinkle it over the compost. Others are confident enough to scatter seed direct from the packet with a series of gentle taps. Cover the seed with a thin layer of compost or vermiculite, which many gardeners find much better and easier to use as a seed covering. Vermiculite is a

lightweight mineral rather like mica that retains moisture but also drains quickly. Perlite, made from expanded granules of volcanic minerals, has the same qualities. You do not have to worry about the exact depth of a covering of vermiculite as you do if you are using compost. Water thoroughly before sealing the pot in a cocoon of clingfilm or placing a sheet of glass over the top to prevent the compost drying out. If you have a propagator like the one shown opposite, you can stand the pots in that.

Once the seed has germinated, take the cover off the pot, keep the compost damp but not saturated and turn the pot around regularly as seedlings always tip themselves toward the light. Damping off may be a problem with seedlings raised inside. They suddenly collapse at the point

where stem meets soil and whole pots of seeds may be affected. Overwatering is the most common cause, but it may also arise from using old compost in dirty pots.

Large seeds, such as those of melons and cucumbers, can be sown in single 7cm (3in) pots, setting one or two seeds on edge in each pot. If you sow two, remove the weaker of the two seedlings once they have germinated. Seeds sown in this way can stay in their pots until planted outside.

PRICKING OUT

Seedlings grown *en masse* in a 12cm (5in) pot need to be pricked out, that is moved on to fresh quarters, sooner rather than later. Growing close together, as they do in the initial seed pot, seedlings quickly get leggy – too much stem to top – and

SOWING

1 *Fill the seed tray or pot with compost and firm it down gently. In trays, use a piece of wood to do this. Compost in a pot can be firmed using the base of a second, empty pot.*

2 *Scatter the seed as evenly and thinly as you can over the compost. The thinner you sow, the better the chance of producing healthy seedlings with good, sturdy stems.*

3 *Cover the seed with a thin layer of compost or vermiculite and water in carefully with a fine-nozzled can. Cover with clingfilm or a sheet of glass to stop the compost drying out.*

SIMPLE PROPAGATOR
A unit like this fits neatly on to a windowsill and can be used for germinating seeds or to protect seedlings that have just been pricked out.

then keel over at the slightest disturbance. One evening when you feel in need of some calming, therapeutic activity, fill some full-sized seed trays with compost, gently firm down the surface and, with your forefinger, poke a grid of holes in the compost, 6 along the long side and 4 along the short. With a lollipop stick, or similar implement, gently ease up a few seedlings at a time from the pot. Pick each one up by one of its lowest leaves and drop it into one of the holes you have made in the compost. Set the seedlings deep, so that the first pair of leaves sits on the surface of the compost. Firm the compost around them gently with your fingers. When the whole tray is planted, water thoroughly with a fine-nozzled can.

Seedlings of tomatoes that have spent the first part of their lives in a 12cm (5in) pot should be pricked out into 7cm (3in) pots, one plant in each pot. Fill the small pots with compost, make a hole in the centre with your forefinger and drop in the seedling, setting it deeper than it was

originally growing. Gently firm the compost around the stem.

Plants that resent having their roots disturbed, such as Chinese cabbages, can be pricked out into modules. These are specially modified planting trays divided into separate small compartments. You can improvize by using cardboard egg boxes. Sow in the lid and prick out seedlings into each of the compartments. The advantage of modules is that roots do not have to compete with one another for nutrients and are less easily disturbed when being transplanted. You can also sow 2 or 3 seeds direct into modules and thin them after they have germinated.

HARDENING OFF

The compost in the modules or the tray into which you have pricked out plants should contain sufficient food for the seedlings to live on until the time they can be planted out, usually in late spring. Watering is important, as is hardening off

the plants, getting them acclimatized to the real world. Do this gently, putting the trays out on warmish days and bringing them in at nights until the plants seem sturdy enough to be planted out.

You can help to harden off plants inside by brushing them over the top with the edge of a piece of card. Do this for about a minute each day, brushing in different directions. This flexing of the stems strengthens them, simulating the effect of wind. But even if you brush your plants, you will still have to acclimatize them gradually to lower temperatures outside. If you intend to grow plants such as melons and cucumbers in a greenhouse, you will not need to harden them off. They will be living their entire lives in luxurious warmth and shelter.

TRANSPLANTING

Planting out vegetables such as courgettes or tomatoes that you have been growing under cover in pots is not usually as detrimental to a plant as transplanting it from a drill or seedbed outside (see overleaf). Ease the rootball out of the pot without disturbing the roots and, if you water them in well, these plants will not usually be too badly checked. In general, the earlier seedlings can be transplanted to their permanent quarters, the better. Move lettuce when they have about 4 leaves, and cabbages and other brassicas when they are about 10cm (4in) high.

PRICKING OUT

1 *Seedlings are vulnerable when being pricked out so handle them as gently as possible. Pick them up by their first leaves rather than their stems, which are easily damaged.*

2 *Prick out the seedlings into a tray or, as here, modules. First make a grid of holes in the compost, then ease in the seedlings with the help of a lollipop stick or fine dibber.*

TRANSPLANTING
When planting outside, make the hole large enough for the seedling to be set a little deeper than it was growing in its pot.

SOWING OUTSIDE

VEGETABLES ARE MORE OFTEN grown from seed sown directly in the ground than by any other means. Seed of frost-tender vegetables such as courgettes and tomatoes is sown inside in order to give as long a growing season as possible, but many vegetables do not need this treatment. Some vegetables are sown in short rows in seedbeds and transplanted later to their final growing positions. Brassicas and leeks are often treated in this way, although in very exposed situations both could be raised under cover and grown in pots and trays for planting out later. Other vegetables such as parsnips and peas are sown in the positions they will occupy for the whole of their growing lives. Remember this when preparing the site for sowing. Do not expect seeds to hoist great clods of soil on their backs in their struggle to reach the light.

SOWING

PREPARING THE GROUND If you are sowing outside, good preparation of the seedbed is the single most important factor in getting seed to germinate. On sandy soil, you may only have to clear the soil of weeds and rake it in order to create the fine, crumbly tilth that a seed likes to lie in. On clay, you will hope that frost will have helped during winter to break down obdurate clods of earth. Banging with the back of a rake also helps. The smaller the seed, the finer the tilth should be.

SOWING IN A DRILL This is the most usual way to grow vegetables from seed. Peg out a line to make a straight row (see right) and take out a drill using a hoe or the back edge of a rake. The depth of the drill should depend on the size of the seed, shallow for small seed, deeper for large seed. Scatter small seed as thinly as possible along the drill to try to avoid, as far as possible, the need for thinning. Seed such as beetroot or parsnip can be sown "at stations", that is in little groups of 2 or 3 seeds spaced at intervals. Leave only the strongest seedling to grow on at each station. Cover the seed carefully with soil. If the ground is very dry, water the drill before sowing, otherwise water afterwards with a fine-nozzled can.

SOWING IN A WIDE DRILL Use wide, flat-bottomed drills for vegetables that grow in broad rows such as peas. Make the drill roughly 23cm (9in) wide (see right), using either a hoe or spade. Space the seed evenly along the drill. Cover with the earth you have removed and smooth it over carefully. You can also use shallow, wide drills for growing bands of cut-and-come-again crops, but when sowing these, broadcast the seed as thinly as you can.

SOWING IN A DRILL

1 *Stretch out a line, usually twine attached to a short stake or peg at either end, and take out a drill as close to it as possible using the corner of a hoe or the back edge of a rake.*

2 *Scatter seed along the drill as thinly as you can. Carefully pull back the soil over the seed with a rake and firm it down with the flat back of the rake. Water carefully along the drill.*

SOWING IN A WIDE DRILL

1 *Peg out some twine to mark a straight line. Make a flat-bottomed drill, about 23cm (9in) wide, either by pushing the soil out with a spade or pulling it along with a hoe.*

2 *Space large seed evenly along the drill, but thinly broadcast small seed. Cover with the earth you have removed and carefully smooth it over. Protect peas from birds with wire netting.*

BROADCASTING SEED

1 Rake the soil over the whole area to produce a fine tilth before sowing. This is essential if the seed is to germinate well. Then scatter the seed over the patch as thinly as you can.

BROADCASTING SEED To broadcast seed is to scatter it over a relatively wide area. It is a technique that is most useful where you have a series of deep beds (see page 166) each bearing a different crop, or want to grow blocks of crops in the beds of a potager. It is also the method to use when sowing saladini, a mixture of salad leaves such as loose-leaf lettuce and rocket, or oriental brassicas. Grow the plants as a cut-and-come-again crop, picking the leaves when they are at the seedling stage.

2 Carefully rake the soil in the opposite direction to cover the seed and firm it down very lightly with the back of the rake. Water the area well using a fine-nozzled can.

THINNING

Seed that is sown direct, such as carrots and beetroot, may need to be thinned to allow each plant a chance to develop its full potential. If you practise the art of sowing thinly, you can escape this wasteful task. Pests and diseases will do their own grim thinning, so carry out yours in stages, nipping off tiny seedlings rather than uprooting them and disturbing the roots of neighbours. It is particularly important

to try to avoid thinning carrots, because the smell of bruised seedlings will act like a magnet for the carrot fly and the tiny holes give it ready-made points of entry.

TRANSPLANTING

Vegetables such as leeks, Brussels sprouts and other brassicas are often grown in nursery seedbeds. These are small patches of ground where you can rake the soil to a mouthwatering tilth and use it to sow seeds in short drills. At some stage, the plants will need to be moved to their final growing positions. Try to do this when the soil is damp and the weather overcast, so that the uprooted plants will not have to struggle too much to find their feet.

Trowel up the plants with as much soil as possible around the roots and replant them in a hole which takes the rootball comfortably. Replant brassicas deeper than they were growing in the seedbed, so that their lowest leaves are level with the soil. Leeks should be dropped into holes made with a dibber. Thinnings of crops such as lettuce may be transplanted with success if the soil is moist and the temperature moderate, but you cannot transplant tap-rooted vegetables such as parsnips or carrots successfully.

THINNING SEEDLINGS
All plants need sufficient space to develop to their full size. If you sow sparsely enough, there may be no need to thin seedlings. However, if thinning is necessary, nip off the unwanted plants at ground level and remove them to avoid unnecessarily encouraging diseases or pests.

TRANSPLANTING LEEKS
Make a hole at least 15cm (6in) deep with a dibber and drop in the seedling so that as the plant grows it develops a good length of white stem. Water in well to wash soil over the roots.

PLANTING BRASSICAS
When transplanting, set plants a little deeper than they were before. Brassicas need to be planted with their lowest leaves at soil level.

PROPAGATION

PROPAGATION CAN EASILY BECOME an obsession. There is no more wildly parental feeling than seeing your first cutting turn into a grown-up bush. In the kitchen garden, cuttings will mostly be of soft fruit such as blackcurrants, gooseberries or blueberries. When you become more ambitious, you may turn your hand to figs. Fruit such as blackberries and loganberries require no effort at all, for wherever the growing tip of a stem touches the ground, it will produce a fresh plant. Several of the shrubby herbs will obligingly start growing extra roots if soil is piled around the stems, a technique known as mound layering. Vegetables are mostly grown from seed, but rhubarb and globe artichokes are perennials and produce offsets around the edge of the clump. A sharp spade is what you need here, to separate the siblings from their parent.

DIVIDING

RHUBARB Dividing is one of the easiest ways of increasing your stock of plants and, in the kitchen garden, rhubarb is a prime candidate for this particular type of propagation. Wait until the leaves die down in autumn before taking the spade to it (see right).

GLOBE ARTICHOKES You need to replace these on a regular basis since old plants tend to become woody and unproductive. As artichokes start into growth in spring, they produce a circlet of offsets around the woody crown, each offset made up of a plume of leaves sprouting from the same point. Drive a sharp spade down alongside the clump to detach the offset, which may or may not have embryo roots (if not, it will quickly grow some). Plant the offset in fresh ground, burying it only just sufficiently to keep it standing upright and water it frequently. The outer leaves will die back, but the plant will renew itself very quickly. Leave about 1.2m (4ft) between newly planted offsets.

TAKING CUTTINGS

SOFT FRUIT BUSHES In order to propagate currants or gooseberries, you need a spare patch of ground where you can line out cuttings for a year. Propagate red and whitecurrants and gooseberries by taking hardwood cuttings in mid-autumn from vigorous, clean, well-ripened stems (see right). Remove the lower buds that would normally produce shoots, as these bushes are grown with a short main stem. Blackcurrants are dealt with slightly differently. A blackcurrant bush should constantly renew itself by sending up

DIVIDING RHUBARB

1 When the foliage dies down in autumn, lift the plant or scrape away the soil to expose the buds. Drive a spade down between them, making sure that each section has a good bud.

2 Replant the sections in their new quarters, spacing them about 1m (3ft) apart. Set them so that the bud just shows above the soil. If necessary, replant the parent plant.

HARDWOOD CUTTINGS

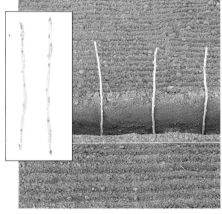

1 Take 30–38cm (12–15in) long hardwood cuttings in autumn. For gooseberries and red and whitecurrants, remove all but the top 4–5 buds and insert the cuttings 15cm (6in) deep in a narrow slit in prepared ground. Firm the soil.

2 By the following autumn, the cuttings will have produced roots. Carefully lift the new plants and transplant them to a freshly prepared plot. On windy days, roots dry out quickly. Protect them, if necessary, with a plastic bag.

stems from below ground level. In autumn, take hardwood cuttings 20–25cm (8–10in) long and leave all the buds intact. Bury the cutting so that only 2 buds show above ground. With luck, each buried bud will produce a shoot, so that when you dig it up the following autumn it will have 3–4 good stems.

FIGS These take longer to find their feet. For cuttings, choose 30cm (12in) sections of well-ripened wood (not from a growing tip) and bury them up to half their length in well-drained soil in a sheltered, sunny spot. After 2 years, transplant the new young tree to its final growing position.

BLUEBERRIES These are propagated from softwood cuttings taken from tips of stems in early summer. Choose growth 10–20cm (4–8in) long and strip off all but the top 3 leaves. Set each cutting in a 7cm (3in) pot of sandy, acid, ericaceous compost. Water, then cover the pot with polythene, or put it in a propagator at a temperature of 18°C (65°F). Rooting will take 3–6 weeks. As the cuttings begin to grow, harden them off and pot on into larger pots of lime-free compost. Plant out in autumn.

LAYERING

CANE FRUIT Blackberries, loganberries and other hybrid berries like tayberries are easily propagated by tip layering (see below).

HERBS Many shrubby types such as sage, rosemary and thyme can be propagated by mound layering (see right). In spring, pile free-draining soil over the base of the plant. If your soil is sticky, mix it with sand or compost. Replenish the mound with fresh earth through the summer, if necessary. This treatment stimulates new roots to grow on the branches covered with soil. Hyssop, lavender, cotton lavender (santolina) and winter savory can also be propagated by mound layering.

STRAWBERRIES These increase by means of runners (see page 143). All summer, mature plants send out long stems that, when they find a piece of bare ground, will produce a small plantlet that quickly grows into a new plant. If you have just planted a strawberry bed, you must spend the first 3 years nipping off the runners as the plants need to concentrate on producing fruit. But strawberries lose vigour after 3 years and then you should leave enough runners in place to produce new plants. The lazy (but effective) way is to let the runners root themselves where they will. Alternatively, you can sink 7cm (3in) pots of compost into the ground and peg down a runner into each. Whichever method you choose, you need, in early autumn, to cut the young plants from their runners and plant them out in a new bed of fresh, well-fed ground. Old plants should be destroyed.

MOUND LAYERING THYME

1 *In spring, pile free-draining soil over the base of the plant, leaving only the tips exposed. Replenish, if necessary, in summer.*

2 *By late summer or autumn, new roots will have formed on the stems. Carefully scrape away the earth and cut off the sections of rooted branch to plant out in well-prepared ground.*

TIP LAYERING A BLACKBERRY

1 *To propagate blackberries, loganberries and other hybrid berries, poke the growing tip of a stem into the soil with the tip pointing down. Bury it about 10–12cm (4–5in) deep. This is best done in summer.*

2 *In a few weeks a new growing tip will emerge, roots will form and, in autumn or early winter, you can sever the new plant from its parent to set out in its new position. If necessary, pot it for planting out later.*

CHOOSING FRUIT TREES

TRAINED FRUIT TREES WILL GIVE MUCH PLEASURE in a decorative kitchen garden, perhaps curving to make a tunnel of blossom over a path, or splayed out on walls to make geometric espaliers and fans. Use lines of cordons to screen off one part of the garden from another, or set low hedges of stepover apples (see opposite) around your salad plot. These low apple hurdles look equally good stretched out in front of a flower border. Fans of peaches and apricots are practical as well as beautiful for, spreadeagled on a sunny wall, the blossom is protected from frost and the fruit has the best possible chance of ripening. The simplest route to success is to buy fruit trees that are ready-trained in the shape you want.

FINE FIG FAN
Whether fanned out over a crisp, white greenhouse wall or basking outdoors in a warm, sunny site, figs have an architectural quality unmatched by any other fruit.

TREE STYLES

CORDONS These are the answer where quality rather than quantity of fruit is the goal. A cordon is a single-stemmed tree that is usually planted at an angle of 45 degrees to reduce vigour and produce as much fruiting wood as possible. Cordons should be tied into parallel wires stretched between posts. They are normally grown on dwarfing rootstocks and different cultivars of apples and pears can be grown together to make a fruitful screen. Double cordons are grown upright, the two arms making a goblet shape.

BUSH TREES Bushes start fruiting when they are very young, are easy to pick and spray, but difficult to mow under.

HALF-STANDARDS AND STANDARDS These are the apple trees of picture books. Half-standards have a clear stem of at least

1.2m (4ft), while full standards go up to 1.8m (6ft) before the branches break from the trunk. Their height makes spraying and picking slightly more difficult to manage, but they are infinitely more pleasing to look at than a dwarfed bush. When you plant a half-standard, you dream of picnicking in its shade, or of slinging a hammock from its branches. There is no such romance with a bush.

FANS These are more often used for cherries, plums, peaches and pears than they are for apples. The name explains the shape, which looks particularly good against a stone or brick wall. The branches are best trained on rigid canes of bamboo and, as with all trained fruit trees, summer pruning is essential.

ESPALIERS An espalier is trained to make several flat tiers of branches, like a wedding cake. It may have two, three or four sets

of parallel branches, depending on the space available. Naturally, espaliers take up more space than cordons, but can be used in the same way to make a screen. The branches need to be tied in regularly as they grow, and careful pruning is imperative if the espalier is to keep its formal, two-dimensional shape.

GUIDE TO TREE STYLES
From slanting cordon to tall-stemmed standard, the different styles of fruit tree all have a role to play in the decorative kitchen garden. Cordons will squeeze into the smallest plot, standards

look romantic in flower-strewn grass, and pruning espaliers and fans can become a strangely satisfying and rewarding task.

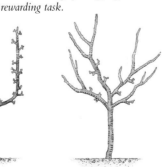
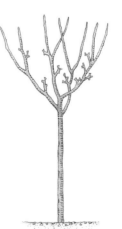

CORDON **DOUBLE CORDON** **BUSH** **HALF-STANDARD** **STANDARD**

If the main trunk is trained on a hoop over a path, espaliers make beautiful fruit tunnels.

STEPOVER A stepover tree is a miniature espalier, with one set of arms growing out about 30cm (12in) above the ground.

The style of tree you choose must be considered hand-in-hand with site, cultivar and rootstock. Some of the most aristocratic dessert pears, such as 'Marie-Louise' and 'Glou Morceau', are best grown as fans or espaliers against a wall, but an apple such as 'Bramley's Seedling' would be too vigorous. If you have poor soil, then you are unlikely to succeed with dwarfing rootstocks. They are demanding things and need weed-free ground as well as careful feeding and watering.

ROOTSTOCKS

Fruit trees are usually grafted on to rootstocks to control the rate at which they grow as well as the size they reach. As a rule, dwarfing rootstocks bring a tree into production earlier but are more demanding in terms of growing conditions. Good grafts are imperceptible. Bad ones are like a crooked elbow. Sometimes the rootstock makes a bid to take over the graft. This is called suckering and, if it happens, the suckers should be cut or pulled out as soon as you see them.

Good nurserymen will offer fruit trees grafted on to more than one type of rootstock, so once you have chosen the cultivar, you can buy it on a rootstock that suits your soil and the style of tree you want. You might want to grow the dessert apple 'Discovery'. This is of medium vigour, so you would not generally want it on the extremely dwarfing M27 stock. As a cordon in a restricted situation on good soil, you might choose M9. On poor soil, you would do better with MM106. This would also be the best choice for growing 'Discovery' as an espalier or fan, but if you wanted to grow it as a half-standard you need to look for a tree grafted on to MM111 stock.

BACK TO THE WALL
Any stretch of wall, whether on the house or part of a boundary, can be used to train a fruit tree. The blossom of this old pear has enhanced the mellow red brick for many a season.

ROOTSTOCKS

APPLES

M27 Extremely dwarfing. Produces trees up to 1.8m (6ft) high and wide and crops at 2–3 years. Can, with care, be grown in tubs. Only succeeds in very fertile soil and needs permanent staking.

M9 Very dwarfing. Produces trees from 2–2.5m (7–8ft) high and wide. Crops at 3–4 years. Slightly more tolerant than M27, but needs good soil and permanent staking.

MM106 Ideal for the average garden. Produces trees from 3.5–4.8m (12–16ft) high and wide. Crops at 4–5 years. Does not need permanent staking. Vigorous even on poor, sandy soils.

MM111 Vigorous. Produces trees from 4.5–5.5m (15–18 ft) high and wide. Used for standards and half-standards. Trees do not start fruiting for 6–7 years.

M25 Ideal for orchard and specimen trees, forgiving of poor conditions. Produces trees from 4.8–5.5m (16–18ft) at maturity.

PEARS

QUINCE C Produces trees about 3m (10ft) high and wide that start fruiting earlier than those on Quince A. Only suitable for very fertile soils or for cordons.

QUINCE A Semi-vigorous. Good all-round performer. Produces trees from 3.5–4.5m (12–15ft) high and wide. Said to be more frost-resistant than Quince C.

PEAR ROOTSTOCK Pears on pear roots, not necessarily their own, grow slowly to produce beautiful trees. Only suitable for standards or half-standards.

PLUMS

PIXY Dwarfing. Produces trees 3–4.5m (10–15ft) high and wide. Only suits very fertile soil. Trees need permanent staking.

ST JULIEN A Semi-vigorous. Produces trees up to 6m (20ft) high and wide. Compatible with all cultivars.

BROMPTON Good for standards in orchards. Produces trees 7.5m (25ft) high and wide.

PEACHES AND NECTARINES

ST JULIEN A Semi-vigorous. Produces fans 3.5–4.5m (12–15ft) wide.

BROMPTON More vigorous. Produces fans 4.5–6m (15–20ft) wide.

APRICOTS

ST JULIEN A Produces fans about 4.5m (15ft) wide or similar-sized bush.

CHERRIES

INMIL Most dwarfing rootstock, slowly becoming available. Produces trees little more than 1.8–2m (6–7ft) high and wide. Needs to be well looked after.

DAMIL Semi-dwarfing. Produces trees 3–4.5m (10–15ft) high and wide. Slightly more tolerant of poor conditions than Inmil.

COLT Old and reliable. Produces trees from 4.5–6m (15–20ft) high and wide.

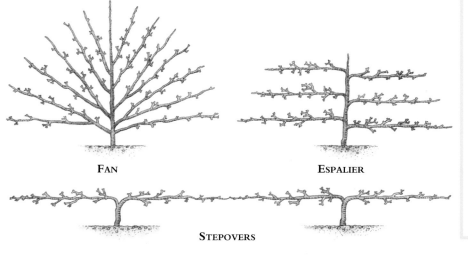

FAN

ESPALIER

STEPOVERS

PLANTING & POLLINATION

TAKE TIME TO PLANT A FRUIT TREE. It deserves your full attention, for it has the potential to be one of the longest-serving features in your new kitchen garden. That potential is unlikely to be realized if you cram it into a measly little hole with its roots coiled around as dizzily as vipers in a basket. Excavate generously, remain oblivious to the siren calls of the telephone, the coffee pot or any other distraction, and do not leave the tree's roots drying in the wind while you dig. Give some thought, too, to your tree's sex life. Some fruit trees are self-fertile, which relieves you of any further worry on this score. Others need to have suitable pollinating partners not more than a bee's hop away.

PLANTING A FRUIT BUSH

1 *Dig a hole larger than the bush's rootspan. Spread out the roots evenly in the hole and lay a cane across to indicate the soil level. Make sure the bush is neither too high nor too low.*

PLANTING

If your fruit tree comes in a container, do not plant the pot as well as the contents. There is a certain logic in doing so (plant easier to move if you have made a mistake, roots not disturbed, job quicker) but it does nothing for the plant's long-term future. Roots must run. Autumn is generally the best time to plant, when trees are dormant. They can settle in and get their roots firmly plugged into supplies before having to fuss about flowering.

Make a hole bigger than the one you first thought of and have a bucket of compost mixed with bonemeal standing by. Settle the tree into the hole so that the stem sits at the same level in relation to the ground as it was in the pot. Put in a short stake to stand about 50cm (20in) above the ground for half-standard and standard trees. You should also stake bushes on very dwarfing rootstocks. Make sure the join of the graft is above soil level, otherwise the plant that has been grafted may try to make its own roots and the benefit of the rootstock will be lost. Spread the roots out comfortably, so that the main ones go off in different directions, and fill in first with the compost, firming it around the roots, then with soil. Water the plant thoroughly – a drench, not a sprinkle. If it is very dry, mulch around the base of the tree after watering.

POLLINATION

Many fruit trees need to be cross-pollinated if they are to produce fruit. The job is usually done by insects, who transfer pollen from the anther of a flower on one tree to the stigma of a flower on another. Some fruit trees, such as the 'Morello' cherry, are self-fertile, in which case you can expect fruit even if it is the only tree in the garden. Some trees, such as the 'Conference' pear, are technically self-fertile, although this will set fruit more readily if it is also cross-pollinated by another type of pear. Where trees need to be cross-pollinated, the pollinator obviously needs to be in bloom at the same time as the tree it is pollinating.

Most specialist nurseries number the fruit trees in their catalogues to indicate the different flowering seasons (see opposite). The early-flowering apple 'George Cave' might, for instance, be

2 *Fill in the hole, first with compost mixed with a little bonemeal, working it around the roots, then with soil. Firm it down, so that there are no air pockets, and water well.*

PLANTING A FRUIT TREE

1 *Dig a hole large enough for the roots to spread out comfortably inside. If planting half-standard or standard trees, drive in a short stake. Lay a cane across the hole to check the planting depth. The graft (inset) must be above it.*

2 *Work some compost mixed with a little bonemeal in around the roots, then fill in the hole with soil and firm it down, especially around the trunk. Use a tree tie to attach the stake to the tree, and water in thoroughly.*

HAND-POLLINATION

Peaches and nectarines flower before most insects are about, so help pollination by using a small, soft brush to transfer pollen from one flower to the next. Repeat as new flowers open.

paired with another early-flowering cultivar such as 'Egremont Russet', and the 'Beurré Hardy' pear with 'Doyenné du Comice', both late-flowering. Whereas most fruit trees are diploids, with two basic sets of chromosomes, a few are triploids with three and this makes them sterile. These need to be pollinated by two different cultivars. 'Ribston Pippin' and 'Bramley's Seedling' are triploid apples, 'Jargonelle' is a triploid pear.

The other vital factor in pollination is a good supply of insects. Commercial growers hire hives of bees to move into their fruit orchards. Others release specially bred bumblebees to work in their glasshouses. Bees have suffered appallingly from the thoughtless use of insecticides. Think before you spray.

Both peaches and nectarines are self-fertile, so you do not have to plant different cultivars to ensure pollination. But to bring about a good set of fruit, you can pollinate with a paintbrush, as above. Unless doors are left open, trees grown in greenhouses will always have to be hand-pollinated. Traditionally, this job was done at noon and the floor damped down afterwards to help the fruit to set.

POLLINATION GROUPS

APPLES

Early flowering: 'Baker's Delicious', 'Beauty of Bath', 'Christmas Pearmain', 'Crispin', 'Discovery', 'Egremont Russet', 'George Cave', 'George Neal', 'Idared', 'Lord Lambourne', 'Red Melba', 'Rev W. Wilks', 'Ribston Pippin', 'St Edmund's Pippin', 'Sunset'.
Mid-season flowering: 'Arthur Turner', 'Ashmead's Kernel', 'Blenheim Orange', 'Bramley's Seedling', 'Charles Ross', 'Chiver's Delight', 'Cox's Orange Pippin', 'Crown Gold', 'Early Victoria', 'Elstar', 'Fiesta', 'Greensleeves', 'Grenadier', 'Howgate Wonder', 'James Grieve', 'Jester', 'Jonagold', 'Jonagored', 'Jupiter', 'Katja', 'Kidd's Orange Red', 'Laxton's Epicure', 'Laxton's Fortune', 'Malling Kent', 'Merton Knave', 'Queen Cox', 'Rosemary Russet', 'Rubinette', 'Sanspareil', 'Sturmer Pippin', 'Tydeman's Late Orange', 'Wagener', 'Worcester Pearmain'.
Late flowering: 'American Mother', 'Annie Elizabeth', 'Crawley Beauty', 'Edward VII', 'Ellison's Orange', 'Gala', 'Golden Delicious', 'Golden Noble', 'Harvey', 'Lane's Prince Albert', 'Laxton's Superb', 'Lord Derby', 'Monarch', 'Newton Wonder', 'Orleans Reinette', 'Pixie', 'Suntan', 'Winston'.
Triploids: cultivars needing two pollinators include 'Blenheim Orange', 'Bramley's Seedling', 'Crispin', 'Jonagold', 'Jupiter', 'Reinette du Canada', 'Ribston Pippin', 'Suntan', 'Warner's King'.

PEARS

Early flowering: 'Louise Bonne of Jersey', 'Marguérite Marillat', 'Ovid'.
Mid-season flowering: 'Beth', 'Beurré d'Amanlis', 'Concorde', 'Conference', 'Dr Jules Guyot', 'Durondeau', 'Fertility Improved', 'Fondante d'Automne', 'Glow Red Williams', 'Jargonelle', 'Joséphine de Malines', 'Merton Pride', 'Nouveau Poitou', 'Packham's Triumph', 'Williams' Bon Chrétien'.
Late flowering: 'Beurré Hardy', 'Bristol Cross', 'Catillac', 'Doyenné du Comice', 'Glou Morceau', 'Gorham', 'Marie-Louise', 'Onward', 'Winter Nelis'.
Incompatible cultivars: despite overlapping flowering times, some pears are not compatible. 'Fondante d'Automne', 'Louise Bonne of Jersey' and 'Williams' Bon Chrétien' will not pollinate each other. 'Conference' is self-fertile, but sets a better crop given another pollinator.

Triploids: cultivars needing two pollinators include 'Beurré d'Amanlis', 'Beurré Diel', 'Bristol Cross', 'Catillac', 'Jargonelle', 'Merton Pride', 'Pitmaston'.

PLUMS, GREENGAGES AND DAMSONS

Some of the plum family, such as 'Belle de Louvain', 'Czar', 'Denniston's Superb', 'Early Transparent Gage', 'Marjorie's Seedling', 'Merryweather', 'Ontario', 'Opal', 'Ouillins Gage', 'Reine Claude de Bavay', 'Victoria' and 'Warwickshire Drooper' are self-fertile, but crops are much improved if you provide a suitable pollinator. Some plums are incompatible. 'Jefferson' and 'Coe's Golden Drop', for example, will not pollinate each other.
Early flowering: 'Coe's Golden Drop', 'Denniston's Superb', 'Farleigh Damson', 'Jefferson', 'Ontario', 'Reine Claude de Bavay', 'Warwickshire Drooper'.
Mid-season flowering: 'Anna Spath', 'Czar', 'Early Laxton', 'Goldfinch', 'Kirke's Blue', 'Merryweather', 'Opal', 'Reeves Seedling', 'Rivers's Early Prolific', 'Victoria'.
Late flowering: 'Belle de Louvain', 'Cambridge Gage', 'Count Althann's Gage', 'Early Transparent Gage', 'Marjorie's Seedling', 'Old Greengage', 'Ouillins Gage'.

PEACHES AND NECTARINES

Both peaches and nectarines are self-fertile but may need hand-pollinating if there are no insects on the wing to do the job.

APRICOTS AND CHERRIES

Apricots are self-fertile, but may need hand-pollinating. The acid cherry 'Morello' is self-fertile and will pollinate sweet cherries such as 'Bigarreau Napoléon' and 'Bigarreau Gaucher' that flower at the same time. With the exception of 'Stella', sweet cherries are not self-fertile. 'Governor Wood' and 'Merton Bigarreau' will pollinate each other. 'Merton Heart' will pollinate 'Early Rivers'.

MELONS, KIWI AND PASSION FRUIT

Pollinate melons by stripping the petals from a male flower and pushing it into a female flower. The females are the ones with slight swellings just underneath the flowerheads. One male flower will pollinate at least four females. Pollination is best done at midday. Female kiwi plants will only set fruit when there is a male plant growing close by. The passion fruit is self-fertile.

PRUNING & TRAINING TREE FRUIT

PLANTS DO NOT DIE if they are not pruned. There is no ghostly pruner in the wild, flitting about with secateurs to get hedgerow blackberries into shape or to trim up the hawthorn. Gardeners prune fruit trees to enhance fruiting, to maintain the style or shape of a tree that is growing in a particular way, as with a cordon or an espalier, or simply because they are tidy-minded. Accept that the diagram in your manual will never look like the tree that confronts you in the garden. Try to master the principles. Once you understand these, the practice is easier to carry out.

PRINCIPLES OF PRUNING

You cannot rely on pruning alone to contain the size of a tree. If an apple has been grafted on to M25 rootstock, it will always have the urge to do what destiny dictates: grow into a big, beautiful, prize-fighter of a tree. Heavy pruning will lead only to renewed efforts on the tree's part to fulfil the imperative of its genes. If you want a small tree, choose a cultivar that is only moderately vigorous and match it with the right rootstock (see page 175). If you buy a tree trained as a cordon, espalier or fan, the appropriate rootstock is likely to have already been chosen for you.

Most apples and pears produce their fruitbuds on new shoots which develop from short, woody clusters known as spurs. These are called spur-bearing trees.

A few cultivars, such as the apples 'Bramley's Seedling' and 'George Cave' and the pears 'Jargonelle' and 'Joséphine de Malines', are tip bearers, producing their flowerbuds on the ends of 2-year-old shoots. If you are constantly cutting these back, there is little chance of getting any fruit. Tip-bearing cultivars are not a wise choice for cordons or espaliers.

Before you home in, brandishing a pruning saw, remind yourself why you want to prune. It may be to maintain the tree in a particular form, to increase vigour, to encourage more fruitbuds to form, to improve the quality or quantity of the fruit, to cut out diseased or dead wood, or to thin out overcrowded branches (which will in turn help prevent diseases). Just as you need to balance suitable rootstocks with particular styles of

tree, so you should regulate your pruning to the vigour of the cultivar. Winter pruning stimulates a tree to produce more growth, so the more vigorous a tree is, the more lightly it should be pruned. Conversely, if a tree has weak, droopy branches, it can be pruned hard.

APPLES AND PEARS Trees growing as bushes, half-standards and standards will need only winter pruning, if you prune them at all. They will grow and fruit quite happily, although not at maximum potential, if you leave them alone. If you prune, do it on the replacement principle. Encourage new growth by cutting back some of the old growth at the ends of the branches, making the cut where there is a new shoot waiting to take over.

On trees growing as single or double cordons, espaliers and fans, summer pruning is more important than winter pruning as it is by this means that you control the amount of growth that the tree produces. To summer prune, cut back the new leafy shoots that have been produced during spring and early summer. If the shoot is growing directly from one of the main arms of the tree, cut it back to the third leaf above the basal cluster of leaves. Leave the cluster itself intact. If the shoot is springing from a knobbly spur formed by previous pruning, cut it back to

PRUNING AND TRAINING A SINGLE CORDON

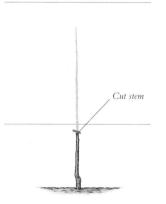

Thin spurs

Cut back to 3 leaves

Cut back spur shoots to 1 leaf

1 *In winter, thin out buds on spurs that have become congested, especially on old trees. Tighten or loosen ties if necessary.*

2 *In summer, cut back shoots from spurs to 1 leaf above the spur. Cut back other shoots from the main stem to 3 leaves.*

MAKING A DOUBLE CORDON

Cut stem

Tie shoots to canes

1 *In winter, cut a very young, single-stemmed tree to 25cm (10in) from the ground, just above 2 good buds, one at either side.*

2 *As the shoots grow, tie with twine to bamboo canes fixed to wires, first at an angle and then vertically. Prune as single cordons.*

just 1 leaf above the cluster. Do this in mid to late summer, when the greenish stems of the shoots have started to turn brown. In winter, you may have to shorten any other long shoots that have grown since summer pruning.

A fan is slightly less rigid in its underlying structure than a cordon or espalier. You can continue to tie in sideshoots springing from the main branches, until all the space between them is filled. After that, you must summer-prune sideshoots, cutting them back to 1 leaf above the basal cluster. If one of the main stems starts to outgrow its space, cut it back to a strong replacement shoot, which you can tie in in its place.

PLUMS, GREENGAGES AND DAMSONS
Free-standing trees require little pruning. Simply take out dead wood and thin, overcrowded growth. Any cutting should be done in late spring or summer. This reduces the risk of spores of silverleaf getting into the system (see page 193).

Fans require more attention. Shoots sprouting from the main framework should be nipped out in two stages. In midsummer, pinch back all sideshoots to leave about 6 leaves. These will be the shoots that bear fruit in the subsequent summer. When they have fruited, cut back these sideshoots by half, to about 3 leaves. Any shoots that are pointing directly forward or backward into the wall should be taken out entirely.

PEACHES AND NECTARINES These can most conveniently be grown as fans. Make life easy for yourself by buying a ready-trained tree. The fruit is borne on the shoots produced in the previous season. Take out any shoots that you do not want (including those pointing forward or back) in spring, leaving 3 growth buds on each lateral branch. In early summer, prune back each of these 3 shoots to 6 leaves. When you have picked the fruit, cut out the shoot that bore it and tie in a replacement shoot. On free-standing trees, trim out crowded or crossing branches in summer. In mid-spring, prune back any shoots killed by winter frost.

APRICOTS Fan apricots are treated in a similar way to peaches. Aim to build up a series of fruiting spurs about 15cm (6in) apart all the way along the branches. Do this by pinching back the lateral growths in early summer, leaving about 7cm (3in) of each growth in place. Any growths

springing from these laterals should be pinched back, leaving just 1 leaf. Keep tying in the new growth to maintain the fan shape. No regular pruning is needed for established bushes.

CHERRIES Sweet cherries growing as standards or half-standards do not need pruning. Simply cut out any dead wood and remove crossing branches. 'Morello' cherries only fruit on new wood, so you must prune to force the tree to produce

plenty of the necessary growth. When a wall-trained tree has fruited, cut out the long growths at its extremities so that it will make new shoots in the centre or the tree will bear fruit only at the tips of its branches. Tie in as many new shoots as you can fit in among the main branches.

CITRUS FRUIT Citrus trees do not need regular pruning. Trim new growth in early spring, if necessary, to keep the plants balanced and shapely.

PRUNING AND TRAINING AN ESPALIER

APPLES AND PEARS
Train new branches to form horizontal tiers. In summer, cut back shoots from the main stems as inset below, and cut back those arising from spurs to 1 leaf above the spur.

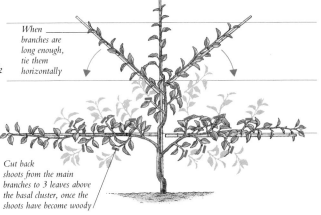

When branches are long enough, tie them horizontally

Cut back shoots from the main branches to 3 leaves above the basal cluster, once the shoots have become woody

PRUNING AND TRAINING A FAN

PLUMS
In midsummer, cut back all sideshoots from the main framework to 6 leaves. After fruiting, cut them back further to 3 leaves. These shoots will bear the following season's fruit. Cut out entirely shoots growing forward or backward.

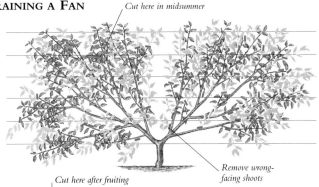

Cut here in midsummer

Remove wrong-facing shoots

Cut here after fruiting

MORELLO CHERRIES
In late summer, cut off growths at the extremities of the branches to encourage the tree to produce new shoots in the centre. The following season's fruit will be borne only on new wood. Cut out entirely shoots growing forward or backward.

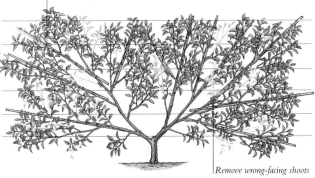

Remove wrong-facing shoots

PRUNING & TRAINING SOFT FRUIT & VINES

WITH SOFT FRUIT, as with tree fruit, you can grow canes or bushes in a decorative manner. Train blackberries to make garden dividers, or grow a standard, mop-headed gooseberry on a 1.2m (4ft) stem to rise up among your annual flowers. Redcurrants respond to being trained, too. You can turn them into double cordons, which grow in the shape of a wine glass, the two stems trained out and up from a single trunk. Of this group, vines need the most careful pruning. In good soil, they tend to develop too much leaf and you must prune to remind them to flower and fruit. Where you are growing a vine to cover an arbour you need not be too particular about the pruning. Greenhouse vines are more demanding.

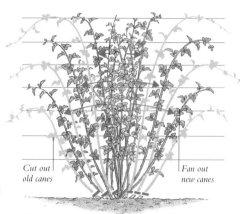
Cut out old canes | *Fan out new canes*

TRAINING BLACKBERRIES
Keep the new canes bunched in a fountain in the centre. After cutting out the fruited canes in autumn, fan out the new growth and tie it in.

CANE FRUIT

RASPBERRIES These need pruning every year, but this is a simple process. After summer cultivars have fruited, cut out the old canes close to the ground and thin the new canes, leaving no more than 5 or 6 strong stems growing from each original clump. Tie in the new canes to supporting wires, if using the post and wires system. In late winter, cut off the top of each cane just above the top wire. Autumn-fruiting raspberries need slightly different treatment as they carry fruit on canes formed earlier in the same season. Cut the old, fruited canes to the ground in late winter and thin out the new growth gradually as it grows during the season.

HYBRID BERRIES If you are training hybrid berries such as loganberries or tayberries on wires to make a screen, fix the first wire about 1m (3ft) from the ground, with several parallel wires above. Tie the growths securely to the wires, keeping the new canes bunched up in the middle and the older, fruiting growths trained along the wires away from the centre (see training blackberries above). After picking the fruit, cut out the old canes, unbundle the new ones and tie them in where the old ones were.

BLACKBERRIES These are treated in the same way as hybrid berries. Cut out the fruited canes each year after the crop has been gathered. With a late-fruiting cultivar such as 'Himalaya Giant', this may not be until mid-autumn. Fan out and tie in the new canes to replace the old. With 'Himalaya Giant', which does not produce canes quite as freely as other blackberry varieties, a proportion of the old wood may be left in place each season.

SOFT FRUIT BUSHES

BLUEBERRIES Bushes can be trimmed, rather than severely pruned. Start in winter by cutting out dead or damaged branches together with a proportion of old wood. In spring, shear over the tops of the bushes to keep them compact.

CURRANTS Although redcurrants and whitecurrants are pruned in the same way, you need to treat blackcurrants differently. While red and whitecurrants fruit on spurs made on old wood, blackcurrants fruit on young, one-year-old wood. When they have finished fruiting, cut out at least a third of the old, dead wood, leaving as much of the new, light brown growth as possible to bear the following season's fruit. As red and whitecurrants fruit on old wood, pruning can be less drastic. After fruiting, or during the autumn and winter, shorten branches by about a third to keep the bushes shapely and compact. On red and whitecurrants grown as cordons, cut the lateral branches back to within 3cm (1½in) or so of the main stem.

Redcurrants are especially good trained as double cordons (see page 178). Allow a rooted cutting to grow up as a single stem, without any side branches. It needs to be planted against the parallel wires that will support it. When it is growing well and about 75cm (30in) high, cut the stem back to about 25cm (10in) from the ground, leaving a strong bud on either side below the cut. These 2 buds will break into sideshoots, which you should train on canes set at an angle of 45 degrees. When

TRAINING RASPBERRIES

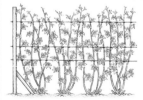

POST AND WIRES
This method of support takes up the least space. The posts need to stand 1.8m (6ft) high, with 3 parallel wires stretched between, the first 75cm (30in) from the ground.

PARALLEL WIRES
Canes need no tying in with this system. Put up 2 rows of posts 75cm (30in) apart with 2 wires along each row. Criss-cross twine between them.

TYING IN
Tie in the strongest of the new canes as soon as the old ones have been cut down. Twist the twine around and along the wire to hold them in place. This method stops canes from coming loose in wind.

Cut out old stems

PRUNING BLACKCURRANTS

After fruiting, cut at least a third of the old, dead stems to ground level. Prune off any excess side growth to keep a fairly upright shape.

PRUNING GOOSEBERRIES

1 *Cut out a proportion of old stems each year in late autumn or winter to prevent the centre of the bush from getting congested, and shorten any stems that are unnecessarily long.*

2 *Prune until the bush has an open centre. This will allow air to circulate between the branches and so deter gooseberry mildew. It will also make picking the fruit a less prickly task.*

PRUNING A CORDON GRAPEVINE

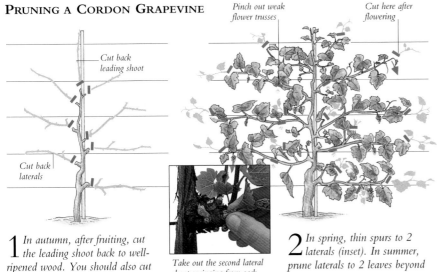

Cut back leading shoot

Cut back laterals

Pinch out weak flower trusses

Cut here after flowering

1 *In autumn, after fruiting, cut the leading shoot back to well-ripened wood. You should also cut all laterals back to 2 buds so that spurs develop at each of these points.*

Take out the second lateral shoot springing from each spur when the first one is growing well

2 *In spring, thin spurs to 2 laterals (inset). In summer, prune laterals to 2 leaves beyond the last cluster of fruit. Pinch out any weak flower trusses.*

the tips of these shoots are at least 45cm (18in) apart, lower the training canes to an angle of 30 degrees and attach more canes vertically to the wires. Continue to train the shoots in the new vertical position. Prune them as you would a single cordon.

GOOSEBERRIES These will bear fruit even if they are not regularly pruned, but it is easier to pick the fruit if you remove some stems each year, to keep the centre of the bush open, and shorten long branches that may be weighed down by berries. Shorten the side growths on cordons to 3 buds, and cut the branches of standards back by at least a third to keep a well-shaped head.

GRAPEVINES

CORDONS When grown under glass, vines should be trained on wires set about 30cm (12in) apart and at least 15cm (6in) away from the glass itself. The leading shoot should be trained vertically, and the laterals horizontally along the wires. When the vines have flowered, prune the laterals back, leaving 2 leaves beyond each cluster of fruit. Any subsequent shoots breaking from the laterals should be pinched out, leaving 2 leaves at most. After fruiting, cut the leading shoot back to well-ripened wood, and cut the laterals back to 2 buds.

WALL-TRAINED VINES Train vines on walls by allowing, at most, 3 or 4 main stems to develop from a single rootstock. After the first season's growth, cut back the branches by two-thirds and repeat in early autumn each year until all the available space is filled. On young plants, tie in the laterals and grow them to about 60cm (24in) before stopping them by pinching out. On mature plants, the laterals should be stopped just beyond the clusters of flowers, leaving no more than 2 leaves. Sub-laterals (shoots springing from sideshoots) should be stopped at 1 leaf.

THE GUYOT SYSTEM Vines growing outside can also be trained according to the Guyot system, named after its inventor. For this, you need parallel sets of wires spaced 30cm (12in) apart, stretched between posts or fastened to a wall. After planting the vines in the dormant season in late autumn, cut the previous season's growth hard back, leaving no more than 2 buds. During the first summer, train a single shoot vertically up the wires, tying it in at regular intervals. Prune away any other shoots that develop. In autumn or early winter, cut back this shoot, leaving about 75cm (30in) of growth. Undo the ties and retie this stem horizontally along the bottom wire.

The following season, several shoots will break from this stem. Train them vertically up the wires. When the grapes have been gathered, cut out all except 2 shoots nearest the original rootstock. Shorten these to about 75cm (30in) and tie them along the bottom wire. As before, train the new summer shoots vertically up the wires, then repeat the process of cutting out most of the growth and selecting new shoots to tie in on the lowest wire every autumn or early winter.

GROWING IN GREENHOUSES

THE CHIEF BENEFITS OF A GREENHOUSE are the extra warmth and shelter it will give to plants, although it can also be decorative in its own right. Under glass, you can extend the growing season of all plants and grow fruit and vegetables that may not survive outside in the garden. Unfortunately, greenhouses provide ideal living conditions for pests as well as plants. Be prepared for armies of whitefly and red spider mite. The planting options available will depend on the type of structure you have. Old-fashioned kitchen gardens will have lean-to greenhouses built against a sunny wall, where apricots, peaches and nectarines can be trained in fans. Protected from frost, trees blossom fearlessly and fruit ripens easily. Vines, too, benefit from the shelter of a greenhouse, but the rootstock is best planted outside, with the trunk leading in through an opening in the side.

HEADY DAYS OF SPRING
Peaches and nectarines put on a sumptuous display in this traditional greenhouse long before the rest of the garden has sprung into action.

CHOOSING A GREENHOUSE

Free-standing aluminium greenhouses, glassed to the ground, are one of the most popular options for amateur gardeners. Although maintenance is minimal and the design allows maximum light to reach the plants, this type can be cold, and condensation may be greater than in a similar house made of wood. But wood, even cedar, needs looking after.

The cheapest option is a polytunnel, made from plastic sheeting stretched over big metal hoops. Unfortunately, these add nothing to the decorative value of the garden and even polythene that has been treated against ultraviolet light rarely lasts for more than three years and is easily punctured or torn in high winds.

Whatever type of greenhouse you choose, make sure that it can be well ventilated. You need to have roof ventilators equal in area to at least 20 per cent of the floor space. If you are away from home for a good deal of time, it may be wise to invest in automatic ventilators. These are designed around a cylinder of sensitive wax that expands or contracts according to the temperature. The cylinder moves a piston rod attached to the ventilator. All automatic ventilators should be marked with the weight they

can lift. Check that you have got one that is man enough for the job.

The heating in your greenhouse will depend on your purse, but, in any case, arrange the space so that you can partition off part of it to keep frost-free in winter. Electricity is reckoned an expensive

IN SIMPLE STYLE
A greenhouse can be an attractive as well as a practical feature. Wooden structures are more harmonious but they need regular maintenance.

option, although installing it is relatively cheap. Remember that maintaining a minimum winter temperature of 10°C (50°F) costs twice as much as maintaining one of 8°C (45°F). Paraffin heaters are cheap, but not so precise as electric ones. Insulation is the best way to save on heating costs. Use heavy-duty bubble polythene fixed with clips to the inside of the greenhouse frame.

GREENHOUSE CROPS

Even in an unheated greenhouse you can extend the growing season of basic crops such as carrots and lettuce. Tender vegetables such as aubergines, cucumbers, peppers and tomatoes will grow outside, but cannot be set out until all danger of frost is past. In a greenhouse, they can be planted earlier and so will start cropping sooner. Frost-tender herbs such as basil also benefit from the extra warmth and grow extremely well in polytunnels. Some vegetables, such as endive, chard and certain oriental brassicas, may be hardy, but will be more succulent if they are grown under cover during winter.

Your greenhouse or polytunnel can also function as a nursery in which to bring on seedlings of lettuce, courgettes or sweet corn that you intend to plant out later on. You can raise seedlings on a windowsill indoors, but light levels are unlikely to be as good as those in a greenhouse and the temperature may be too warm. Both these factors could induce the seedlings to become leggy and weak.

Grow tomatoes in a greenhouse as cordons rather than bushes, setting a short, strong cane, about 60cm (24in) high, by the side of each plant, and train them as shown right. Stop the leading shoots by pinching out in late summer, or when 6 trusses of fruit have formed, if that is sooner.

Damping down helps keep pests at bay. Some of the most troublesome, such as red spider mite, thrive in hot dry conditions. Hose down the floor every day during hot weather to keep the air inside moistly humid. If the weather itself is moistly humid, you need to keep air moving through the greenhouse to prevent plants rotting.

PLANNING THE SPACE

You can use the space inside a greenhouse more economically if you grow crops in earth borders on either side of a central path. Where greenhouses are set on a solid base in a backyard, all crops will have to be grown in grow bags or containers. In the main, borders are easier to manage in terms of watering and feeding, but they have an important disadvantage. If you grow the same crop year after year in the same soil, a build-up of salts can occur, causing "soil sickness". This means that crops will not continue to thrive in that position unless the soil is sterilized or replaced. If you have three greenhouse borders, one at either side of a central path and one at the end, you can practise a simple crop rotation. See the plan below for one way of organizing the growing area and taking full advantage of the space available in winter as well as summer.

TRAINING TOMATOES
Set a cane by the side of each tomato plant and tie a double string between the cane and the greenhouse roof. As the plants grow, twist the string around the stems to support them.

GREENHOUSE PLAN: *for a house 3 × 2m (10 × 7ft)*

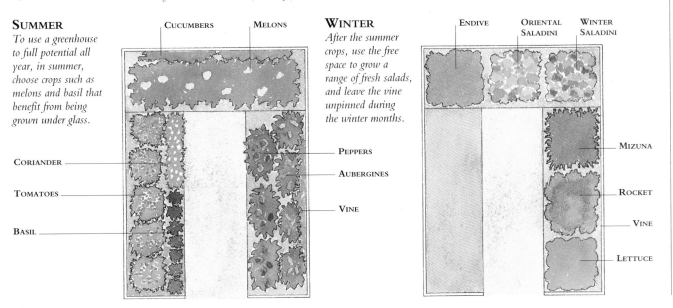

SUMMER
To use a greenhouse to full potential all year, in summer, choose crops such as melons and basil that benefit from being grown under glass.

CUCUMBERS   MELONS

CORIANDER

TOMATOES

BASIL

WINTER
After the summer crops, use the free space to grow a range of fresh salads, and leave the vine unpinned during the winter months.

PEPPERS

AUBERGINES

VINE

ENDIVE   ORIENTAL SALADINI   WINTER SALADINI

MIZUNA

ROCKET

VINE

LETTUCE

COLD FRAMES, CLOCHES & LIGHTS

IF YOUR GARDEN IS TOO SMALL for a greenhouse, you can still arrange useful protection for vegetables and fruit by investing in a cold frame, a set of cloches or individual lights. A cold frame is a kind of doll's greenhouse, unheated as the name suggests, and built with a low, sloping glass roof that you slide on and off depending on the weather. Old-fashioned cloches were always made of glass, which allows the maximum amount of light through on to the crops beneath. Modern cloches may be made from Perspex or plastic of different types, and can be either transparent or translucent, ridged or smooth. Victorian lantern lights, or modern replicas, are attractive and easy to move around the garden, but expensive to buy. Considerably cheaper are jam jars or chopped off plastic bottles that can be used to cover seeds or newly emerging plants.

COLD FRAMES

The warmest type of cold frame has walls of brick or wood rather than glass. Use it to harden off plants raised from seed, before planting them out. Set the young plants as close as possible to the top of the frame by raising the seed trays or pots on piles of bricks or similar support. Do not leave the frame closed on hot, sunny days, as the temperature will rise dramatically and plants will suffer. In the tricky days of late spring, when sudden frosts can wreak havoc, give the frame extra protection by covering the top with sacking, newspapers, old carpet or any other material that will provide insulation.

If you do not have a greenhouse, use a cold frame to grow crops such as peppers, chillies, aubergines and melons. Position the frame so that it catches maximum sun, and is protected from cold winds.

CUSTOM-MADE COLD FRAMES
Cold frames can be bought in kit form, straight off the garden centre shelf, but if you want to add a certain idiosyncratic charm to the garden, *try building one yourself. Secondhand materials are ideal: use old windowframes, if you can find them, and reclaimed timber or bricks.*

A LOW POLYTUNNEL
Mini-polytunnels, made to whatever length you need, are a cheap method of producing early crops and warding off pests. The polythene needs to be fairly tough and the hoops should be made of galvanised wire.

MAKING THE TUNNEL

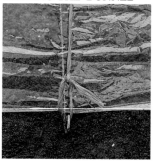

1 *Stretch the polythene over the wire hoops, pushed into the ground at 1m (3ft) intervals. Keep it in place by taking some twine over the top and attaching it to the loops at the base of each hoop.*

2 *Bunch up the polythene at the ends and tie it to a stake driven into the ground at an angle. When ventilation is needed, push up the sides of the tunnel between the hoops and the twine.*

OPEN-ENDED CLOCHE

A cloche like this will give temporary protection to a patch of seedlings or a short row of plants. Leave the ends open for daytime ventilation, but close them with a propped-up sheet of glass on cold, frosty nights.

LANTERN LIGHT

Old-fashioned lights look very pretty, will give cover to reasonably large plants and are easily moved around the garden.

RECYCLE A BOTTLE

A plastic bottle, chopped in half and placed over seeds or seedlings will provide warmth, light and protection from slugs and mice.

You can also use a frame to grow early crops of vegetables such as carrots, lettuce or radishes. Fork over the soil inside to a depth of at least 15cm (6in) before direct sowing. "Soil sickness" can as easily build up in a cold frame as in a greenhouse. Vary the crops that you grow and keep the soil in good heart by mulching areas that are free of crops in the late autumn and winter.

LOW POLYTUNNELS

The cheapest way of protecting vegetables is to grow them under a low tunnel, made by stretching polythene sheeting over wire hoops (see opposite). These are usually available as kits and provide a protected growing area of whatever length you want, but usually no more than 30–45cm (12–18in) high. Tunnels of this kind are ideal for protecting strawberries and carrots. The strawberries ripen more quickly and the tunnel keeps them safe from birds. Carrots do not need extra heat to grow well, but a covering of some kind prevents them from being attacked by carrot fly (see page 190).

CLOCHES

Cloches can be made of plastic or glass and used singly or put together to form a row. The simplest style is tent-shaped and you can easily make these yourself, either from two sheets of glass held together with a specially designed clip, or from polythene stretched over batons, held together with a bulldog clip. For bulkier crops, barn cloches are a better shape. These have tent-shaped roofs supported on two slightly slanting side-pieces. Place them end to end to protect a whole row, but leave a little space between each one for ventilation.

Plastic does not hold on to heat as well as glass, and temperatures under a glass cloche will usually be 2–3 degrees higher. Glass cloches do not deteriorate with age as plastic does, but they are more fragile – and heavier to move. Sometimes, though, this is an advantage. Wind can get under a light plastic cloche and whirl it away in a fashion that obliterates not only the cloche but also the crop underneath. You do not have to move cloches to water crops. Water over the tops of them so that the water drips down and soaks in either side. The roots of the plants underneath will reach out to find it.

Use cloches to warm up and dry out soil before planting and to protect emerging seedlings. With such protection, crops should be ready to harvest 2–3 weeks early. Warming the soil is as valuable as any other benefit of a cloche, for seeds sulk and may rot in cold, wet ground. Cloches are particularly valuable during the last month of winter and the first one of spring, when temperatures fluctuate in a way that is not favourable to young seedlings. Beetroot, carrots, lettuce and peas will all benefit from protection.

Later on in the season, use cloches to help along tender vegetables such as French beans, sweet corn, outdoor cucumbers and tomatoes. In cold areas, use them to warm the soil before transplanting brassicas such as cauliflowers. Leave the cloches in place as long as possible, until the cauliflowers outgrow the space. You can also use them to good effect with peas. You may find that the only way to bring a late-sown crop to fruition in cold areas is to cover it with cloches. This would only be possible with a dwarf cultivar. In early autumn, you can extend the growing season by giving protection to carrots and lettuce sown in late summer. You can also use cloches to hasten the ripening of bush tomatoes or to protect onions drying off for storage.

LIGHTS, BOTTLES AND JARS

Old lantern lights make attractive covers for plants or patches of seedlings and are easy to remove during the day and replace at night. But for the cheapest covers of all, use upturned jam jars or cut the bottoms off clear plastic drink bottles. Put these over seeds of plants such as cucumbers, sweet corn and courgettes while they are germinating. Keep them over the seedlings until the nights have warmed up.

HARVESTING & STORING

VEGETABLES AND FRUIT GATHERED FRESH from the garden nearly always taste better than produce that has been stored, however carefully. The exceptions are apples and pears, some varieties of which need to be stored to finish ripening (as with pears) or to develop full flavour (as with late-season apples). By trial and error you will sort out those crops that you are most likely to use and those that store most successfully. Handle all produce carefully as cuts and bruises quickly lead to disease. The freezer has revolutionized the whole business of preserving vegetables and fruit. Few people now preserve peas by drying them, but once these were a winter staple. And if there was a glut of tomatoes, you bottled them in preserving jars. You can still do this, but it is easier to freeze them. Frozen whole with their skins on, they maintain an excellent flavour.

VEGETABLES

Leafy vegetables such as lettuce and spinach deteriorate fast, but root vegetables can be stored successfully for months given the right conditions. Where you have a range of different-sized vegetables, try to store them so that you can use the smallest first.

LEAF & SALAD VEGETABLES Harvest soft leafy vegetables such as salad crops, oriental brassicas and spinach early or late in the day, when they are at their coolest. On sunny days a lettuce may have heated up considerably by midday. Store in a cool place (for most people, the salad box of a refrigerator), in a polythene bag, loosely folded over. Red and white cabbages that are not frost-hardy need to be stored on wooden slats (see below) or trimmed and hung in nets in a cool, frost-free place. Other winter cabbages and chard are harvested as they are needed.

FRUITING & FLOWERING VEGETABLES Late crops of frost-tender vegetables such as courgettes, cucumbers, aubergines, peppers and chillies can be stored in a cool place in polythene bags, loosely folded over. Sweet corn can also be stored but the flavour soon deteriorates. Tomatoes keep successfully in a cool place. Marrows, pumpkins and winter squash should be "cured" by leaving them to dry and harden in the sun. They will keep for several months in a cool, frost-free store. Chillies dry successfully. Pull up plants and hang them upside-down before picking the chillies and putting them in jars or threading them on a string.

PODDED VEGETABLES Pick French and runner beans before frost can get to them and store in a cool place in polythene bags, loosely folded over. They will only keep for a few days. Haricot and lima beans, peas and southern peas can be dried. Pull up the plants whole when the pods are mature and hang them in a cool, airy place. When they are completely dry, shell and store in jars.

BULB & STEM VEGETABLES Leeks can be wrapped in newspaper and kept in a cool place if the ground is likely to freeze hard. Onions, shallots, garlic and celeriac can all be stored successfully. Proper harvesting is the key to keeping onions, shallots and garlic. Make sure that bulbs are thoroughly dried off before storing in shallow trays in a well-ventilated, frost-free place. You can also hang them in nets or tie or plait them in strings. They need drier storage conditions than other vegetables. Damp starts them into growth again. Onions with thick necks will not keep for long.

ROOT VEGETABLES Harvest potatoes when the ground is dry, so that they are not covered in mud, and store in thick paper sacks, not polythene which makes them rot. Tie the neck of the sack to exclude light as this stimulates the poisonous alkaloids that make green

STORING RED CABBAGES
Pull up red (and white) cabbages whole and store on slatted shelves, with a little straw if you want, the roots dangling through the slats.

HARVESTING SQUASH
Both squash and pumpkins should be picked with a piece of stalk still attached. Summer varieties of squash will keep for 2–3 weeks.

STRING OF GARLIC
The most decorative way of storing garlic, as well as onions and shallots, is to make a plait or string, and hang it in a cool, dry place.

patches on the tubers. Leave carrots, beetroot, turnips, swedes, parsnips, winter radishes, salsify and scorzonera in the ground for as long as possible. Covering them with straw will make lifting easier in frosty weather. They can also be stored in layers in boxes of damp sand, in a cool place. Twist the foliage off first. If you have enough space you can make a clamp, the traditional method of storing root vegetables. Kept like this, they should last through most of the winter. Put down a 20–30cm (8–12in) layer of straw on the floor of a cool store-room, cellar or outhouse, and pile the vegetables in a tidy heap on top. Cover them with another layer of straw at least as thick as the first and finish by adding a layer of earth 15cm (6in) deep. Vegetables in a clamp are, of course, much easier to get at than ones stuck firmly in frozen ground, but they may attract vermin.

FRUIT

Soft-fleshed fruit such as peaches and plums deteriorate quickly once harvested, so the most important fruit to store are those such as apples and pears.

APPLES The ideal store is one that is free of frost and mice with a temperature of 3–5°C (37–40°F). In practice, it is difficult for ordinary gardeners to keep stores as cool as this. Aim for a steady 8°C (45°F). Pick apples when the stalk parts easily from the branch. Early-maturing cultivars such as 'George Cave' should be eaten straight from the tree. Other apples can be stored in wooden boxes, laid out on slatted shelves or packed into polythene bags that can hold 2–3kg (4–6lb) of fruit. Tie the bags loosely and punch holes in them so that air can circulate freely. Keep fruit as far as possible from anything strong-smelling, such as creosote, onions and paint, that may taint the flavour.

PEARS The same general principles apply as for apples. The lower the temperature, ideally 0–1°C (32–34°F), the longer they keep. Do not wrap them as they need picking over frequently. Pears are at their best for a very short period. Bring them a few at a time into a warm room to finish the ripening process. Do not store in polythene bags as it encourages rot.

QUINCES & MEDLARS Store quinces on trays in a cool, dark place where they will keep for up to a month. Keep them as far as possible from other fruit, which may pick up their strong aroma. Medlars must be stored until soft (see page 133).

CITRUS FRUIT Citrus fruit last a long time provided they are cool and dry. Store fruit in boxes or on slatted shelves.

STORING APPLES
Apples can be stored in wooden boxes or laid out on slatted shelves in a cool place where they are never in danger of freezing. They keep better if individually wrapped, but the gain must be weighed against the extra work involved.

FREEZING

The quality of frozen produce is greatly affected by the rate at which it has been frozen. If food is frozen slowly, large ice crystals form and these spoil the texture of the vegetables and fruit. Fast-freeze produce (the instruction booklet that comes with the freezer will give details of how to do it) and do not try to do too much at the same time. If you know that you are going to freeze crops, choose cultivars that have been specially selected for the process.

VEGETABLES

- Broad beans: best frozen while small and not yet starchy.
- Broccoli and calabrese: cut the florets into suitable lengths.
- Brussels sprouts: choose small, firm sprouts, trim off outer leaves.
- Cauliflower: break into florets about 5cm (2in) across.
- French beans: pick beans while still small and freeze them whole.
- Peas: freeze only young peas. Shell them first.
- Spinach: wash thoroughly, drain and trim the stems.
- Sweet corn: remove the husks and tassels before freezing.
- Tomatoes: freeze whole. To use, slip off skins under the tap.

HERBS

- Mint and basil: freeze leaves in small polythene bags.

FRUIT

- Apples: freeze after cooking to a pulp or purée.
- Apricots, nectarines, peaches and plums: cut in half and stone the fruit. Freeze halves in light syrup.
- Blackberries, hybrid berries, mulberries and raspberries: spread the fruit on trays to fast-freeze before packing it in containers.
- Acid cherries: stone first.
- Currants: strip fruit from the bunches before freezing.
- Gooseberries: top and tail first.

PESTS & DISEASES

SOME PEOPLE ONLY SEEM TO SEE their gardens in terms of its pests and diseases, a battlefield where a long war of attrition has to be waged by the gardener against mangold fly, mustard beetle, blight and rust. These are probably the same people who write complaining letters to their local newspapers and as a matter of principle challenge their bills in a restaurant. Gardening does not have to be confrontational in this way. In mixed plantings of herbs and flowers, vegetables and fruit, there is little likelihood that crops will be completely wiped out by bugs. That is a problem that comes with monoculture, when large areas are covered with single crops, such as potatoes or peas. Diseases can best be prevented by attending to the conditions in which plants grow. If they are growing strongly and enjoying life, they are much less likely to succumb to illnesses.

BEAT THE BIRDS
Birds are often intent on plundering the strawberries. This pleasing frame has been made from netting attached to young, pliant hazel stems that have been bent over the row.

NATURE'S BALANCE

Bugs exist to feed other creatures. If you annihilate them with insecticides, their hungry predators will have to go elsewhere. Then, when the pests come back, they will not have any enemies. The reason for the existence of diseases such as grey mould/*Botrytis* is not so clear to the gardener but, with plants as with humans, the best strategy is prevention rather than cure. Disease is much less likely to strike plants that are thriving. In Part Two of this book (see pages 50–149), we have

included under each type of fruit or vegetable, a list of the most common pests and diseases to which that plant is prone. There, too, you will find the names of some fungicides and insecticides that may help with specific problems. They are given in recognition of the fact that some gardeners like to know what potion they can turn to if the aphids get out of hand, or what preventative sprays they can use in a season when blight is most likely to strike the potatoes and tomatoes. But serenity in the garden is more easily achieved if you learn to be tolerant of

pests and diseases. Up to a point . . . There is no need to fling the netting off the raspberries and invite the birds in for a feast. But it is not the end of the world if the cabbages have a few outer leaves nibbled by caterpillars, or if a slug has taken an *hors d'oeuvre* from the lettuce.

Now that we buy, rather than grow, so much of our food, we have come to expect an almost unreal perfection in the appearance of fruit and vegetables. A supermarket lettuce may have been sprayed as many as 11 times before it leaves the glasshouse for the supermarket shelf. No insects lurk in the folds of its leaves. No downy mildew disfigures its appearance. We would complain bitterly to the manager if it did. But there is a price to pay for this: a suspicion that what we are putting in our mouths is not altogether good. When you grow your own fruit and vegetables, you eat them confident in the knowledge that you have been the sole arbiter of what they should or should not receive by way of medicine. If the price to pay for that is occasional

STAY SANGUINE
Some damage may be inevitable, but a few slug or caterpillar holes in the outer leaves of a cabbage hardly spell disaster. The leaves will, in any case, probably be discarded in the kitchen.

PREVENT AND PROTECT

Young brassicas, left, are being protected from two different pests. The netting deters birds from pecking the leaves, while the square collars at the base of the plants will stop the cabbage root fly from laying its eggs around the stems. When the maggots hatch, they eat the roots.

FRUITFUL HARMONY

If the soft fruit patch needs a fruit cage, try building one that is as attractive to the human eye as it is off-putting to the birds. Here, the supports are arranged like the spokes of a wheel. The netting is fixed to the top and sides.

WIRED UP

Plants are at their most vulnerable to attack by birds while they are small. Lengths of chicken wire arched over rows or patches of seedlings will give all the protection that is necessary.

root fly damage to cut out of a carrot when you are preparing it, or a few strawberries lost to grey mould, then that is a price worth paying.

It may sometimes seem to the gardener that there are more baddies than goodies in the garden. There are not, but the goodies are slower on the uptake and the gardener's patience is limited. Aphids (greenfly and blackfly) are the most common horrors and it *is* offputting when you go to gather broad beans to find the plant seething with blackfly. You could spray them, but you can just as easily snap the tops off the plants – blackfly always congregate on the juicy growing tips – and put them in the dustbin. It is in artificial environments such as greenhouses, often without natural predators, that you may feel most need to reach for a bottle. But you could equally well reach for an *Encarsia* wasp (see page 195), which can dispatch prodigious numbers of whitefly.

In the natural cycle, a build-up of pests is followed by a build-up of predators. It is the gap between that is nerve-racking, but, gradually, you learn to trust in nature, which has a longer overview than fidgety humans. The cycle is not helped by the introduction into the food chain of unnatural numbers of predators such as cats. In towns and cities, where there are more cats than could star in a million musicals, there are relatively few species of birds. This, in turn, has an effect on the numbers of insect pests.

BOTTLED REMEDIES

Insecticides work in several ways. The simplest are those that kill by contact. You spray the bug. It drops down dead. Other insecticides leave a deposit on the leaf that is then eaten by the creature. Caterpillar killers work in this way. Systemic insecticides are more devious. These are absorbed by the tissues of the plant and then get into the sap. The insects are killed by feeding on the plant that you have sprayed. Sap suckers such as greenfly and blackfly are usually tackled in this way. The least dangerous times to spray are early in the morning (say before 10am) or in the evening (after 6pm), when there are fewer beneficial insects on the wing and bees are less likely to be working flowers. Millions of bees, which do only good in the garden and are essential for pollination, are killed each year by reckless spraying. Spray when foliage is dry and when there is no wind. But remember your allies. If you must spray, avoid using kill-all insecticides that get rid of friends as well as foes. Choose chemicals that are as specific as possible to the problem in hand.

Fungicides can be used to fight against a wide range of common diseases. They can combat powdery mildew, which is particularly prevalent in hot, dry summers, and are also effective against grey mould/ *Botrytis*, which attacks strawberries and many other plants. Leaf spots, such as chocolate leaf spot on broad beans, may also be controlled by a systemic fungicide.

Like insecticides, fungicides work in different ways. The systemic types are absorbed through the leaves into the plant's sap, there killing any fungus spores. Contact fungicides work by making a barrier between the leaf surface and any external spores. They will only be effective if applied regularly, usually at 10–14 day intervals. All fungicides are better at prevention than cure. Unfortunately, most gardeners are better at reacting than predicting. Your best defence is to grow your plants in well-nurtured soil and in the kinds of situation that nature intended for them. They will then be less prone to any kind of disease.

PESTS, DISEASES & MINERAL DEFICIENCIES

PESTS AND DISEASES SORT THEMSELVES quite clearly into the general, such as aphids and grey mould, which are attracted to a range of plants, and the specific, such as asparagus beetle or cane spot, which are particular about their targets. Generally the latter are less of a problem than the former, although where they attack, they may inflict more damage. A gardener also needs to distinguish between problems that can be controlled and those that cannot. Usually pests are more easily dealt with than diseases. There is no sure treatment, for instance, for honey fungus and violet root rot.

PESTS

APHIDS

Aphids – or greenfly and blackfly as they are more usually known – share with slugs the dubious honour of being the most commonly complained about pests in the garden. About 550 different kinds of aphid thrive in northern Europe. They breed prodigiously because, for the whole summer, all aphids are female. Their young grow up in a week and then start to breed themselves. Do not even *think* about it. It is too frightening. Greenfly are sap suckers and therefore spreaders of virus diseases that can be more of a problem to the gardener than the pests themselves. Their enemies are ladybirds, lacewings and hoverflies. Blackfly are most likely to be a problem on cherry trees, where they congregate on the growing shoots, and on broad beans, where they also favour the juicy tips. Pinching out the tops of broad bean plants is the simplest way of getting rid of them on this crop. On a small cherry, you can also pinch out growing tips regularly, both to keep the tree compact and to deter aphids. Most aphids overwinter on different host plants to those that they attack in summer. The black bean aphid often overwinters on euonymus. As well as the problem of their introducing virus diseases, aphids can also reduce a plant's vigour and distort its growing tips. They excrete a sticky liquid known as honeydew that, in its turn, attracts sooty mould. You can help to keep aphids in control by encouraging their natural predators (see page 195). You can also treat them with insecticide.

SHOOT DAMAGE BY APHIDS

BLACKFLY ON BROAD BEAN

ONION FLY

If your onions suddenly turn yellow and keel over then you may well have this fly on your patch. The adults look like small houseflies and in late spring lay their eggs in the soil around onion or leek crops. The creamy maggots eat the roots of onions and leeks, then burrow into the bulbs themselves and continue to fatten themselves up at the gardener's expense. The most dangerous time is in early and midsummer, when young plants may be killed by the onion fly's grubs. The flies themselves overwinter in the ground as pupae. There is no effective treatment against the problem. Remove and destroy any plants that are affected by this pest. Your best strategy for outwitting it is to shift your onion and leek beds each year; in other words to practise an organized rotation of crops.

WHITEFLY

Whitefly are a particular problem in greenhouses, where they congregate on crops such as aubergines, weakening plants. They lay eggs, usually on the backs of leaves, which hatch into tiny, scale-like, sap-sucking creatures. The scale pupates, hatching into a fly, and the grisly cycle starts again. Yellow sticky traps are effective, as is the parasitic wasp *Encarsia* (see page 195). You can also clear whitefly on the wing with a car vacuum cleaner.

WHITEFLY NYMPHS   ADULT WHITEFLY

CARROT FLY

The adult fly is inconspicuous. It is its progeny that does the damage. Small underground grubs nibble at carrot roots, causing the tops to wilt or discolour. The first generation of flies hatches in late spring, so damage is most obvious in early summer. As the adults are incompetent fliers, you can protect crops with barriers of polythene about 75cm (30in) high, or cover rows of seedlings with a fleecy film (see page 166). You can also time sowings to avoid the peak hatching period: sow in early summer rather than late spring.

CARROT FLY DAMAGE

CELERY FLY

Tiny white grubs, similar to carrot fly grubs, tunnel into the leaves of celery, causing pale blotches which later turn dry and brown. Spring attacks, when celery plants are still young, are the most dangerous. Pick off and destroy affected leaves or spray with a systemic insecticide.

CABBAGE ROOT FLY

The small white grubs of the cabbage root fly feed on the roots of brassicas – from cabbages and cauliflowers to kohl rabi – causing the plants to wilt. Young plants may be killed altogether. Several generations of the fly hatch in a single season, usually appearing in mid-spring, midsummer and late summer. There is no cure, but collars fixed around plant stems (see page 57) provide an effective deterrent.

ASPARAGUS BEETLE

These yellow and black beetles are easy to identify. Both beetles and their larvae feed on asparagus foliage and may completely defoliate plants. They are active from late spring to late summer, and overwinter as pupae in the soil. Spray with a contact insecticide and clear away all debris from asparagus beds.

BEETLE LARVAE

ADULT ASPARAGUS BEETLE

SCALE INSECTS

These small, brown, flat creatures may colonize the stems of plants such as apples, cherries, peaches, figs, vines, citrus and bay trees. They are rarely troublesome, but a winter tar wash will kill insects and eggs.

SCALE INSECTS

RASPBERRY BEETLE

The maggots of the raspberry beetle may also attack loganberries, tayberries and blackberries. The adult beetles hatch from pupae in the soil from mid-spring onward and lay eggs in the flowers. The grubs eat the centre of the fruit as it develops. When it is ripe, they return to the soil to pupate. You can prevent damage by spraying with a contact insecticide before raspberries begin to change colour. Loganberries and tayberries should be sprayed as the petals start to fall, and blackberries before the flowers open.

RASPBERRY BEETLE DAMAGE

RED SPIDER MITE

Red spider mite is a problem in summer in the greenhouse. It can only be seen through a magnifying glass, but can produce threads like a spider's web. Affected leaves are flecked with yellow and turn brown before dying. Crops such as aubergines, cucumbers and melons are worst affected, but in hot summers the mite moves outside on to strawberries and vines. Damp down greenhouses to maintain a humid atmosphere and disinfect them in winter. *Phytoseiulus* is an effective biological control in greenhouses (see page 195).

RED SPIDER MITE DAMAGE

COWPEA CURCULIO

A curculio is a weevil with a long snout, and this type is particularly prevalent on southern peas (cowpeas). Shake the adult weevils on to newspaper spread under the crop and destroy them. The young spend their entire lives inside the seeds and are a major nuisance while crops are in storage.

FLEA BEETLE

Brassicas of all kinds, including turnips, radishes, rocket, pak choi and mizuna, as well as cabbages and Brussels sprouts, may be attacked by these tiny beetles which pepper the leaves with holes and leap into the air when disturbed. Seedlings and new transplants are most at risk. The beetles overwinter in plant debris, so clear this away at the end of the growing season. Derris is an effective control.

FLEA BEETLE DAMAGE

MEALY BUG

Mealy bug is a tropical pest that attacks greenhouse crops and vines. The bugs are small, white and covered with a waxy-looking wool. They are a nuisance both as adults and larvae. They feed on sap and excrete a sticky liquid that in turn attracts sooty mould. Tucked into places like leaf axils, they can be difficult to dislodge. You can pick them off with a paintbrush soaked in methylated spirits or use the ladybird *Cryptolaemus* (see page 195) as a biological control in a greenhouse.

BIRDS

In the summer, soft fruit such as strawberries, raspberries and currants will need protection. Pigeons may attack winter brassicas and pea seedlings. Both can be protected quite easily with nets, wide-meshed for the brassicas, small-meshed for the soft fruit. Bullfinches sometimes strip buds from fruit trees and starlings are partial to cherries, but full-sized trees are difficult to protect.

MICE

Beans and peas are the most likely crops to attract mice. They burrow down to eat the seeds sown in spring. Netting or chicken wire provides a partial deterrent, so does a scattering of holly leaves along the row. But the only sure way to catch mice is to set traps, baited with something they like even better than legumes.

MOLES

Gourmet moles can set themselves up in asparagus patches where they crunch the succulent stems underground, but they are rarely a major problem in vegetable gardens. They are difficult to dislodge as their underground tunnel systems are extensive, but you can flood the runs using a hosepipe, which discourages them.

CUTWORMS

Lettuce seedlings seem most often to be attacked by cutworms, which are actually moth caterpillars rather than worms, unpleasantly plump, brownish-cream in colour and about 3cm (1½in) long. They nibble through the base of young plants which, even if not severed completely, quickly wilt and die. Cutworms emerge from the soil to feed at night. You can collect and destroy them by torchlight if you are not squeamish. Alternatively, you may choose to drench the ground with a soil pesticide. They are more of a problem in new gardens than old.

CUTWORM

POTATO CYST EELWORM

Potato cyst eelworm is a baddy with no redeeming features, as is its close relative pea cyst eelworm. It is a soil-borne pest that hatches out from an egg protected by a tough brown cyst. Young eelworms home in on the roots of plants and, in the worst cases, the whole plant dies. Crop rotation is the best defence. Do not grow maincrop potatoes in the same place more than once every 5 years. Cultivars such as 'Cara', 'Concorde', 'Maris Piper', 'Morag' and 'Penta' have partial resistance.

EELWORM CYSTS ON ROOTS

CABBAGE CATERPILLARS

You could forgive cabbage caterpillars if they were content with feasting on the outside leaves of cabbages, cauliflowers and Brussels sprouts. But they get where we want to be – right in the heart of the plant. Caterpillars may be of three different kinds: those of the large cabbage white butterfly are yellow and black and hairy; those of the small cabbage white are pale green and velvety; while those of the cabbage moth are yellowish-green and scarcely hairy at all. Try picking off caterpillars by hand (chickens are very partial to them), or dust the plants with derris or pyrethrum.

CABBAGE CATERPILLARS

SLUGS AND SNAILS

The most bothersome pests in a fruit and vegetable garden are slugs and snails. Although they may not look as impressive as the big, overground monsters, small, black, keeled slugs are the worst offenders, attacking a wide range of crops, including potatoes, tomatoes and strawberries. But many other crops are at risk, particularly when young and succulent. Thrushes and hedgehogs feed on slugs and snails. If these are not in evidence, try nematodes, a biological control, or use a slug killer based on aluminium sulphate.

SLUG AND
SNAIL DAMAGE

DISEASES & MINERAL DEFICIENCIES

BACTERIAL CANKER

Apples, cherries and plums are the fruit trees most often affected by bacterial canker. It invades the stems through leaf scars or wounds. Drops of amber-coloured gum may ooze from the affected areas. The stem, then foliage and flowers begin to wither. Control by cutting out and burning the affected branches. Spray the trees with a copper-based fungicide when the petals fall. You will need to follow that up by spraying 3 more times at weekly intervals from late summer onward. Help prevent canker by supporting heavily laden branches of fruit.

BLOSSOM END ROT

Tomatoes, and occasionally green peppers, are most commonly affected by blossom end rot, which is caused by a deficiency of calcium. Underwatering is often the cause and so it is perhaps not surprising that plants in grow bags, pots or hanging baskets are susceptible. Sunken, blackish patches discolour the base of the fruit and it may rot as a consequence. There is no cure. Prevent it by attending to the correct watering and feeding.

BLOSSOM END ROT

CHLOROSIS

Chlorosis is particularly noticeable in acid-loving plants, such as blueberries, which may be growing in soils that are too alkaline for their tastes. Plants are unable to take up enough manganese and iron from the soil and leaves turn yellow, particularly between the veins. Prevent it by matching plants to the right growing conditions. You can hold it in check by watering with a solution of sequestered iron and using an acidic mulch.

CANE SPOT

Small purplish spots may appear in late spring or early summer on the canes of raspberries, loganberries and other hybrid berries. The spots eventually split open the canes, and new shoots springing from them may die back. Control by cutting out the worst affected canes. Spray with a systemic fungicide every 2 weeks if necessary from the time the flowerbuds start to open to petal fall. The fungus overwinters on old canes.

BLIGHT

This is most troublesome on potatoes and their cousins, tomatoes. It is particularly prevalent in damp summers, when spores of the fungus *Phytophthora infestans* cause blotches on foliage and tomato fruit. It can spread rapidly, completely rotting foliage. Brown patches on potatoes spread into the hearts of the tubers. The best way to prevent it is to grow blight-resistant cultivars of potato, such as 'Wilja'. You can also spray with a copper fungicide at 2-weekly intervals from midsummer on.

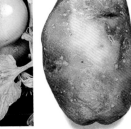

TOMATO BLIGHT POTATO BLIGHT

CHOCOLATE LEAF SPOT

Fungus spores cause chocolate-coloured spots on broad bean foliage and stems may discolour. It is rarely fatal. Spring-sown crops are less likely to be infected. Grow beans in fertile, well-drained soil and destroy badly affected plants. Avoid fertilizers with too much nitrogen.

VIOLET ROOT ROT

This will attack asparagus, beetroot, carrots, parsnips and, occasionally, swedes, turnips, potatoes and celery. Leaves wilt and turn yellow and a purple fungus covers the roots. Spores remain in the soil for a long period and there is no cure. Destroy plants and move crops to fresh ground.

CLUBROOT

The spores of clubroot can remain active in the soil for up to 20 years, causing galls on the roots of the cabbage family (which includes swedes and turnips). Roots become distorted and swollen and may rot. Leaves turn yellow, red or purple. There is no cure; crop rotation is the best defence. Do not compost roots, and lime soil to create a pH of 7–7.5 (see page 161).

CLUBROOT

DOWNY MILDEW

Many crops, including spinach, cabbages, onions, peas, vines and especially lettuce, may be affected. In humid conditions, fluffy white fungal growths develop on the undersides of leaves and growth is stunted and discoloured. Ventilate greenhouses to circulate air through crops. Lettuce such as 'Avondefiance' have some resistance.

DOWNY MILDEW

WHITE BLISTER

This is disfiguring but not fatal. Green blisters turn into shiny white, warty clusters on the undersides of the leaves of brassicas, salsify and scorzonera. It may occur where plants are growing too close to each other. Adjust spacing and rotate crops.

SILVER LEAF

Cherries, peaches and plums are most likely to be affected by this disease, which causes a silvering of the leaves and can eventually kill the tree. Spores infect the tree through wounds or cuts. Prune in summer, when there is less risk of this occurring. Cut away infected branches, making the cut at least 30cm (12in) below affected foliage. Take care not to damage the tree with strimmers or mowers.

GREY MOULD/*BOTRYTIS*

Many fruit and vegetables, including courgettes and marrows, peas and beans, greenhouse tomatoes, lettuce, figs, vines and especially strawberries, may be affected by this disease. It is worse in damp summers. Buds, fruit, leaves and stems can all become covered with grey, fluffy mould. It often attacks plants already suffering from diseases such as downy mildew. Some strains are resistant to fungicides, but you can try spraying soft fruit at flowering time, repeating every 2 weeks.

GREY MOULD/*BOTRYTIS*

HONEY FUNGUS

This is a soil-borne parasite that attacks the roots of trees such as apples, causing slow decay and eventual death. A creamy fungal growth gathers under the bark at the tree's base. Strong, healthy plants can usually resist attack. Destroy affected plants, including all traces of root. Avoid members of the *Rosaceae* family when you replant.

SOOTY MOULD

Sooty mould forms on the sticky liquid that aphids excrete. It weakens a plant because it blocks out light from leaves and prevents the plant from photosynthesizing. You can wash it off with soapy liquid.

PARSNIP CANKER

The shoulders of affected parsnips discolour and rot. The disease may also spread into the root, especially where there are lesions caused by carrot fly. The disease, which shows as black or orange patches on the flesh, is worse in wet seasons. There is no cure, but you can prevent outbreaks by rotating crops, improving drainage and planting canker-resistant varieties such as 'Avonresister', 'Cobham Improved Marrow', 'Gladiator' or 'White Gem'.

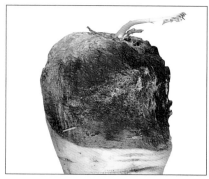

PARSNIP CANKER

LEAF BLOTCH

Occasionally affects medlars, producing large brown blotches on the leaves. The disease may spread from leaf to shoot, causing them to wilt. As the fungus overwinters on fallen leaves, the best defence is to collect and burn leaves when they fall. Quinces may be affected by a similar disease.

PEACH LEAF CURL

Peaches, nectarines and almonds may all be attacked by spores of the fungus *Taphrina deformans*. It distorts and blisters foliage, which drops and is replaced by a second healthy crop of leaves. Repeated attacks weaken trees. Protect wall-trained trees from midwinter to mid-spring with a light polythene shelter to keep off rain that contains the spores. Spray with a copper-based fungicide in autumn after leaf fall, then again as the buds swell from late winter.

PEACH LEAF CURL

SCLEROTINIA

This may attack Jerusalem artichokes, carrots, parsnips and celery. White fluffy mould gathers on the bottoms of the stems of artichokes. Affected plants should be dug up and destroyed. The mould is most likely to attack carrots and parsnips while they are in store. Keep stored crops cool and dry. On celery plants, *Sclerotinia* is most likely to form on the crown. There is no cure. Destroy affected plants and practise a strict rotation of crops.

POWDERY MILDEW

Powdery mildew attacks a wide range of crops, including cabbages, courgettes, peas, beans, apples, pears, cherries, gooseberries, peaches, plums, vines and strawberries. The mildew, which coats leaves and stems, is most likely to be a problem in hot, dry seasons. Do not plant too closely. The only certain control is to spray with a systemic fungicide before the disease appears and to continue at 2-week intervals.

POWDERY MILDEW ON FRUIT AND SHOOT

RUST

Powdery brownish spots or streaks appear on leeks and, more rarely, chives, but the disease is rarely fatal. Destroy affected leaves and water at the base of the plant rather than over the leaves. In hot, dry summers, apricots may also be affected by rust, but it is rarely serious.

RUST ON LEEKS

SCAB

Apples, pears and citrus fruit can all develop scab. It appears as black, scabby patches on fruit and foliage, and fruit may remain small and distorted. It is worse in mild, damp summers. Plant scab-resistant varieties such as the apples 'Sunset' or 'Winston' and pears 'Beurré Hardy' or 'Conference'. Clear away fallen leaves in autumn. Potato scab produces corky growths on tubers and is most common on light soils. Avoid susceptible varieties such as 'Maris Piper'.

SCAB ON APPLES

STEM ROT

Stem rot is most likely to be a problem where cucumbers and tomatoes are grown in greenhouse borders. Brown, sunken patches appear on the stems at ground level and the plants wilt. It is most likely to occur in cold, damp conditions. Rotate crops in greenhouse borders or grow crops in grow bags to prevent the build-up of soil-borne diseases. Spores can remain in the soil for long periods and reinfect future crops.

REVERSION DISEASE

This virus-like disease may be spread by big bud mites feeding on blackcurrant bushes. The plants become markedly less vigorous and crop less well. The leaves may be narrower than usual and the flowers smaller and a brighter pink. There is no cure. Dig up affected bushes and burn them. Buy fresh, certified virus-free stock and plant it in ground as far away as possible from the old site.

CUCUMBER MOSAIC VIRUS

The virus also attacks courgettes, marrows and melons and is spread by sap-sucking aphids. Foliage is mottled with yellow and the fruit may also be affected, with stunted growth. There is no cure. Destroy any badly affected plants and keep on top of aphids that transmit the virus from plant to plant in the garden.

BIOLOGICAL CONTROL

THERE IS RATHER A GHASTLY FASCINATION in peering through a magnifying glass at a purposeful little ladybird hoovering up mealy bugs and cramming them into its mouth with all the delight of a five-year-old at a birthday tea. The brown and black ladybird called *Cryptolaemus montrouzieri* is one of several predators that, given the right conditions, can be most effective in demolishing pests such as whitefly, red spider mite and mealy bugs. The predators work best in a controlled environment such as a greenhouse, which is where pest attacks are often most severe.

ENCARSIA FORMOSA
This tiny wasp, which lays its eggs in whitefly larvae, will control the pest in a greenhouse, but it is only effective in the right conditions.

To use biological controls effectively, you have to understand the life cycle of the pest as well as the predator. Whitefly have young offspring that suck in sap at one end and excrete a sticky syrup called honeydew at the other. Only a day or two after maturing, the adult whitefly starts to lay a frightening number of eggs. Having hatched, the larva plugs into a leaf vein to feed, and stays at the same trough until it pupates and itself becomes a fly. Then the whole ghastly cycle starts again.

ENCARSIA FORMOSA, a minute wasp, is the most effective control against whitefly. Its method of attack is grisly. The adult lays its eggs inside the larva of the whitefly and the young eat their way out from inside, emerging after about three weeks as fully fledged wasps. To operate productively, the wasp needs night temperatures above 10°C (50°F) and it is most effective in day temperatures of 18°C (65°F) and above. If the temperature is low, the wasp cannot breed as fast as the whitefly. *Encarsia* works best if introduced three times at fortnightly intervals in spring (such predators are available by mail order, see page 201). Then the wasps attack the whitefly where it hurts most – right in the middle of its reproductive cycle. The wasps are powerless against clouds of whitefly on the wing, the point at which most gardeners start to think about biological control.

PHYTOSEIULUS PERSIMILIS, a mite, will control red spider mite and feeds on its prey at any stage, juvenile or adult, but, as with *Encarsia*, the conditions have to be right for it to keep up with its prey.

COMMON LADYBIRDS, whether adult or in their larval form, can dispatch prodigious numbers of aphids – biological control can work with indigenous predators as well as with introduced ones.

HOVERFLIES, and their larvae, will help to keep down aphids. Plant marigolds to attract them to the vegetable patch.

LACEWINGS are more likely to visit gardens with a wide range of plants. Their larvae will devour huge quantities of aphids.

ICHNEUMONS are a type of leggy, four-winged wasp that preys on caterpillars. You can encourage them to the garden by planting golden rod and herb fennel.

CENTIPEDES like a diet of slugs, but will make do with other pests.

GROUND BEETLES are also keen on slug breakfasts. Remember these friends before you start spraying your foes. If you must spray, use an insecticide specific to the job.

LADYBIRD

LADYBIRD LARVA

LADYBIRDS
Adult ladybirds eat huge numbers of aphids, but their larvae have an even greater appetite and will make short shrift of 50 aphids a day.

LACEWING

LACEWING LARVA

LACEWINGS
Lacewing larvae are voracious aphid eaters. If you grow flowers among the vegetables it will help to attract the adults to the garden.

HOVERFLY
Hoverflies provide their young with a ready meal by laying their eggs within aphid colonies. Increase the numbers of hoverflies visiting the garden by planting marigolds.

WEEDS

NEW GARDENERS NEED TO KNOW WHAT WEEDS look like, especially in their seedling or underground forms. Bindweed roots look quite important if you are a novice and you may be tempted to replant them tenderly in finely sifted earth. If you do, their gratitude will be boundless, as will the time you spend weeding.

On the other hand, if you think a plant is pretty, keep it, even if know-alls tell you it is a weed. Corydalis, the weed with ferny leaves and yellow flowers that grows in walls, is a case in point. Daisies are enchanting. So, in the proper place, is speedwell. Call it by its proper name, veronica, if it makes you feel better about it.

PERENNIALS

GROUND ELDER
Aegopodium podagraria
The worst weeds are perennial ones such as ground elder, which thrives in a wide range of soils and often arrives entangled in the roots of the clumps of michaelmas daisy or golden rod that gardeners give away in suspiciously large quantities. It spreads both by seed and by means of its shallow network of creeping rhizomes. These will manage to sprout new plants from any small piece that you have left in the ground. Digging and pulling weakens it eventually, but it can be difficult to control among permanent plantings, for instance in a fruit garden.

GROUND ELDER

CREEPING THISTLE
Cirsium arvense
Creeping thistle is another horror that often arrives woven, unnoticed, through the roots of other plants. A systemic weedkiller is the most effective way of attacking it. Systemic weedkillers travel down through leaves and stems into the roots of pernicious weeds. They do not work immediately, but they are very effective. The active ingredient breaks down rapidly in the soil. They work best if you apply them when the target weed is growing strongly. Holding fire in this way tests the nerves, but is the most effective strategy.

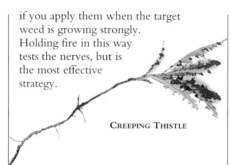

CREEPING THISTLE

BINDWEED
Convolvulus arvensis
Bindweed makes its presence known in the second half of summer. Having hauled itself unnoticed through raspberry canes, it opens a succession of trumpet flowers. If it were not such a bully, it would be a very decorative climber. It dies down each winter to a tangle of fleshy, white roots that travel yards in a season. Dig it out or kill it with glyphosate. If digging, be sure to extract every last piece, as tiny lengths of root will grow into new plants.

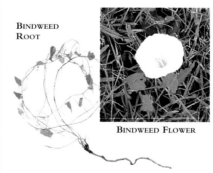

BINDWEED ROOT

BINDWEED FLOWER

COUCH GRASS
Elymus repens
Couch grass, which can grow up to 75cm (30in), is supported by a deep subterranean network of rhizomes, by which it spreads rapidly through the ground. It flowers in late summer and can also spread by seed. Its greatest friend is the rotavator, which chops up its rhizomes and spreads them about very efficiently. Dig out every piece of rhizome, which will sprout afresh if left, or use a non-residual weedkiller, if necessary.

COUCH GRASS

DOCK
Rumex sp.
Docks are well anchored with long tap roots. Once dug up, they are done for, but if you merely snap off the roots, they will resprout, as will dandelions. There is immense satisfaction in drawing a large dock intact from the soil. Do not allow it to set seed, which it sheds prolifically, and tackle docks when young, before the root is too entrenched. There is little need to use herbicide.

DOCK

PERENNIAL STINGING NETTLE
Urtica dioica

Plants are a sign of fertile ground and have some use in the garden as fodder for moth and butterfly caterpillars and nettle aphids, on which predatory ladybirds feed. Nettles can also be turned into a liquid feed. Soak about 1kg (2lb) of them in a barrel of water. You can use the liquid after three weeks. If you cannot learn to love them, dig them out or spray them with glyphosate when they are in flower.

PERENNIAL STINGING NETTLE

ANNUALS

SHEPHERD'S PURSE
Capsella bursa-pastoris

Annual weeds are not so sinister as perennials as they can be kept in check by hand-weeding or hoeing. Shepherd's purse, with its distinctive triangular seedpods, may be in flower all year and is a prolific self-seeder. Try to deal with plants before they set seed.

SHEPHERD'S PURSE

HAIRY BITTERCRESS
Cardamine hirsuta

This is a landcress which, when young, you can mix in salads. It has a peppery taste, not unlike watercress. That is one way of keeping on top of it. It has a staggeringly explosive mechanism for dispersing seeds. Catch it before it lets fling. Its roots are not usually difficult to pull from the soil.

HAIRY BITTERCRESS

ANNUAL MEADOW GRASS
Poa annua

This is most likely to be a problem where there are grass paths through a kitchen garden, but it is easy to pull out. It can be suppressed to a large extent by heavy mulching. As with most annual weeds, the trick is to deal with it before rather than after it has seeded.

ANNUAL MEADOW GRASS

GROUNDSEL
Senecio vulgaris

Each plant of groundsel, with its yellow flowers, can produce up to 500 seeds, so the best time to pull or hoe it is before it sheds them. Hoeing is best done in hot, dry weather, when plants die quickly. You do not have to uproot annual weeds, just cut off their heads.

GROUNDSEL

FAT HEN
Chenopodium album

Fat hen, with its succulent leaves and green bobbly flowers, can carry up to 28,000 seeds on one plant. Weed seeds germinate in the top 5cm (2in) of soil, so mulches need to be deeper than that if they are going to suppress weeds.

FAT HEN

COMMON CHICKWEED
Stellaria media

Common chickweed is one of the most persistent weeds in vegetable gardens, flowering for most of the year. Seeds will germinate in autumn and the plants continue to grow all winter in a mild year. Control it by hand-weeding or hoeing.

CHICKWEED

SPEEDWELL
Veronica persica

The common field speedwell is one of the large family of speedwells which, although very pretty, may spread rapidly to become a weed in the kitchen garden. Control it by pulling or hoeing.

SPEEDWELL

THE KITCHEN GARDEN CALENDAR

SPRING

	EARLY SPRING	MID-SPRING	LATE SPRING
THROUGHOUT SPRING • Hoe regularly between crops to keep down weeds. • Mulch around plants, trees and bushes to suppress weeds and conserve moisture in the soil. • Water if necessary, especially newly planted crops.	**VEGETABLES** • Sow broad beans, Brussels sprouts, calabrese, carrots, cauliflowers, lettuce, parsley, parsnips, peas, radishes, rocket, spinach and spring onions outside when conditions are suitable. • Continue to force Belgian chicory. • Sow aubergines, celeriac, celery, cucumbers, leeks, lettuce, parsley, peppers and tomatoes in a frost-free greenhouse or indoors. • Plant out Jerusalem artichokes, asparagus, onion sets and seedlings, early potatoes and shallots. **FRUIT** • Finish planting fruit trees and bushes. • Finish pruning fruit trees and bushes. • Where mildew has been a problem, spray gooseberries just before the flowers open and continue at fortnightly intervals. • Hand-pollinate wall-trained fruit such as peaches and apricots if insects are not on the wing. • Prune out some of the old wood on 'Morello' cherries if not already done. • Prune blueberries. • Check blackberries, loganberries and tayberries. Tie in to wires as necessary. • Mulch young trees, raspberry canes and fruit bushes. • Set out young plantlets grown from strawberry runners.	**VEGETABLES** • Earth up early potatoes. • Pull up stumps of Brussels sprouts and burn them. • Sow beetroot, broad beans, broccoli, Brussels sprouts, winter cabbages, calabrese, carrots, cauliflowers, kohl rabi, leeks, lettuce, spring onions, parsley, parsnips, peas, radishes, red chicory, rocket, salsify, scorzonera, spinach, swedes and turnips. • Plant out Jerusalem artichokes, onion sets and potatoes. • Sow aubergines, courgettes, cucumbers, French and runner beans, squash, sweet corn and tomatoes in a frost-free greenhouse or indoors. **FRUIT** • Pick flowers off new young strawberry plants, which should not be allowed to fruit in their first year. • Finish planting raspberries, if this was not done in late autumn. • Check fig trees, and prune and tie in new growth if necessary. • Hand-pollinate wall-trained peaches and nectarines if necessary. If the weather is very dry, spray the trees with a fine mist of water that will help the fruit to set.	**VEGETABLES** • Plant globe artichokes and cardoons. • Stake peas. • Earth up potatoes. • Sow beetroot, winter cabbages, carrots, calabrese, cauliflowers, chard, courgettes, endive, French and runner beans, kohl rabi, leeks, lettuce, parsley, parsnips, peas, radishes, red chicory, rocket, spinach, spring onions, swedes and turnips. • Sow cucumbers, courgettes, squash, and sweet corn in a frost-free greenhouse or indoors. • Plant out Jerusalem artichokes, aubergines, celeriac, celery, peppers, potatoes, French and runner beans, sweet corn, and outdoor tomatoes. • Transplant well-developed seedlings of cauliflowers. **FRUIT** • Start to pick gooseberries. • Pull out any new young raspberry canes that come up a long way from the original rows. • Continue to water if necessary, especially wall-trained trees. • Weed strawberries and put straw around the plants, together with a sprinkling of slug pellets if slugs are known to be a problem. • Put netting over soft fruit. • Start to thin out new shoots on wall-trained peaches, apricots and plums.

SUMMER

	EARLY SUMMER	MIDSUMMER	LATE SUMMER
THROUGHOUT SUMMER • Hoe regularly between crops to keep down weeds. • Mulch around plants to suppress weeds and conserve moisture. • Water if necessary, especially newly planted crops.	**VEGETABLES** • Sow beetroot, calabrese, carrots, chard, chicory, courgettes, cucumbers, endive, Florence fennel, French and runner beans, kohl rabi, lettuce, parsley, peas, radishes, rocket, spring onions, squash and swedes. • Plant out aubergines, celeriac, celery, courgettes, cucumbers, peppers, sweet corn and outdoor tomatoes into prepared ground. • Transplant broccoli, Brussels sprouts, cauliflowers and leeks.	**VEGETABLES** • Watch for blight on maincrop potatoes and spray if necessary. • Earth up Brussels sprouts and other brassicas on exposed, windy sites. • Nip out sideshoots and the tops of outdoor cordon tomatoes when 4 or 5 trusses have set fruit. • Lift garlic and dry off the bulbs. • Sow beetroot, calabrese, carrots, chard, chicory, endive, Florence fennel, kohl rabi, lettuce, parsley, peas, radishes, rocket and turnips.	**VEGETABLES** • Lift onions and shallots and dry them off before storing them. • Cut off and burn the top growth of maincrop potatoes if it is blighted. • Sow kohl rabi, oriental salad leaves, radishes, spinach and turnips. • Sow curly endive under glass.

SUMMER CONTINUED	FRUIT	FRUIT	FRUIT
	• Pick strawberries, raspberries, currants and gooseberries regularly. • Train in new shoots of blackberries, loganberries and other hybrid berries. • Tie in selected shoots of wall-trained peaches and nectarines, and thin the fruit if necessary. • Remove strawberry runners unless needed to make new plants. • Pinch out shoots on wall-trained plums and 'Morello' cherries that are growing in the wrong direction. • Pick off sawfly caterpillars if they attack gooseberry bushes.	• Train in the canes of blackberries and hybrid berries. If you want to propagate them, tip layer shoots. • After fruiting, cut the leaves off strawberry plants and remove the straw. Weed between the rows. • Thin apples if they have not already thinned themselves naturally. • When raspberries have fruited, cut out old canes and tie in new ones. • Continue to train and tie in tree fruit growing against walls. • Branches of plum trees that are very heavily laden may need support. • Give citrus fruit a high-nitrogen feed.	• Continue to cut out old raspberry canes that have fruited and tie in the new canes. • Prune wall-trained apples and pears as necessary. • Plant out well-rooted runners in new strawberry beds. • Prune damsons and plums, if necessary, when they have fruited and cut out any damaged branches. • When peaches and nectarines have finished fruiting, cut out the stems on which the fruit was borne and tie in new shoots to replace them.

AUTUMN

	EARLY AUTUMN	MID-AUTUMN	LATE AUTUMN
THROUGHOUT AUTUMN • Store root vegetables such as beetroot, carrots, swedes and turnips as you lift them. Keep them in a cool, frost-free place. • Dig and manure ground once it has been cleared of crops.	VEGETABLES • Cure pumpkins and winter squash before storing them. • Continue to earth up brassicas. • Sow oriental salad leaves, winter radishes and spinach. FRUIT • After fruiting cut out at the base old canes of blackberries and other hybrid berries. Tie in new canes. • Weed well around fruit trees growing in grass. • Cut off and burn any mildewed top growth on gooseberries. • Order new fruit trees and bushes. • Finish summer pruning of wall-trained apples and pears. • Cut out dead wood on wall-trained 'Morello' cherries and tie in new shoots.	VEGETABLES • Plant garlic. • Sow broad beans and winter radishes. • Clear away bean sticks, tomato stakes and rotting vegetation. • Cut down stems of asparagus and Jerusalem artichokes. FRUIT • Store sound fruit in a cool frost-free place. • Take cuttings, if necessary, from gooseberry and currant bushes. • Prepare ground for planting new trees and bushes. • Tidy up alpine strawberry plants, removing dead leaves. • Prune gooseberries and currants after the leaves have fallen.	VEGETABLES • In cold areas, protect crowns of globe artichokes by packing them with straw or bracken. • Sow broad beans and peas. • Plant garlic and rhubarb. FRUIT • Finish picking apples and pears. • Plant new trees, bushes and raspberry canes as soon as possible after leaf fall. • Spray peaches and nectarines against peach leaf curl just after leaf fall.

WINTER

	EARLY WINTER	MIDWINTER	LATE WINTER
THROUGHOUT WINTER • Finish digging and manuring ground whenever conditions are suitable, and prepare it for spring planting. • Force plants such as Belgian chicory and rhubarb from midwinter onward. • Inspect stored apples and pears regularly and take out any fruit that is starting to go rotten.	VEGETABLES • Store carrots, turnips and swedes in a cool, frost-free place. FRUIT • Check stakes and ties on fruit trees and loosen ties where necessary.	VEGETABLES • Order vegetable and flower seeds, seed potatoes and onion sets. • Sow crops such as chicory and onions in a frost-free greenhouse or indoors. • Start planting shallots. FRUIT • Prune apples and pears if frosts are not too hard. • Continue to plant fruit trees and bushes if weather permits.	VEGETABLES • Prepare seedbeds for early sowings. • Set out potatoes in boxes to 'chit'. • Sow peas outdoors in mild areas. • Sow aubergines, celeriac, leeks, lettuce and onions in a frost-free greenhouse or indoors. FRUIT • For an early crop, cover strawberry plants with cloches. • Prune hazels when the catkins are fully open.

STAR PLANTS

SOME VEGETABLES AND FRUIT in Part Two of this book (see pages 50–149) are starred, to show that they are particularly good choices for a decorative kitchen garden. This list acts as a quick reference to these star plants and includes some other cultivars recommended for their looks.

VEGETABLES

CABBAGES Savoy types 'Julius' or 'Ice Queen': swirling outer leaves. 'January King Hardy Late Stock 3': shades of plum and grey. Red cabbage 'Ruby Ball'.
ORIENTAL BRASSICAS Mizuna: deeply cut leaves. Pak choi: shiny foliage on snow-white stems.
KALE 'Chou Palmier': elegant, upright black leaves. 'Dwarf Green Curled': spreading, curly leaves. 'Russian Red': purple leaves with red ribs.
CHARD 'Rhubarb Chard': scarlet ribs. 'Burgundy Chard': purplish-red stems.
LETTUCE 'Little Gem': small semi-cos. 'Iceberg': crunchy texture. 'Lollo Rossa': frilly leaves tinged with red. 'Red Salad Bowl': lasts well if picked regularly.
CHICORY AND ENDIVE 'Alouette'/'Chioggia': red and white leaves. 'Palla Rossa': neat, wine-red leaves. 'Variegata di Castelfranco': wonderfully decorative old cultivar with green, red and white leaves. 'Wallonne': French curled endive with large, tightly packed head.
COURGETTES All are decorative, especially 'De Nice à Fruit Rond', pale green, round fruit; and 'Gold Rush', yellow fruit.
PUMPKINS AND SQUASH All are decorative, especially 'Turk's Turban', intricately shaped and marked.
CHILLIES 'Yellow Cayenne': good in containers. 'Jalapeño': bullet-shaped fruit. 'Apache': prolific cayenne type.
SWEET CORN All are decorative.
GLOBE ARTICHOKES AND CARDOONS All are decorative.
TOMATOES All are decorative, especially 'Tigerella', with striped fruit, and 'Yellow Perfection', with bright yellow fruit.
RUNNER BEANS All are decorative, especially 'Painted Lady', with red and white flowers, and 'White Achievement', with pure white flowers.
FRENCH BEANS 'Purple Queen': purple pods. 'Kinghorn Wax': yellow pods. 'Blue Lake': climbing variety.

PEAS 'Waverex Petit Pois': makes a low hedge. 'Carouby de Maussane': purple-flowered mangetout.
BROAD BEANS All are decorative, especially 'Red Epicure', with red flowers followed by bronze beans.
LEEKS All are decorative, especially purplish-blue 'Bleu de Solaise'/'St Victor'.
FLORENCE FENNEL All are decorative.
ASPARAGUS All are decorative.
CARROTS All are decorative.
BEETROOT All are decorative, especially 'Bull's Blood', with dark lustrous leaves.

FRUIT

APPLES All are decorative, especially when trained as cordons and espaliers or grown as standards or half-standards as specimens in a lawn.
PEARS All are decorative, especially when trained as cordons, fans and espaliers or grown as specimens in a lawn.
PLUMS Decorative trained as fans.
PEACHES AND NECTARINES Decorative trained as fans.
APRICOTS Decorative trained as fans.
CITRUS FRUIT Decorative in large tubs.
FIGS Decorative trained as fans on a wall.
MULBERRIES Decorative in a lawn.
MEDLARS AND QUINCES Good lawn specimens.
HAZELNUTS Decorative in early spring, covered with catkins, and in autumn, with butter-coloured leaves.
BLACKBERRIES 'Oregon Thornless': leaves deeply cut like parsley.
STRAWBERRIES 'Baron Solemacher': neat alpine type that does not produce runners.
REDCURRANTS Decorative trained as double cordons.
GOOSEBERRIES Decorative grown as mop-headed standards.
GRAPES All vines are decorative in leaf.
MELONS Decorative in fruit.
KIWI AND PASSION FRUIT Decorative trained against supports; the kiwi has particularly good foliage.

BIBLIOGRAPHY

Baker, Harry: *The Fruit Garden Displayed*, London, 1986

Bunyard, Edward: *The Anatomy of Dessert*, London, 1929

Bunyard, Edward: *The Epicure's Companion*, London, 1937

Bunyard, George: *The Fruit Garden*, London, 1904

Consumers' Association: *The Gardening from Which? Guide to Pests and Diseases*, London, 1991

Creasy, Rosalind: *The Complete Book of Edible Landscaping*, San Francisco, 1982

Davidson, Alan: *Fruit*, London, 1991

HDRA: *The Fruit & Veg Finder*, Coventry, 1995

Hogg, Robert: *The Fruit Manual*, London, 1875

Larkcom, Joy: *Vegetables for Small Gardens*, London, 1995

Larkcom, Joy: *The Vegetable Garden Displayed*, London, 1992

Larkcom, Joy: *Oriental Vegetables*, London, 1991

Lord, Tony (ed): *The Plant Finder*, Whitbourne, England, 1995

McHoy, Peter: *The Gardening Which? Guide to Successful Pruning*, London, 1993

McVicar, Jekka: *Jekka's Complete Herb Book*, London, 1994

Morgan, Joan: *A Paradise out of a Common Field*, London, 1990

Phillips, Roger and Rix, Martyn: *Vegetables*, London, 1993

RHS: *Award of Garden Merit Plants*, London, 1995

Robinson, William: *The Vegetable Garden*, London, 1905

Sanders, Rosanne: *The English Apple*, Oxford, 1988

Wilson, Alan: *The Story of the Potato*, 1995

USEFUL ADDRESSES

Listed below are some gardens that have particularly interesting displays of fruit and vegetables, suppliers of more unusual plants and seeds, and some general horticultural organizations. Check before visiting gardens or nurseries as some have very limited opening hours. Remember to send a stamped, addressed envelope if you require a reply.

GARDENS

Barnsley House
Barnsley
Nr Cirencester
Gloucestershire GL7 5EE
One of the first potagers in Britain

Bourton House Garden
Bourton-on-the-Hill
Gloucestershire GL56 9AE
Small formal salad beds

Château de Hex
Hex
Nr Tongeren
Belgium
Kitchen garden remodelled on the turn-of-the-century original

Château de Villandry
Villandry
Nr Tours
France
The grand-daddy of potagers

Glenbervie House
Drumlithie
Stonehaven
Kincardineshire
AB3 2YA
Old-fashioned walled garden, splendid cabbages

Hadspen Garden
Nr Castle Cary
Somerset BA7 7NG
Bold combinations of vegetables and flowers in curved walled garden

Hatfield House
Hatfield
Hertfordshire AL9 5NQ
Excellent vegetable garden arranged with raised beds

Heale Gardens
Middle Woodford
Nr Salisbury
Wiltshire SP4 6NT
Magnificent apple tunnels

Hexham Herbs
Chesters Walled Garden
Chollerford
Northumberland
NE46 4BQ
National collections of thyme and marjoram

Kinoith
Shanagarry
Midleton
Co Cork
Ireland
Exuberant kitchen garden

Lake House
Northington
Alresford
Hampshire SO24 9TG
Beautifully trained fruit in formal kitchen garden

Miromesnil
Tourville-sur-Arques
76550 Offranville
Seine Maritimo
France
Fruit trees with peonies, and carrots among the flowers

Prieuré St Cosme
37520 La Riche
Nr Tours
Indre et Loire
France
Apple, apricot and plum trees decorate the potager

Prieuré Saint-Michel
Crouttes
61120 Vimoutiers
Orne
France
A monastic potager with good vegetables

Shepherd House
Inveresk
Nr Musselburgh
East Lothian EH21 7TH
Good small potager

Stowell Park
Yanworth
Nr Northleach
Gloucestershire GL54 3LQ
Classic walled garden and exceptional glasshouses

Woodpeckers
The Bank
Marlcliff
Nr Bidford-on-Avon
Warwickshire B50 4NT
Ornamental kitchen garden

SEED SUPPLIERS

Chase Organics Ltd
Coombelands House
Addlestone
Weybridge
Surrey KT15 1HY
Suppliers of organic seeds and biological insect predators; issue HDRA's mail order catalogue

Chiltern Seeds
Bortree Stile
Ulverston
Cumbria LA12 7PB
Extraordinary range, including oriental vegetables and herbs

James Henderson & Sons
Kingholm Quay
Dumfries DG1 4SU
Potato specialist

S.E. Marshall & Co Ltd
Wisbech
Cambridgeshire PE13 2RF
Down-to-earth supplier with interesting range of starter plants as well as seeds

W. Robinson & Sons Ltd
Sunny Bank
Forton
Nr Preston
Lancashire PR3 0BN
Unusual vegetables, especially tomatoes and French beans

Seeds by Size
45 Crouchfield
Boxmoor
Hemel Hempstead
Hertfordshire HP1 1PA
Extensive list including 175 varieties of cabbage and 80 varieties of tomato

Suffolk Herbs Ltd
Monks Farm
Coggeshall Road
Kelvedon
Essex CO5 9PG
Superb range of vegetables as well as herbs

NURSERIES

Michael Bennett
Long Compton
Shipston-on-Stour
Warwickshire CV36 5JN
Specialist supplier of asparagus crowns and artichoke offsets

Chris Bowers & Sons
Whispering Trees Nursery
Wimbotsham
Norfolk PE34 8QB
Good range of fruit trees

Buckingham Nurseries
14 Tingewick Road
Buckingham MK18 4AE
Hedging specialists

Global Orange Groves UK
PO Box 644
Poole
Dorset BH17 9YB
Wide range of citrus trees

Highfield Nursery
School Lane
Whitminster
Gloucestershire GL2 7PL
Excellent trained trees, including standard gooseberries

Keepers Nursery
446 Wateringbury Road
East Malling
Kent ME19 6JJ
Wide range of unusual fruit trees and soft fruit

Ken Muir
Honeypot Farm
Rectory Road
Weeley Heath
Essex CO16 9BJ
Specialist in soft fruit

Michael Paske Farms Ltd
Estate Office
Honington
Grantham
Lincolnshire NG32 2PG
Asparagus crowns, artichoke offsets and thongs of sea kale

Reads Nursery
Hales Hall
Loddon
Norfolk NR14 6QW
Vines, figs, citrus, unusual fruit and nuts

Scotts Nurseries
(Merriott) Ltd
Merriott
Somerset TA16 5PL
Excellent trained fruit trees

Clive Simms
Woodhurst
Essendine
Stamford
Lincolnshire PE9 4LQ
Nuts and unusual fruit

J. Trehane & Sons Ltd
Stapehill Road
Hampreston
Wimborne
Dorset BH21 7NE
Blueberries and cranberries

J. Tweedie Fruit Trees
Maryfield Road Nursery
Maryfield
Nr Terregles
Dumfries DG2 9TH
Wide range of fruit

ORGANIZATIONS

Brogdale Horticultural
Trust
Brogdale Road
Faversham
Kent ME13 8XZ
2000 different apples and the national collections of pears, plums and bush fruit

HDRA
Ryton Organic Gardens
Ryton-on-Dunsmore
Coventry
West Midlands CV8 3LG
Europe's largest organic organization (Henry Doubleday Research Association), with seed library of threatened cultivars

The Herb Society
134 Buckingham Palace
Road
London SW1W 9SA
Seminars, workshops, magazine and newsletters

INDEX

Page numbers in *italics* indicate illustrations or photographs with captions.

ACKNOWLEDGMENTS

AUTHOR'S ACKNOWLEDGMENTS
Without the generosity of garden owners, this book could not have come into being. I would particularly like to thank Tim and Darina Allen at Kinoith; Dr and Mrs A. J. Cox at Woodpeckers; Christine Forecast at Congham Hall; Rupert Golby and *Country Living* magazine for photographs of their garden at the Chelsea Flower Show; John and Caryl Hubbard at Chilcombe; Stewart and Jill Macphie at Glenbervie; Mr and Mrs R. Paice and their gardener Paul Williams at Bourton House; Nori and Sandra Pope at Hadspen Garden; Malcolm Seal and Anna Jamieson at Hill Cottage; and Lord and Lady Vestey and their gardener Neil Hewertson at Stowell Park, who have all allowed their gardens to be photographed. The design for the herb garden on pages 48–49 is adapted from one at Coton Manor, by kind permission of Mr and Mrs Ian Pasley-Turner. I would also like to acknowledge a debt to Rosemary Verey of Barnsley House, a pioneer of potagers, and to Joy Larkcom, whose writing has done so much to increase our knowledge of unfamiliar vegetables, particularly those from the orient.

Finally, I would like to thank the staff at Dorling Kindersley, particularly Thomas Keenes, for the clarity of his design, and Pamela Brown whose determination, good humour and expertise have made her an exemplary editor.

DORLING KINDERSLEY would like to thank Serena Dilnot, Nell Graville and Heather Jones for editorial assistance; Claire Naylor, Joanne Long and Laura Owen for design assistance; Dorothy Frame for the index; Sarah Ashun for photographic assistance; Suttons Seeds and Hyams & Cockerton for supplying plants, fruit and vegetables for photography.

PICTURE CREDITS
Additional commissioned photography by Steve Gorton: 4-5, 52-3, 59tl, 61, 63bl, 65tr, 81cl,tc, 85, 89cl,tr,bc, 101tr, 103br, 104tr, 116-7, 137tr, 157tr, 157tr, 159, 162, 196bc,tl,tr; and Andy Crawford: 7, 83cl, 87cl,bl, 88br

Additional photography: Peter Anderson, Andy Crawford, Geoff Dann, Philip Dowell, Andreas Einsiedel, Neil Fletcher, Frank Greenaway, Dave King, David Murray, Tim Ridley, Karl Shone and Clive Streeter.

Dorling Kindersley would like to thank the following for their kind permission to reproduce their photographs:

Bruce Coleman Ltd: Dr Frieder Sauer 195bc/Kim Taylor 195crb
Elsoms Seeds: 21tr, 40bl, 54bl
Eric Crichton: 79br
Mary Evans Picture Library: 34bl, 46bl
Garden Picture Library: Gillian McCalmont 135tr/Howard Rice 118-9c/Gary Rogers 44br, 119tr/Juliette Wade 109tc
John Glover: 182b
Holt Studios International: 192bl, 193l,cl,tc,cr,cl,bc
Jacqui Hurst: 68bl, 122, 141, 143tc, 184, 186br, 189cr
National Institute of Agricultural Botany: 103bl,cl
Oxford Scientific Films: J.A.L. Cooke 195tr/Mark Hamblin 197br
Photos Horticultural: 26tr, 27t, 166bl
Harry Smith Horticultural Collection: 71bc, 83tc, 136bl, 140br
Suttons Seeds Ltd: 67tl
Steven Wooster: 42br, 153tr

Key to illustration positions: t = top; b = bottom; l = left; r = right; c = centre

Picture Researcher: Lorna Ainger